Rio Grande
Sand in
Your Shoes

Enjoy!

Isabel Ziegler

The material in this book has been adapted from

For The Soul Is Dead That Slumbers
The Adventures of a Surgeon
And His Family
In
Northern New Mexico
(1946–1996)

A Memoir
By
Samuel R. Ziegler, MD
and
Isabel H. Ziegler

As Told To
Norman P. Ziegler, PhD, RN

RIO GRANDE SAND IN YOUR SHOES

A Memoir
by
Isabel Ziegler
as Told
to
Norman Ziegler

SUNSTONE PRESS

SANTA FE

Sunstone books may be purchased for educational, business, or sales promotional use.
For information please write: Special Markets Department, Sunstone Press,
P.O. Box 2321, Santa Fe, New Mexico 87504-2321.

Book and Cover design ›Vicki Ahl
Body typeface › Adobe Caselon Pro ‹›› Display type › Trajan
Printed on acid free paper

Library of Congress Cataloging-in-Publication Data

Ziegler, Isabel H.
  Rio Grande sand in your shoes : a memoir / by Isabel Ziegler as told to Norman Ziegler.
     p. cm.
  Includes bibliographical references.
  ISBN 978-0-86534-804-2 (softcover : alk. paper)
  1. Ziegler, Samuel R., 1914-2000. 2. Ziegler, Isabel H. 3. Physicians--New Mexico--Biography.
  4. Physicians' spouses--New Mexico--Biography. 5. Surgeons--New Mexico--Biography.
  6. Medicine--New Mexico--History--20th century. 7. Espanola (N.M.)--Biography
  8. Community health services--New Mexico--Espanola--History--20th century.
  9. Espanola (N.M.)--Social life and customs--20th century.
  10. Community life--New Mexico--Espanola--History--20th century.
  I. Ziegler, Norman. II. Title.
  R154.Z46Z54 2011
  610.92'2789--dc22
                                      2011001193

Published in

WWW.SUNSTONEPRESS.COM
SUNSTONE PRESS / POST OFFICE BOX 2321 / SANTA FE, NM 87504-2321 /USA
(505) 988-4418 / ORDERS ONLY (800) 243-5644 / FAX (505) 988-1025

FOR SAM

CONTENTS

PROLOGUE

I knew that marrying a doctor would involve a life filled with caring and concern for others, and with some hardship and uncertainty along the way. I also saw it as a life filled with adventure. Dr. Sam Ziegler provided me and our family with all of this, for his was a life guided by a true sense of compassion and purpose. During World War II, we were a transitory family at first, managing endless moves from Ohio to Georgia and then California with our two young sons. Eventually, Sam was ordered overseas. He served as a medical officer in the Philippines and later in Japan, during the Occupation. While Sam was overseas, I stayed in California with my parents and our children.

Sam's entire tour of duty seemed to renew a deep-seated aspiration to devote his life and medical career to mission work. Much of this purpose was inspired by the work of his father, Rev. Samuel G. Ziegler, General Secretary of Foreign Missions for the United Brethren Church. Sam had often talked about Africa and the mission work of David Livingstone and Albert Schweitzer. Coincidentally, Sam's father mentioned in several of his letters a great need for medical care in northern New Mexico. He told Sam that Arthur and Phoebe Pack of Ghost Ranch in Abiquiu were interested in building a hospital in the area under the supervision of the United Brethren Church.

While still overseas, Sam received yet another letter from his father saying the Packs were very serious about building a hospital, and noted that the site would be in a "frontier area of the old west." Sam's interest seemed to grow, and after his discharge from the service, we agreed to meet the Packs to discuss the creation of a much needed hospital facility.

It was clear to me that the opportunity being offered to Sam was very important to him. He could not contain his enthusiasm when telling me that here was a chance to be of service in a meaningful way and to play a major role in the development of a community hospital from its inception. It would also allow him to establish his own practice in an area vitally in need of medical services. Sam said we would be going to a small town called Española. He qualified this statement by saying that the town was located just "north of Santa Fe."

I was not certain the challenge offered Sam was as inviting to the other members of the Ziegler family! The village of Española I saw in 1946, on our first trip west, was a small assemblage of several cantinas, a gas station or two, one mercantile and one small grocery. This was a very different community from the one to which I was accustomed, having grown up in the college town of Westerville, Ohio. We then met with Arthur and Phoebe Pack. Their enthusiasm for the hospital project and their sense of well-being in the area provided me with a more positive outlook for our future.

The tale that unfolds in this book emerged from our decision to settle in Española. Over the years, Sam and I became involved not only with the hospital, but also with the community of Española and the surrounding area, and we had many adventures and came to know many wonderful people along the way. We often considered writing a memoir, and we finally commenced this work in 1987 with the help of our son, Norman, and his wife, Judy. That memoir became the story of our families and of our upbringing, with much about our lives before coming to New Mexico. It was first printed in June of 1999 in a limited private edition under the title *For The Soul Is Dead That Slumbers.*

Sam is now gone, having passed away in July of 2000. Since his death, I have been concerned with shortening that large original volume to a manageable size suitable for the general reader, with a focus on our lives and activities in Española and northern New Mexico. However, I did not really know how to get started. The task seemed daunting to me all by myself. My son, Norman, who had worked so hard pulling the original Memoir together, said he now needed time to devote to his own family and work. The Memoir thus sat dormant for some time.

Over a year ago now, two good friends, Hal and Mary Beth Shymkus, who were interested in the history of northern New Mexico and Rio Arriba, read the original 660-page Memoir. They learned of my desire to rework the material, and while at lunch one day, casually inquired if I were still interested. I said that I was. Hal and Mary Beth then offered to help. They were both genuinely interested in the work, and felt that it made a real contribution to the history of our area. They also believed that the material itself and the story it told were worthy of publication.

I then contacted Norman to ask how he felt about this development. He was busy working full-time and much involved with his own family in Denver, Colorado. He said that it would be fine for us to proceed ahead. He would need to be involved again only with the final reworking of the text, after selection had been made of material to be included.

So began a long labor with Hal and Mary Beth. I was delighted to work with them. I knew something of Hal's background in journalism. He had been the editor of a local newspaper in his hometown in Illinois, and for many years advertising director for a large company by the name of Cummins in Columbus, Indiana. In addition, he had done a good deal of fiction and non-fiction writing for publications such as *Sports Afield, Field & Stream,* and *New Mexico Magazine.* Mary Beth herself had a professional background as a marketing and public relations director. I felt I would be in good hands working with them.

At Hal's direction, I provided him and Mary Beth with copies of the material from the original Memoir which focused on our lives and activities in New Mexico. They read through this material once again and chose sections they felt were most important and interesting. When their initial work was complete, they brought this material to me, and we began to meet weekly and sometimes twice a week, for several hours at a time. We decided early on, at Hal's suggestion, that the edited book should speak with one voice only, which would be mine. The original work speaks with two voices, Sam's and mine, as we both had much to say from our own perspectives. Mary Beth was wonderful throughout all our discussions in making notes and providing reasoned judgments about what material should be included.

These edited chapters were then typed into a "coherent" book with which I could work. Annie Lovato, an attractive young woman whom I had met, helped with this initial work and also typed a more finished manuscript. Annie was working as a pharmacy technician while pursuing her degree in pharmacy, but she found time to help and was very dependable and capable.

Another person who came to my aid was my great-grandson, Patrick Day. He is a handsome and intelligent fourteen year-old who solved my computer problems about how to handle the manuscript. Patrick also joined in some of the early proofing of the material being typed.

With a "revised" manuscript in hand, I then contacted Norman again with questions about how to proceed from this point. He was now in a different place in his life and said he would be happy to help get the book ready for publication. We worked steadily together, mostly by computer and e-mail, over the next several months. There was still a good deal of reworking and editing of material to be done, along with the final polishing of the writing itself. This was really Norman's work to do, because he had put so much work into the original chapters and he knew the material so well.

The volume at hand offers a picture of Sam's and my activities as we settled in Española and became involved with the community and its people, with whom we have been privileged to be associated over these many years. My hope is that this work offers a contribution to the historical literature of northern New Mexico, and recognizes many of the people who have contributed to its development.

—Isabel Ziegler

*Samuel R. Ziegler, MD and Isabel H. Ziegler, As Told To Norman P. Ziegler, PhD, RN, *For The Soul Is Dead That Slumbers: The Adventures Of A Surgeon And His Wife In Northern New Mexico (1946-1996), A Memoir* (3209 West 70th Street, Shreveport, LA 71108: K's Kopy It, First Printing, June, 1999, Copyright TX-5-195-139, April 17, 2000).

ACKNOWLEDGEMENTS

Many wonderful people have contributed to this work. I would like first to acknowledge those who have helped to bring this current volume into being. These individuals include Hal and Mary Beth Shymkus for their diligence in reading and helping to edit down the original Memoir, Annie Lovato for her typing skills, Patrick Day for being a computer whiz kid, my son, Norman, for his continued energy and skill with words in helping to polish the final manuscript, and Norman's wife, Judy, for helping with final editing and proofreading.

I am also aware of the generous help Sam and I received from many individuals during the writing of the original Memoir, *For The Soul Is Dead That Slumbers*. I want to include mention of these people in these Acknowledgements as well. They all took an interest in the subject matter of the book. Their contributions ranged from assisting with information about local history, people, civic events and family genealogy, to the location of important documents, the identification of people in old photographs, and the lending of a "collective" memory about things that happened in the past in order that our memories be better and more complete. I thank all of these individuals for their help. Included in this group are:

Helen Akes, Mary Agnes Anderson, Jose V. (Butch) Archuleta, Martha Bell, Gertrude Brashar and her sister, Margery Falkenbach, Adelle Davis Carpenter, Ramona Vigil Chavez, Lois Coover, Irene Cole, Jim Cleary, Richard Cook, Darryl Froman, Janet Fowler, Pres Garcia, Lee Gerlach, Janice Harvey Hamrick, Suzette Hausner, Mildred Healy, Art and Joyce Houle, Elizabeth Margulis Hendryson, Elberta Honstein, Kue Hunter, C. L. Hunter, Janet Harvey Hussong, Ann Lilystrand, Theresa Lonewolf, Ralph and Elaine Marshall, Barbara Martin, Robin McKinney Martin, Roberta McDaniel, David and Linda Meyer, Dora Giron Mitchell, McGee

Mortuary, Phoebe Pack, Sandra Pomeroy, Natalie Powers, Evelyn Boren Sadlier, Kathy and Gilbert Sanchez, Terry Sanchez, Catherine Scheutzel, Olga Velasco Scott Newsom, Pauline Toeves, Duddy Wilder, and Dr. Merle and Anna Mae Yordy.

I appreciate the help Sam and I received from Tony Montoya, Chairman, Rio Arriba County Republican Party, David Roybal, columnist for *The New Mexican*, staff at the City Library of Santa Fe, Lupé Martinez with the New Mexico State Library in Santa Fe, Orlando Romero, New Mexico Palace of the Governors historian, Janet Johnson, University of New Mexico Medical Center Library historian, Marilyn Fletcher of the University of New Mexico Newspaper Project, Marilyn Reeves, Library Director of the Española Public Library, and Bob and Ruth Trapp of the *Rio Grande SUN*, in locating information from newspapers and other local publications.

I send a special thanks once again to Carol Rachlin of Oklahoma City, Oklahoma who took on the role of editorial consultant with the original Memoir and worked closely with my son, Norman, on a range of tasks necessary to bring that work to completion.

Finally, I share my appreciation for members of my family and the roles they played in helping with the original Memoir:

My grandson, Samuel T. Ziegler, for his contributions as a reader;

My daughter, Julia Ziegler Langille, for review of content, help in remembering, and continued moral support through the long labor of that work;

My son, Sam Ziegler, Jr., for assistance with format and content, and for his fine work with the printing of that book;

My son, Norman Ziegler, for his diligence and energy in seeing that this work was first begun and then completed and for his skill as a writer, and my daughter-in-law, Judy, Norman's wife, for her contributions as a reader and editor, and her technical expertise with computers, in helping with the production of a manuscript.

If I have omitted mention of anyone who should be recognized, the error is unintentional and I humbly apologize.

1

THE TRIP WEST

In early May of 1946, Sam and I set out from Dayton, Ohio on our trek across country. We had with us in our little Model A Ford coupe just our two sons, Sammy and Norman, and our few meager belongings.

We arrived in Santa Fe late one afternoon, about the time we needed to find someplace to eat and settle down for the night. Our Duncan Hines Lodging book, which we used a good deal, displayed an interesting advertisement for The Bishop's Lodge, located north of town on Bishop's Lodge Road. We set out with some anticipation in search of it. We drove for what seemed quite a distance, not really knowing where we were, when we spotted some riders on horseback and stopped to ask directions. They said to turn the car around and follow them. They were headed directly for the Lodge.

We spent our first night at Bishop's Lodge, and it was a lovely introduction to New Mexico. The accommodations were excellent, and we had both dinner that evening and breakfast the next morning in the lodge dining room. Mrs. James Thorpe, Sr., owner, was a most gracious host. There were plenty of grassy, wide open spaces for the boys to run and play, and we managed a trip to the corral to talk with the wranglers. This was our first close look at the adobe houses common to northern New Mexico.

The next day we drove north to Santa Cruz and McCurdy Mission School. I was not prepared for the area that greeted us. It was a hot day. The land was dry, dusty, and without grass. We turned off the two-lane paved highway from Santa Fe and made our way along a bumpy, unpaved dirt road barely two lanes wide. We saw no one except the lone figure of a little, stooped Hispanic woman trudging along beside the road. She was wearing a long black dress with a black shawl draped over her head. The adobe buildings along the way all appeared in varying states of disrepair, some with plaster falling off the walls. The area seemed to me a foreign land not welcoming in any way. I remember saying to Sam half seriously, half in jest, "Sam, please don't stop. Just keep going."

A staff member at McCurdy School directed us to the Española State Bank in the nearby community of Española where we were to meet with Clarence Brashar, the bank manager. He was to give us directions to Ghost Ranch. We drove the few miles from Santa Cruz across the Rio Grande into town.

The main street of Española, Oñate Street, was a broad, two-lane paved road lined with large, old cottonwood trees that made a canopy over the street. There were several large homes with large front lawns along the street. The street ran for half a mile west from the river and then divided at a "Y" intersection. One branch turned south toward Santa Clara Pueblo and then continued on to Los Alamos. The other branch moved north, running another half mile through town to the community of Hernandez and then on to Abiquiu.

A few commercial buildings were in evidence—a local bar named Lalo's and the Granada Hotel, a nice looking hard plastered, adobe colored building situated on the north side of the street near the center of town. Nearby at the west end of town was the Hunter Motor Company and across the street from it, Cook's Española Mercantile and Simpson's Food and Meat Market.

The Bond Willard Mercantile was situated along the west side of the "Y." It was a flat white front, rather non-descript building with a post office attached. We went in the store to use the post office and were confronted with an old style general mercantile store. Stacks of canned goods, fabrics and items of all kinds and sizes from safety pins to wood burning stoves lined the shelves and counters and walls. A small grocery store was part of the general store, and out back was a lumber yard. We saw a number of local men, Indians as well as Hispanics and an occasional Anglo, standing around talking and leaning on the counters. Most were munching on food or smoking, and conversing in small groups. Everyone paused to inspect us, their stares making us feel conspicuous.

A railroad station for the Denver and Rio Grande Railroad sat along the north branch of the "Y" just up the street from Bond Willard Mercantile and across from Hunter Motor Company. We later learned from Arthur Pack that the railroad was known locally as the "Chili Line." Arthur Pack himself called it the "Dangerous and Rough Going Line." It was built in the days of the railroad wars to compete with the Santa Fe Railroad. Its bed followed the route of U.S. Highway 285 south from the Colorado border to Tres Piedras, then turned into the canyon of the Rio Grande near Embudo. It paralleled the river down to Española, then traveled in a circuitous route on south past the Santa Clara Pueblo to Santa Fe. Its narrow gauge tracks ran north and south through the west end of town. Just to the north of the station was the United Brethren Church, an ancient, rundown two story structure badly in need of repairs.

Across from the station and on the south side of main street, the Española State Bank was housed in a long narrow building, not far from the train tracks. Salazar's Bar and the Rio Grande Café were at the west end of town along the Los Alamos Highway. The café was run by Bernie Archuleta and known for its excellent northern New Mexico food. Beyond the café was a large, old adobe building used as a meeting place for the Women's Club and for various town meetings.

Clarence Brashar was one of the first people we met in Española, and our introduction at the bank began a close and valued friendship that lasted many years. Clarence welcomed us with a warm smile and pleasant inquiries about us and our trip. He had been expecting us, he said, and made every effort to be helpful.

The bank was an antique structure with a single entrance into a narrow interior, with two barred teller cages to one side and a pair of tellers wearing green eye-shades like in a movie from the 1920s. They were busy behind their teller cages, spotlighted beneath the glare of close overhead lamps. A thin veil of cigarette smoke filled the air as occasional customers shuffled in and out the lone, narrow front door.

I felt as if we were on a western movie set as we stood there in the bank. I half expected a bank robber to burst on the scene or at least a stage coach to arrive with dust flying and a guard leaping down, rifle in hand, to dash inside with the money bags. The entire environment depicted a quaint little western town, something quite unique to us.

We were soon on our way to Ghost Ranch. Our path led along the narrow road north past Hernandez, Medanales and Abiquiu. I continued to have mixed feelings as we drove, but I knew Sam was quite excited.

We viewed the fields of alfalfa and small orchards with apple, plum and cherry trees along the Chama Highway. We occasionally saw a man leaning on a shovel in the middle of a large field. We later learned that this man was out irrigating, guiding water into the ditches and channels in the fields.

Though I felt apprehensive, I also sensed growing wonder at this land so new to me. I again voice my concerns to Sam. But he only answered, "Let's just wait and talk with the Packs. Then we can decide."

Much of my disenchantment stemmed from being unprepared for what I saw. None of my friends and acquaintances had known anything about New Mexico. Their only reference to a "Santa Cruz" had been to the resort area of Santa Cruz, California. I somehow reached the illogical conclusion that the Santa Cruz to which we were going was similar. I had spent the long months of the war expecting to return to Ohio, to a place I knew, where we had planned to establish a home and raise our family. I had become accustomed to the idea that we would have access to the opportunities a community like Youngstown or the college town of Westerville, where I grew up, would offer.

In retrospect, I know that I was raised in sheltered and protected surroundings. If I had visited New Mexico or been schooled about its cultures and languages, I would have been better prepared. As it was, having to adjust my whole outlook about my life and hopes in such a short time proved difficult for me.

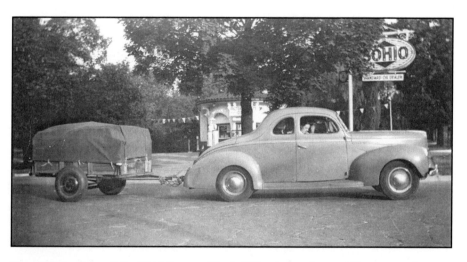

New Mexico bound. In 1946 Sam and Isabel Ziegler, with sons Norman and Sammy, set out from Dayton, Ohio, headed for a new home in New Mexico. Their Ford Cabriolet towed all their belongings.

2

GHOST RANCH WITH
ARTHUR AND PHOEBE PACK

Leaving the village of Abiquiu we rounded a curve and came up a hill where a whole different world came into view. It was a dramatic change of landscape with wide open spaces surrounded by cliffs and sandstone ridges in colors of salmon, purple and yellow. An endless vista surrounded us with a beautiful, turquoise blue sky gracing the land.

We turned off the highway onto a dirt road that took us to Ghost Ranch. At its entrance the Ghost Ranch logo with the skull of a steer greeted us on a weathered wrought iron gate. The skull and the name Ghost Ranch stirred apprehension in me. But after traveling several miles along the dirt road as it wandered up and down across the plain and through arroyo beds and washes, we came upon a welcome sight of what looked like civilization—green alfalfa fields stretching out before a large ranch house set upon a rise overlooking a small valley.

Arthur and Phoebe Pack welcomed us warmly and I soon felt much more at ease. We came to know both Arthur and Phoebe well. Arthur had attended Williams College in Williamstown, Massachusetts. He was brilliant and eccentric at school, the latter characteristic making him unacceptable to many of the more conservative students on campus. He was not invited to join any of the campus fraternities, so he struck out and founded his own fraternity in retaliation, a story he loved to tell.

He became involved in business ventures of his own, following in his father's footsteps. Arthur's father had become a national leader in the promotion of forestry and resource conservation through his involvement with the Louisiana pine lands. He dedicated considerable sums of money from the profits on these lands to these efforts. Arthur launched a new monthly publication called Nature Magazine with his father's backing, which he used as a platform for issues relating to forest conservation and wildlife research.

Arthur's wife, Phoebe, was a lovely, outgoing and energetic woman who could match Arthur's dealings stride for stride. It was she who had implanted the idea of building a hospital in Arthur's mind. Phoebe told us the idea had taken form at the time of her daughter, little Phoebe's, birth in St. Vincent Hospital in Santa Fe.

At this time, Phoebe had asked herself, "Where are the hospitals in Rio Arriba County? They don't exist. Where are the women having their children? At home. No help. Maybe a midwife. There is nothing north of Santa Fe."

When Arthur asked Phoebe what she thought they should do with the money he had inherited, she replied, "Oh, I know what I want to do with it. They need a hospital in northern New Mexico. These people need help!"

I had heard before our first visit to Ghost Ranch that the monies for a hospital were coming from the sale of a stamp collection that Arthur's father had assembled. I knew none of the details about this collection, about its worth or how it was sold to raise money. I have since learned from Arthur's own writing the fascinating story behind these stamps. Arthur wrote:

> All his life, my father had seriously pursued the hobby of stamp collecting, and he accumulated several specialized collections which were exhibited all over the world. At various times some years before his death, he would write me a letter on my birthday or at Christmas, giving to me the completed stamp albums of Australia or Canada or some other country in which he had specialized. And these collections had won, in my name, an assortment of gold medals. Except at exhibition times, the stamps had now lain in a safe-deposit vault in New York for more than ten years. They must be worth something. Actually, their value turned out to be unbelievable, for the German rape of Europe had caused accumulated wealth to take flight and seek investment in works of art and other non depreciable assets, including rare stamps. With the aid of America's leading philatelic dealers, these collections were carefully arranged for private auction sale. In the end, they brought in all the money needed for a complete hospital of thirty beds, together with operating rooms, laboratory, food facility, offices, and nurses' home.
>
> Providence weaves strange pictures. My father had told me

that some of the earliest engraved postage stamps were produced in Australia, where England formerly sent its convicted forgers. These exiled convicts made hand-engraved stone plates, each separate stamp naturally showing slight differences from the next. It had been my father's self-imposed task, by going over thousands of specimens found in pairs and blocks on old envelopes, to reconstruct the original plate; and his years of work, usually in bed after retiring for the night, eventually resulted in an illustrated book about the first half-length portrait of Queen Victoria two pence stamps. This monumental collection was sold to the British Crown. Thus it seemed to me that some forger of long ago had unknowingly laid the cornerstone of a hospital on the other side of the world from his place of exile.[1]

Arthur and Phoebe turned to the United Brethren Church to accomplish the building of the hospital. "We didn't know who to put in charge of the hospital," Phoebe told me. "Arthur's and my idea was that the church would know of someone, and they did."

The Packs were aware of the work of the United Brethren Church in northern New Mexico through its mission schools in Velarde, Alcalde, Vallecitos and Santa Cruz. They sent their children and those of the ranch employees to the McCurdy Mission School in Santa Cruz during the war, when gas was rationed, and were impressed with the quality of education the children received. From our discussions with the Packs, we also learned that the church had already formulated general plans to organize and run a "health center" in the Española Valley. It seemed there could be a meeting of minds. The Packs wanted the church to administer the hospital. They needed only a qualified doctor who was willing to help design and run it.

Sam was very open with the Packs and explained that during the war when he had been close to death, he wondered why he was spared. Then he began to feel that perhaps helping to build this hospital was the purpose for which he had been chosen. Taking care of the wounded under primitive wartime conditions gave him a sense of great accomplishment and value. He would look into the eyes of many soldiers and see the pain and fear in their faces replaced with relief and trust as he cared for them. He wanted to serve now in a similar capacity, where he was needed and where he could use all his training and skills. Building a new hospital offered such a challenge to him.

Sam was convinced that the Packs were good, well-intentioned people, committed to building the hospital. They had the necessary finances and the will to carry forward this task. He gained a better understanding of the need for medical care in the area from talking with them, and of the opportunities available to establish a medical practice of his own.

Arthur and Phoebe were excellent hosts and I knew which way Sam was leaning. At the end of our two-day visit, Sam agreed to take a two year sabbatical from a surgical group in Youngstown, Ohio which he had joined, and come out to New Mexico to help Arthur build his hospital.

I am sure that Sam's thinking was influenced by the beautiful scenery of the ranch grounds and the rustic leisure of the Packs' life. Arthur was also a very persuasive salesman. I realized then that my life was going to change. I had to prepare for new surroundings, unfamiliar people and a far different culture than the conservative environment of Ohio to which I was accustomed. I had never seen Sam so energized and enthusiastic, however, and I began to feel that our move to New Mexico had somehow been predestined. I know that Sam felt that all he had accomplished up to this time had been but a long preparation for what was to come.

Arthur and Phoebe Pack, owners of Ghost Ranch, located north of Abiquiu, provided funding for the establishment of the Española Hospital in 1948.

3

OUR RETURN TO NEW MEXICO

The Packs had promised us a house upon our return and we left the ranch comforted with the knowledge we would have a place to live.

Arthur also said to me, "Now, Isabel, the old saying goes, once you get a little bit of the Rio Grande sand in your shoes, you will never want to leave New Mexico. We are looking forward to your return." He hugged us warmly and wished us God speed.

During our return to Ohio I was incommunicative most of the way. Thinking about picking up our roots and leaving family and friends kept preying on my mind, even though it would only be for a two year sabbatical. Sam recognized my concern and took me to New York for a second honeymoon. I shed more tears of uncertainty on the way, but once there, we both relaxed. New York was a nice, romantic interlude. We stayed at the Henry Hudson Hotel and danced to the music of Vincent Lopez. We took in a lot of the sights of New York. We gave ourselves up to the city and had a wonderful time. That diversion eased my mind and helped me get ready for what was to come.

When we returned to Dayton, Sam contacted Dr. Kilbourne who was a long-standing family friend, about whether there might be a surgeon with whom he could work while he continued to think about his decision to go to New Mexico. Dr. Kilbourne introduced him to Dr. John Austin, a respected general surgeon, with a young associate named Dr. Gene Damstra. They had been looking for a third member for their group who could relieve Dr. Damstra of his role as assistant to Dr. Austin and free him to take more of his own cases. They took Sam in for the several weeks we remained in Dayton. Sam assisted Dr. Austin on a number of his cases.

Dr. Damstra and Sam were about the same age and had much in

common. They got along well. Both Dr. Damstra and Dr. Austin wanted Sam to stay in Dayton and go into practice with them after having worked with him for only a few weeks. They made Sam a reasonable offer, but by then, Sam had firmly decided on New Mexico.

In mid-July of 1946, we packed the few things we had in a small trailer that we pulled behind our little Ford coupe, and got ready to leave for New Mexico. Our belongings consisted of an army footlocker filled with clothing and household goods, and a baby bed. We placed the mattress on top of the jump seats in the back of the car for the boys to sleep, and stacked in an abundance of diapers. We had only two other possessions—a dark walnut Duncan Phyfe coffee table and a small radio.

We arrived back in New Mexico on July 28 and immediately contacted Arthur Pack. He invited us to stay at Ghost Ranch until suitable accommodations could be located in Española. He had been talking with Buck Denton, a local real estate agent, about one of the homes Buck had built. He felt that the house was overpriced at $10,000 and refused to buy it. It was the only house for sale in Española. We agreed, upon inspection, that the price seemed too high for the property.

The lack of other housing was explained by the area. In 1946, most of Santa Cruz and Española was farm land, alfalfa fields, and orchards. The small adobe houses placed here and there on plots near the road were family dwellings that expanded as families grew. When a child was born, a new room was added to accommodate the addition. There was no demand for commercial or rental property such as we needed. The words of an early observer in Española reflect this situation:

> The Española Valley in the early days was the most picturesque valley I have ever seen. No buildings but adobe flat roofs, not many windows, an adobe oven in the yard. Houses were often built in one long string sometimes six or seven rooms. This housed the immediate family and when a son married, he too had a house with his parents.[2]

Arthur put us up in a house at the Ranch called the Johnson House which had been built several years before for R.W. Johnson, president of Johnson & Johnson of New Brunswick, New Jersey. It was a large, two story adobe structure, well designed for a family. The Johnsons used it to escape from all the cares of their busy lives in the East. We really rattled about in that house with only the four of us and our meager possessions. We had more space than we needed, but we enjoyed the luxury of the surroundings and the convenience.

We remained at the ranch for over a month with Sam traveling back and forth to Española and Santa Fe as needed. We had been at the ranch only a few days when Arthur Pack knocked on the door of our house late one afternoon. He said in a distressed voice, "Sam, I need you to come down and look at our ranch foreman, Herman Hall. He seems to be having quite a stomach ache." Sam examined Herman and the signs all pointed to an acute appendicitis. He said they needed to get Herman to a hospital as soon as possible.

Arthur and Sam drove Herman to Santa Fe to the St. Vincent Hospital that afternoon. Sam had not yet taken exams for licensure to practice in New Mexico, and had no hospital privileges. He managed to get in touch with a surgeon by the name of Earl LeGrand Ward. Dr. Ward scheduled Herman for surgery, and he allowed Sam to do the operation. Sam removed a red-hot appendix, a portion of which was gangrenous. He said later that it would probably have ruptured by morning.

Sam and Arthur returned to the Ranch that night, and there was some excitement when Sam made his way back to the Johnson House. I had stayed awake, unable to sleep. Around three o'clock, I heard an eerie howl and footsteps running along the road outside. I realized the steps must be Sam's. I raced downstairs from the bedroom and had the front door open for him as he rushed through. The house was about three hundred yards up the valley from the main ranch house, the dirt path to the house passing along an alfalfa field which was fenced off with some barbed wire. The night was moonlit and full of shadows. I remember Sam saying that about halfway to the house, he heard a sound like someone being strangled and then a blood curdling howl that scared the daylights out of him. He took off a mile a minute racing for the house and was so thankful I had heard him and had the door open. He said he had cold chills running down his spine. It did not particularly comfort either of us to remember that Arthur had said if we heard a sound like a woman being strangled and then a howl, not to worry. It was just a coyote. Sam thought the coyote he heard had not been more than three feet from him across the barbed wire in the field. We came to accept the eerie coyote howling as part of Northern New

Mexico background and missed it when we moved into town.

We met a number of interesting people through the Packs. Georgia O'Keeffe, the artist, was one of the first. She soon chose Sam as her physician, and also became a personal friend of ours.

Arthur, being an avid pilot and having two airplanes of his own, had built a runway at the ranch. People whom he knew would fly in and out from all over the country. We missed meeting Charles A. Lindbergh, the American aviator who made the first solo nonstop flight across the Atlantic Ocean on May 20-21, 1927. He had flown his private plane into the ranch while we were taking care of errands in Española, and then left just as quickly. He had flown in to say, "Hello." Arthur said, on our return, that we had missed him by just fifteen minutes. A sad moment, for we would have considered meeting him special indeed.

The Packs had annual guests who took up residence in the cottages set about the canyon. A woman by the name of Abby Whiteside from New York was one such guest. She was a musician and teacher of piano who came yearly to give lessons to the ranch children. She stayed in the guest house called the Garden Cottage. All of the cottages had their special names. One was called the School House, and another the Ghost House, which had special stories connected with it.

Arthur's original house on the ranch was the Rancho de los Burros, located some three miles away from the present ranch headquarters. It had a wonderful view of the Jemez mountain range and the Pedernal. The house was one he built before he married Phoebe and was the house that he eventually gave to Georgia O'Keeffe. Georgia loved the dry barren atmosphere, and told us many times that its surroundings were perfect for her. She could walk out and collect her rocks and dried bones and pieces of wood. Arthur and Phoebe felt that the house was too isolated, and moved further up into the canyon where they had a better source of water to irrigate the alfalfa fields. They were more centrally located and better able to manage the cattle ranch.

The land was full of beautiful and graceful deer and antelope which Arthur brought in to populate it. Arthur told us, with a pained expression, that people driving along the highway would stop and kill the animals just for the sport of killing, then drive off and leave them lie. It was difficult for me to imagine such behavior.

We became good friends with the staff at the ranch. We got to know the Halls very early because of Herman's appendicitis. Herman's wife, Jimmie, was the ranch cook. She greeted us at each meal and went out of her way to accommodate our wishes for food. Herman was a quiet spoken man of medium height and stocky build, much weathered and toughened from his work with horses and cattle, while Jimmie was a large, husky woman a half-head taller, with a deep booming voice. She had dark auburn hair, lips always bright with red lipstick, and flashing black eyes. She was very much in charge when she was at work in the kitchen, and she let you know it. But her brusque manner hid a very soft well-intentioned interior. Yvonne, their daughter, eventually became Sam's secretary and bookkeeper at his office in Española.

Margaret McKinley was the nursemaid who worked especially with little Phoebe. She had been married to a man named Jack McKinley, who worked as a cowhand on the ranch. Jack had abandoned his family some years before, and during the 1920s and 1930s became the leader of a notorious gang in Rio Arriba County called the Mano Negra (Black Hand) or Night Riders. The gang terrorized northern New Mexico rustling horses and cattle and robbing homes.

Bill Martin, a well-known detective in northern New Mexico who became a friend of Sam's and mine, was responsible for capturing this Jack McKinley and putting him behind bars. McKinley received a sentence of 6 to 30 years in the state penitentiary. Martin described McKinley in his book, *Bill Martin, American*, in the following manner:

> He was a big man, and he wore a big black sombrero. He had on a leather jacket, clean khaki pants, and a red handkerchief about his neck. On his hip rested a single-action six-shooter. I recognized him as a tough hombre and a smooth talker with whom I'd had some dealings in the past.[3]

Martin also noted, however:

> McKinley made a beaded belt for me while he was in prison, hoping, no doubt, I would put in a good word for him. Needless to say, I did nothing of the kind. However, his wife didn't have to wait

fifty years for him, or even thirty. He was out in five years and so were those who had longer minimum sentences.[4]

Margaret stayed on at the ranch with her three children, a younger daughter and two older sons who worked with Herman Hall as wranglers. We often went riding with them and they taught us eastern greenhorns something about handling horses. Later, we would return to the ranch at roundup time and help with the cattle drives. What an experience for us! We quickly came to appreciate the qualities of good cowponies who had a sixth sense about cattle that we did not have.

Maw Burnam, her husband, Blackie, and her daughter, Dorothy, were three of the more colorful members of the ranch community. Maw Burnam was a big strapping woman who had charge of all the laundry. She had a very rough exterior like Jimmie Hall. The way she talked sometimes scared the wits out of me. I needed a lot of help with laundry because of two small children. I had a portable washer only large enough for some diapers and lingerie. I asked Arthur one day if Maw could help me with my washing. Arthur said with a chuckle, "Well, just go ask her. She will try and bite your head off, but she is really a very gentle person and will probably agree to help you." I took my requests to her, and sure enough, she said, "Bring your things on over."

Blackie was a small, quiet man who appeared rather retiring. I think he had to be to live with Maw. He did a little gardening and maintenance around the ranch. I especially liked what Arthur wrote about Blackie, which seemed to explain a good deal about the man. Arthur said that in the early 1930s, shortly after they had moved to the ranch, they heard about a man named "Blackie" who lived up near Copper Canyon. He was supposed to be a poacher and an escaped murderer, and people voiced great fear of him. His house back in the canyon was "a veritable fortress, built mostly underground but with loopholes for his rifle above the surface." Blackie himself made quite a sight, "an unshaven, black-haired little man."

But Arthur noted:

> Blackie turned out to be no bad man, but a little fellow with a dreadful fear of imaginary persons whom he called "them," a spin-

ner of wild tales which he invariably came to believe himself. Part Oklahoma Indian, part Anglo, and part no-one-knows-what, he had fled from his own inability to adapt to reality.

Arthur felt that Maw was a piece of the same cloth, and strong as an ox.[5]

Blackie spent part of his time helping his daughter, Dorothy, who was in charge of the sheep, goats and burros. Dorothy was a pleasant young woman in her late twenties when we first came to know her. She was born with clubbed feet. The Packs helped arrange surgery for her, and afterwards she managed reasonably well with her disability. She had a level sense about animals and yard work, and we became good friends.

Dr. U.P. Hovermale, General Secretary of Home Missions for the United Brethren Church, and his wife came to visit while we were living at the ranch. Phoebe told an amusing story about the Hovermales. Dr. Hovermale and his wife had come out to Ghost Ranch to discuss plans for the new hospital sometime before our arrival. Both were tee-totalers by religious conviction, Mrs. Hovermale in particular very reluctant to accept a gift from Arthur and Phoebe because they smoked and drank. Arthur and Phoebe invited board members of the hospital to a dinner while they were there. Phoebe gave orders to the kitchen to send trays of drinks for the guests, with plenty of juice for the Hovermales in addition to scotch and bourbon for those who wanted it. Phoebe said, as she related the story, "This is my place. They may do what they want and I'll give them what they want. But this is my place and I run it."

Clarence Brashar was one of those present. He sipped on a whiskey and water at dinner, and who should sit next to him but Dr. Hovermale and his wife. Phoebe said to us, "Well, Dr. Hovermale sits down next to me and to Clarence, and he looked at Clarence's drink, and then he leaned over and whispered in my ear, 'I wish I could have one of those, too.'" Phoebe laughed when she remembered this exchange.

Mrs. Hovermale repeated her feeling at dinner that she did not believe the church should accept a gift from anybody who drank liquor or smoked. Phoebe remarked in turn, very tongue in cheek, "Well, Mrs. Hovermale, of course, the Catholic Church would love to have this gift. They are looking for a way to get it. It would be very easy to offer it to them." She heard a yelp as she finished speaking, and realized that Dr. Hovermale had just pinched his wife.

Onate Street in the 1940s was a busy main thoroughfare. Looking east toward the Rio Grande, one sees Hunter Motor on the left. The Granada Hotel was just past it. On the right, barely visible was the popular Zia Club, Cook's Española Mercantile and Española State Bank.

4

STARTING OUT AT McCURDY

Española had no doctor for awhile in the 1890s and the local railroad station agent filled the role with the practice of what was known as Dr. Humprey's Homeopathic Medicine. Mrs. Mary Evans of Española described the situation this way:

> Samuel McBride, the station agent, kept a supply of medicine and knew pretty well how to administer it. This was called homeopathic medicine. It came in a box and there was a chart to show which medicine went with which pain. For instance, if one was suffering with a stomach ache, the chart showed to use pills No. 99. Mr. McBride administered per the chart. If a patient show [*sic*] up with a tooth ache, a pill of a different number was administered.[6]

Sam was constantly on the road to Española while we lived at Ghost Ranch, trying to meet people and figure out how to get his practice started. He also went to Santa Fe to take the state medical examinations in the basic sciences for licensure to practice in New Mexico. He told me about Angus Evans, owner of the Española Drug Store, and his wife, Reecie, and about Jennings Doak, the druggist, and his wife, Verina. I was curious about what brought these people to a town like Española.

We became acquainted with Rev. Paul McFarland and his wife, Jessie. They were involved in the mission field and lived at the McCurdy Mission School where Paul worked as maintenance foreman and served as minister to several of the outlying mission churches. He had a good deal of construction experience and would later become closely involved with the building and administration of the Española hospital.

The McFarlands took us for a drive one Sunday. We went north out of Española toward Taos. We passed through Alcalde and Velarde and then into the gorge of the Rio Grande. The narrow gauge tracks of the "Chili Line" had run along this gorge on the far side of the river. The tracks still remained in the town of Española, but we learned that they were taken up in the gorge shortly before World War II. We crossed an old wooden bridge spanning the Rio Grande near Embudo, and headed north out of the gorge and across the high mesa to Petaca and then on to Vallecitos.

The McFarlands talked excitedly about the beauty of the gorge as we passed through it. The canyon of the gorge was filled with volcanic outcroppings and huge boulders, their colors somber black and gunmetal gray amidst the greens and yellows of the sage, the sparse grasses, and an occasional cottonwood tree. Up on the tableland, the gorge dropped several hundred feet below the level of the plain. The breadth of the land along the high mesa near Taos left me in wonder. The Taos mountains rose hazy blue in the distance, and the gorge formed a dark crevice moving through the center of the plain. The land had an isolated, primitive quality strange to me. We stopped at the mission church at Vallecitos, where a handful of people were attending service.

Miss Lula Clippinger, the missionary there, had been in the mission field since 1920. She told us she had first lived at Alcalde, then moved to Vallecitos. She served as minister in the church, held prayer meetings, taught in the local mission school and acted as counselor for anyone in need. She said she was also a general handyman, providing maintenance for the church and the school. She laughed that she could repair a heating system as easily as a roof. She was a capable person with a difficult task as a Protestant minister in a predominantly Catholic area. I admired her efforts and her devotion to her work.

The Sunday drive with the McFarlands encouraged us to explore further. Our next drive took us to Chimayo and the Sanctuario de Chimayo. The local churches with their thick adobe walls and high ceilings spanned with great vigas (log beams, often hand hewn with an ax) were new to us. This Sanctuario was most impressive and gave us a feeling of warmth and repose. We entered the room by the place of the holy mud, and noticed the niches in the walls filled with baby shoes and crutches and pictures of people who had been healed by the mud. We stood in some awe, trying to comprehend the meaning of this sacred place for the local people.

In the front of the Sanctuario was a graveyard with rows of grave sites, many marked with crude wooden crosses. The crosses were dried and weathered from the elements, and sat in varying degrees of uprightness over the graves. A few graves had small stone markers with the engravings faded and worn. The stone markers were of interest because of the names and dates on them. Many were quite old. Occasional bouquets of artificial flowers adorned the crosses and stones or sat atop a grave mound.

Other grave sites we had seen along the country roads in New Mexico were barren because of the lack of water, the only adornments being wooden crosses laden with bouquets of artificial flowers. All had a compelling simplicity.

We realized how Sam might be able to get his practice started through a happenstance involving the McFarlands. We had driven down to Española one day to go shopping, and as we returned to Ghost Ranch, a storm came up. The three mile drive back from the highway to the ranch headquarters proved treacherous for us. There were several arroyos along the way, the last one before reaching the ranch proper being wide and deep. We found it running high from bank to bank with muddy, foaming water. We knew that we would not be able to ford it, even if we waited several hours for the water to subside. The arroyo bottom would be too muddy and soft for passage until the next day. Seeing no alternative, we returned to McCurdy and asked the McFarlands if we could spend the night there. They smiled knowingly when they heard our story about the arroyos, and welcomed us with open arms. They arranged for us to stay in the McCurdy clinic.

We inspected the clinic closely while we were there. It was a single story rectangular structure, its long side set in a north-south direction some twenty-five to thirty feet back from and parallel to the dirt road that ran through Santa Cruz and past McCurdy school. Its exterior was a rough, grayish white cement stucco. It was divided into nine small rooms inside, with a wide hallway running lengthwise down the middle, and another shorter hallway leading off the center hall to a front door. The front door was set in the center of the east-facing wall fronting the road. Each room measured some 12' x 18'. Four of these were set up as patient wards, with four beds each. A room in the northwest corner served as the school nurse's bedroom. It had a closet and bathroom attached. There was a kitchen and living room. The living room had additional closet space and a bathroom. Lastly, there were two smaller rooms off the entry hallway for offices. A third bathroom with a tub, located off the center hall near the nurse's bedroom, was for patient use.

We began thinking more about the clinic after our return to Ghost Ranch the next day. It seemed unlikely now that Arthur Pack would be able to find suitable housing for us, and I finally suggested that we move to McCurdy. The clinic would provide space for us to live and a place where Sam could work. I thought the school nurse might be able to help him with his patients. Sam agreed and asked the church for permission to move. We made the transition to McCurdy in the middle of August.

We occupied two rooms at the clinic. We converted the small living room with its attached bathroom in the southwest corner into a combination living room-dining room for the four of us, and took over a four-bed ward in the southeast corner of the clinic, directly across from the living room, for a bedroom. This arrangement left three rooms with four beds each for patient care. We reserved one for sick students from McCurdy. The other two were set aside for labor and delivery and for general patient care. We had no idea what the actual needs would be. We had to begin the best way we could under the circumstances.

We organized the remaining rooms in the clinic in the most efficient manner possible. The entry hallway inside the front door served as the waiting room with several chairs placed along the south wall. Adjacent to it was the small open reception area. Sam used an adjoining small room as an examining and consultation room. He had his desk for paperwork, and within a short time we were able to get a telephone hooked up for him there.

The clinic fortunately had a fairly decent kitchen. We shared the kitchen with school nurse, Miss Lillian Moffat, who was quite upset with our coming. We had invaded her space and taken over her living room for our quarters. She allowed us only one small metal cupboard in the kitchen for our groceries and utensils, reserving the remaining cabinets and storage for herself.

I am afraid we disturbed Miss Moffat's private world. She had apparently been content simply to put thermometers into children's mouths and to consider this activity the extent of her involvement with medicine. She refused to have anything to do with Sam's patients.

Sam received a phone call from the Secretary of State's office very soon after we moved into the clinic in late-August of 1946, informing him that he had passed the basic science exams and been granted a temporary license to practice medicine in New Mexico.

The first night after opening the practice was a memorable one. We had finally gotten to bed around midnight after unpacking and arranging things in the clinic, when we heard a knock at the front door.

It was Reecie Evans standing there with a man. Reecie apologized for disturbing us so late, then introduced Buck Voyles, local grocer and butcher, and said they considered coming in the morning, but Buck decided he could not wait any longer. Buck lived just near Reecie and had imposed on her, knowing Reecie was acquainted with us. Buck looked sheepish and stammered something about an infected leg. He told Sam that several days prior, he had been cutting meat at the store when his butcher knife slipped out of his hand and slashed his leg. He had washed the cut with soap and water and then covered it, thinking no further attention necessary. Soon after, he developed fever and chills, and began to have a great deal of pain in his leg. Sam was able to lance an abscess in Buck's thigh which helped to relieve pressure and reduce his pain. After cleaning and dressing the wound, he sent Buck home with orders for continuous hot compresses, bed rest and elevation of the leg along with some medicine he had available. I believe it was penicillin. Buck did well, though it took him some days to heal.

Sam and I came to know Buck and his wife, Lela George, well. Buck was the owner and manager of Voyles Market, and a member of the Española School Board. The market was originally located on Riverside Drive, later on Oñate Street, in downtown Española. It was the best place in town for meats and vegetables. We were always greeted with a friendly, warm, "Hello, what can I do for you today?" whenever we walked into the store. I was a bit wide-eyed about Lela George's name when I was first introduced to her. She smiled broadly and said, "Never mind. My father wanted a boy and got a girl, so he gave me a name for each." Most of us called her "George." The Voyles daughter, Jeanne, was a beautiful girl with a lovely smile and I was privileged to sing at her wedding.

Sam's first emergency had occurred at night. Another happened not long after when we heard a knock at the back door of the clinic around 8 p.m. The back entrance was cloaked in shadow, its only illumination from the back door window. We looked out and saw a small stooped figure of a man with a black hat slouched on his head, partially obscuring a bearded face.

Sam and I were not acquainted with the people of the area yet, nor were we accustomed to their habits. This man's presence placed us in a bit of a quandary. I finally said, "OK, Sam, answer the door." The man standing there very humbly stepped inside, pulling his hat from his head as he entered. He said in broken English that his brother was ill and needed help, and would "*el doctor* please to come."

I realized Sam was uneasy with this situation, but he put on his jacket and said that if he were not back by a certain time, I was to get in touch with someone and organize a search. The man waited patiently as Sam followed him outside to his old truck which he had left running in the yard. Sam was to follow him in our car. Sam said they drove some distance down McCurdy road, with him wondering about his first house call under these strange and very new circumstances.

As Sam later told the story, they pulled into a plot where there was an old adobe house, the only light visible through the windows coming from candles and a lone kerosene lamp. He was escorted into one of the rooms to see the patient, a small, elderly man who lay on a bed in the center of the room, writhing in pain. Several members of the family were crowded around him. Sam was able to do a quick examination of his abdomen. He also took a quick history from family members and learned that the man had similar recurring episodes of pain. The only communication was a quick nod of heads and short phrases in broken English. As Sam worked, the man relaxed somewhat and seemed to be in less discomfort. Sam had only a few basic drugs with him in his medicine bag. He left a suitable one with orders for the man to be given plenty of fluids to drink and for the family to apply a hot water bottle to his abdomen. Sam said he felt very relieved because he was able to assure himself first that the man did not have a hot appendix, but a colicky type of pain.

Sam came to know the patient's family well in time, and took care of other members of his family for many years. They were good people to know.

I thought that these two evening emergency calls might be typical of Sam's practice and was quite close to being right. My own doctoring was limited to soothing Sam with a refreshing drink and positive conversation.

I remember the poem Sam taped in the front of the record book that he kept in his small office. He said it was one he had come across while he was an intern or resident. He felt it helped him to keep things in perspective. It read:

God and the Doctor alike we adore,

Just on the brink of danger and not before.
The danger o're, and all requited,
God is forgotten, the Doctor slighted.

It was amazing how fast the word spread that there was a doctor at the McCurdy clinic in Santa Cruz. Sam's practice grew steadily and the first of many obstetrical patients arrived in early October. We used one of the ward rooms for her, doing the delivery right on a regular bed where the woman labored. Sam did not have a delivery table or any stirrups, and had to call on some of the older female students from the school to come and hold legs.

I was the one who gave drop ether for anesthesia. Many of the women who came to the clinic were primiparas (women having their first child), and they often went through difficult labors. They delivered naturally for the most part. Some pretty fancy obstetrical work was done despite the limitations in the facilities.

We were indeed busy. Sometimes there would be two or three women in labor at the same time along with sick students occupying beds. There became less and less room for the students as more beds were needed for local people and babies, and we then had to move out of our ward room and into the living room in order to make more space available. That made four wards again for patients. We had to reserve some beds for students in case they became sick, so we kept one ward for them. Of the three remaining wards, we set aside one for labor and delivery, with the others serving as combination wards for delivered mothers, babies, and for other types of patients. We sometimes had problems figuring out how to keep the men separate from the women and provide some semblance of privacy, but we managed.

I helped organize a small nursery. We made bassinets for the babies out of orange crates, just like the one our son, Norman, had slept in at Warner Robins, Georgia during the war. Our experience with him gave us the idea of using these crates in the absence of anything else. They worked very well.

We then heard about a delivery table that was available in Gallup, New Mexico. Wayne Corbin, the McCurdy principal, volunteered to go and pick it up. He took a couple of boys from the school and the school truck, and drove to Gallup to get the table from the Sisters of Charity. It cost five dollars. They returned around eleven o'clock that night, just as one of Sam's

———— 37 ————

patients was about to deliver. We quickly washed and cleaned the table and set it up so the woman was able to use it. It was a godsend. Having an old, beat-up table with leg stirrups, brought on a truck late at night, was a very exciting moment in our lives. A lot of babies were born on that table at the clinic.

Sam had clinic office hours on Tuesdays, Thursdays and Saturdays from 10 a.m. to 8 p.m. Mondays, Wednesdays and Fridays were surgical days. I pitched in and helped run the office. Sam had organized his files for patients in a very simple way, combining his history and physical with his charge records all in one. We kept them in a small file in the examining room. I played the part of receptionist, nurse and assistant to Sam as an anesthetist giving ether to women in labor, in addition to trying to take care of two small children. I simply did what was required. It was a matter of necessity. I performed as a nurse because there was no one else to help. I did everything according to Sam's instructions. "Drop the ether faster," he would say. "No, drop it slower." We would laugh, trying to comfort each other and the patient. I also cared for the babies, getting up to tend them and the patients at night.

Our two boys, Sammy and Norman, walked around and played in the hall on their own. They took care of themselves much of the time. They were pretty good about staying in the clinic. I think the patients helped to entertain them. They soon came down with measles, wandering in and out of patient rooms and coming in contact with so many people. After the measles, they caught the chicken pox. They looked like two starving, neglected waifs.

We were cooking our own meals and doing our own laundry. I had to cart the laundry over to the basement of the girl's dorm and do it there along with the teachers and others at the school. We were dependent on a few old-fashioned electric washing machines. I did not have to go back to using plungers (as during the war), but half of the time there was no hot water, and then the washers kept breaking down, so much of the laundry ended up being done by hand. Then, after washing, I had to drag the wet laundry up the steps from the basement and across the parking lot to the clothes lines by the clinic to hang it up to dry.

One gray, dreary day there was once again no hot water for laundry and only one washer to use because the others needed repairs. It was too much for me. I was infuriated at having to put up with such conditions and broke down crying in a state of exhaustion. I wonder now that Sam did not divorce me for all my ranting and raving. Instead, he took me to the New Mexican Room at the La Fonda hotel in Santa Fe for dinner and dancing. What a wonderful support he was to me that night.

I became involved with activities at McCurdy Mission School right after settling in at the clinic. I was amazed that the Pep Club for the school was made up only of girls. I thought some of the boys who were not playing football or basketball should be included. I expressed this opinion in passing to some of the teachers. The school soon asked if I would take charge of the Pep Club that fall. I said that I would.

The Pep Club was comprised of a committee to plan activities, and four cheerleaders. Membership overlapped with Committee members Patty McCracken, Adelita Cordova, Susanna Velarde and Virginia Young, and Cheerleaders Patty McCracken, Adelita Cordova, Barbara McKinley and Cande Cordova. They were all enthusiastic, cooperative and most willing to work to make the club a success.

We began by doing small things like selling soft drinks and popcorn at the school games in order to raise some money. We encouraged boys who were not involved in athletics to join the cheering squad and help support the team, and they seemed glad to have the opportunity to participate. We held the first bonfire and rally the school had ever had the night before the homecoming football game, cheering the players on to victory. The whole team turned out along with the coach and the teachers. It was a successful event, and the kids really loved it.

The end of the school year was upon us almost before I knew it. We had saved a little money and the Pep Club committee met to decide how to spend it for the benefit of the students. The committee thought it would be nice to have a fiesta. They said they could hold it at the school gymnasium, with a fiesta queen to be chosen from the senior class and lots of entertainment for the students.

We presented the idea to the students and teachers. Everyone thought a fiesta would be great. They all seemed excited about entertainment for the students. Suggestions for booths came from all sides with ideas for dart throwing and tossing a penny into a dish that had been placed in a bucket of water. The students also wanted a couple to do the Mexican Hat Dance in honor of the fiesta queen. A boy and girl from among the students said they knew how to do the dance, and there were several boys who could play guitars.

Our enthusiasm was soon dampened, however. The school administration felt that allowing the Mexican Hat Dance would be consenting to "dancing," which was not permitted at the school, and it raised an eyebrow at the penny toss because of concerns about gambling. We had to eliminate these activities completely.

I became upset as I saw our plans being systematically dismantled. I took my concerns to the principal. We exchanged some strong words. I drew attention to the fact that he thought nothing about standing on a chair in the gym raffling off a quilt for the Church Ladies Aid Society, while he would not allow a penny toss at the fiesta. I was not able to change any opinions, and was about to throw in the towel. But Sam said I should go through with the fiesta. So that is what I did.

Helen Sanchez was elected Fiesta Queen. We selected a long white formal dress for her to wear. I sewed sequins on it in order to glamorize it a little. Norman and Sammy, who were four and five years old, were dressed up in Mexican costumes with big Mexican hats and serapes, and they carried the queen's train as she proceeded across the floor of the gymnasium during the ceremony. Toby Atencio, one of the students, played his guitar for the procession. There were game booths set up around the gymnasium and lots of food to eat. The students had a great time, and the fiesta went off very well. It became an annual event at the school.

I enjoyed the students with whom I worked. It was a pleasure to be involved with them. They presented me with a beautiful silver and turquoise barrette for my hair at the end of the year. My hair was long and very dark then, and I wore it in a chignon. The barrette was the perfect accent. I have always cherished this gift.

I met some interesting teachers at McCurdy School. Helen Butterwick was one. She was the Director of Music at McCurdy School and directed the McCurdy Church choir. She had a beautiful soprano voice and handled the music program well. She and I sang solo parts in the cantatas that were given at Easter and Christmas and had a good time singing together. She worked with me to help organize a choir for special performances among the members of the two United Brethren Churches, McCurdy and Valley View.

Irene Cole, who worked in the administrative offices at McCurdy, was another lovely individual. She became McCurdy's school historian when she retired.

I had been acting as receptionist for Sam, but this proved difficult with two small children to care for and other needs at the clinic. Mrs. Mela Velarde from Santa Cruz walked into the clinic one day and said, "I'm here to help in any way I can, and I don't expect to be paid for it." She did help us, and she remained until Sam was able to find someone to act as reception-ist and examining assistant. He eventually hired Lorraine Freestone, who worked out well. We will always be grateful for the help that Mrs. Velarde provided.

I felt we did reasonably well at the clinic, and at least our housing was provided. Many patients paid their bills with chickens, eggs, fresh-caught trout and garden produce, so we had plenty to eat. I remember going to Sam and saying, "Look, we have $49.00 on the books." That amount was pretty good at two bucks an office visit.

We received a small check from the Home Mission Board to help tide us over. They paid Sam four hundred dollars a month, and had an agree-ment with the church to pay this stipend until Sam had enough of a private practice to support our family. In less than a year we notified the Board of Home Missions that their stipend was no longer needed. In October of 1947, Sam opened his own office in Española.

Miss Moffat, the school nurse, was responsible for the care of sick students. She decided to leave the school in the latter part of 1947. Several young, well-trained nurses sent out by the Board of Home Missions had begun to arrive by this time. These nurses lived in the student dorm at McCurdy, and for the most part, were able to adjust to the situation at the clinic and worked out well.

One of the first to arrive was Carol Miller. She came with some stars in her eyes about how things would be, but she was a good clinic nurse and did not mind the long hours that were required. She later took a short training course in Chicago as a nurse anesthetist, and eventually became Sam's anesthetist at the hospital. She did a very credible job.

We also received help from girls at the school. Helen Sanchez and Mabel Gutierrez were very dependable workers. They assisted with deliver-ies, fed the babies and did other general care as needed for the patients.

One other girl who helped at this time was Dora Giron, who later became a special member of our family. These girls often came on short notice, allowing me an occasional moment with Sam when he drove to St. Vincent Hospital in Santa Fe to make his evening rounds. Their willingness to help was a saving grace.

There was so much that Sam and I had to do even with additional help. We did not turn off the coffee pot until two o'clock in the morning on most days, and we averaged about four hours of sleep a night. Patients would often come in and visit with me when I would be in the kitchen trying to fix something to eat or to put the coffee pot on again. They were wonderful to us. One patient gave us a big, live turkey. We also received some goat's buttermilk which I had never tasted before. I must say that drinking it was unusual for me, to say the least.

Some of the patients would sit and talk about things going on locally. There were two women in particular, Mrs. Merhege and Mrs. Richards, who laughed and talked while they waited to see Dr. Sam. They had twenty-three children between the two of them, I think. They were two of the happiest women I have ever been around. They really were fun. I think going to the doctor's office was a special outing for them.

We began to feel a little better organized toward the end of the year, in late November and early December, but we continued to live under rather trying circumstances.

Clyde Hunter was a prominent local businessman we met and liked. Clyde owned the Ford Dealership. We went to see him about a new car soon after we settled at McCurdy. Our 1936 Ford coupe whose tires had been retreaded seven times, was on its last legs. Clyde was concerned that a physician have a trustworthy car. New cars were hard to come by in those days, but Clyde had a shiny new maroon 4-door Ford Sedan delivered to the clinic in a matter of two or three weeks. What an exciting moment it was for us! Clyde went out of his way to help arrange financing with Clarence Brashar and the Española State Bank.

Clyde was a pleasant, outgoing man who was very community minded and ran a flourishing auto dealership. We bought many cars from Hunter Motor Company over the following years. Clyde and his wife, Angie, lived on Oñate Street in downtown Española, directly across from where Sam later had his office.

5

Notes from My Diary

I managed to keep a diary for a short time while at the clinic. I thought that someday my family might be interested in our experiences, especially around the holidays that first year we were there:

Santa Cruz, New Mexico
December 14, 1946

My helper, a young native girl, arrived at 9:00 a.m. to assist with the children and routine Saturday cleaning. Her duties were completed by 3:30 p.m., at which time I bathed the boys in the "twin" rinse tubs—much to their liking.

By 4:30 p.m. we were dressed and ready to join Sam on a few house calls and a hurried trip to Santa Fe hospital to see a patient.

A last minute decision was to take "Bootsy," our cat, in the car with us. This proved to be a mistake as she became carsick.

One visit on a back dirt road to the home of a heart patient was interesting. The road was the worst "washboard" I have been on in New Mexico. However, the view of the mountains was beautiful and the patient, whom we thought would not recover, progressed amazingly well.

We reached Santa Fe by dark. The lights of the city are a beautiful sight in this unpopulated country. Christmas trees lighted here and there intrigued the boys, and questions of Santa Claus immediately followed.

We reached home at 7:30 p.m. As we were to be at the Arthur Gallup's for dinner at 8:00 p.m.—we had to rush. Last minute patients—as usual—so we were late.

Gallup's home sits west of the Bond house up on the hill overlooking Española and the valley, with a fine view of the mountains to the east. Cars were lined up before the house and upon arrival, we were greeted by twelve other people. Included were:

Arthur and Margaret or "Jimmy" Gallup[7]
Frank and Inez Willard[8]
Hubert and Alice Prather[9]
Clyde and Angie Hunter[10]
Howard and Ruth Barbee[11]
Mr. and Mrs. W. P. Cook[12] [Pop and Sarah]

Following a candlelight buffet dinner, the women were given corsages of mistletoe, and then bridge foursomes were started. This was all a new experience for us. In my family, we had our Christmas tree with candles, and family gathering at Christmas time with music and singing. Here we were introduced to a social gathering, one of our first. It was a lovely adobe home. Jimmy Gallup served spiced tea (spiked in the kitchen on request) and sandwiches. The smell of burning piñon in the fireplace was wonderful.

We were introduced to a blending of cultures and learned about Spanish *colchas* and *colcha* embroidery this night. Jimmy and Arthur Gallup had a number of very interesting *colchas*. They brought them out to show along with some Navajo rugs and Hopi Kachinas. They also talked to us about local house construction and the use of vigas (log beams, often hand hewn with an ax) and latillas (made of peeled aspen poles or split cedars placed crosswise on the vigas and fitted carefully together to make an airtight ceiling) for the flat roofs.

The group was congenial and interesting and before we realized, the clock struck midnight.

As the group said "good-night" and started their various ways, we could see the moon high above the crest of the mountains.

Sunday evening, December 15, 1946
Sunday morning and the usual rush for Sunday school and church. We stayed at the church while Sam made house calls.

Following church, we all drove out to Ghost Ranch to spend the afternoon. Our usual relaxing chats with Arthur and Phoebe, and then Arthur took Sam and me for a ride in his new jeep.

Out across the east pasture in search of the antelope. Down over steep rocky slopes, but not an antelope in sight. However, we had an opportunity to observe some of the large rock formations more closely and realize their true beauty. "Ship rock" in particular is quite spectacular.

Shortly after dinner we started for home with two tired little boys who had ridden the burros that afternoon.

December 17, 1946

Christmas dinner and dance of the Lion's Club and Chamber of Commerce of Española. I donned my black formal—a bit extreme, but nice! And with my Japanese comb in my hair and beautiful orchid from my handsome escort—we were on our way.

Dinner practically never arrived, but when it did, it was very good. Music was fair and we danced a few dances.

Wednesday, December 18, 1946

Another busy office day. Sammy and his chicken pox are worse. Norman's case is light, but Sammy is really suffering. Oh, for a good night's rest!

Thursday, December 19, 1946

Have held Sammy practically all day. This is supposedly Sam's day off, but he has been busy all day. Choir practice tonight went off very well.

Friday, December 20, 1946

Christmas program at McCurdy. I sang two numbers with the choir and helped with the Hallelujah Chorus.

Brashars came over following the program and we met their youngest son, Bobby. We had coffee and crackers and cheese and fun talking.

Sunday, December 22, 1946

Sang alto solo part in "A Wondrous Song" at church. I guess it was alright. Sam wasn't there to hear me because of Sammy's being sick.

Norman and I joined the Brashars and drove to El Rito mountains where we cut our greens and Christmas trees. We cooked a dinner over an open fire and had a grand time. Only disappointment—Sam and Sammy couldn't be there, too.

After a quick supper, off to the church to help with the Christmas music for our church program. It was very simple and lovely.

Monday, December 23, 1946

A routine day. In the evening during office hours, a patient visited me. I pray my life will never be as difficult as hers, but may my courage and determination be as great or greater.

While visiting, I dipped my Christmas candies in chocolate. The boys took advantage of my being busy and had a hilarious time with water, etc. It is good to hear them laugh and know that Sammy is better.

Tuesday, December 24, 1946

Patients of Sam's have been very generous.

Canned fruits are always welcome. Our gift chicken caused quite a show. Maybe the doctor's surgery will aid in dispatching the next one. Sammy and Norman were eager and excited spectators and helped to pull the feathers!

After dinner, Santa Claus (Rev. Albert Brandstetter) came all dressed up to see the boys. That was a real treat for me as well as for them. Sammy shook hands immediately and talked with great seriousness!

Sam and I and the Brashars drove out to San Juan Pueblo to see the Indian dances. Not so much excitement as usual we were told, but . . . the governor of the pueblo invited us into his home and had a group of five Indians dance the "Turtle Dance" for us.

It was quite a thrill—their moccasins were heavily beaded and they had turtle shells tied to their legs along with bells. Their chanting was wonderful.

Back to the Brashars for food and coffee and home at midnight.

Wednesday, December, 25, 1946

Christmas day and quite different from last year. The boys awoke at 8:00 a.m. and dashed to see if Santa had been here. They were as pleased as were we.

Breakfast at the McCurdy dorm—then home for a turkey dinner.

Sick calls regardless of Christmas. The boys and I went along.

Sam not feeling too well.

Thursday, December 26, 1946

Out to Ghost Ranch in order for Sam to accomplish some work. I don't seem to know what my job is. I offer to help at the wrong times. Much to my surprise we stayed all night. I was just too tired to join the late discussion with the Packs.

December 27, 1946

Left Ghost Ranch after breakfast. Stopped in town to have hair set and bought new black slacks and shirt steer head design. My first Southwestern outfit from Charlene Hartell's dress shop [The Hart Shop], in Española.

December 28,1946

Formal dinner party at La Fonda [Hotel in Santa Fe] with the obstetrician, Dr. Lathrop, and his wife, the Packs, and close friends of the Lathrops, Mr. & Mrs. Walters. Grand time.

Love the quaint native dances at La Fonda. Varsoviana, schottische, and polka. The local people love to polka!

Sunday, December 29,1946

Sunday school—church. Then took Mr. and Mrs. McFarland to La Fonda for dinner. Afterwards drove out to Black Mesa Ranch to see Mrs. Rachel Lilystrand. She took us through her house which I was delighted to see. A very old adobe. Returned home and Sam made calls.

December 31

Left for Ghost Ranch at 3:30 p.m. Settled ourselves in our cabin. After supper, stayed with boys until asleep and Brashars arrived. Celebrated New Year with smoked turkey, hors d'oeuvres, etc. Quiet, congenial gathering enjoyed by all.

A Note about *Colcha* Embroidery

Sam's and my exposure to *colchas* at the Christmas dinner party with the Gallups greatly impressed us with the quality of the workmanship.

Margaret Gallup had several interesting *colchas*, some quite old and unusual. One had scenes of a Penitente march. These works of embroidery sparked our interest in the Hispanic culture of northern New Mexico.

Fortunately, Sam and I were able to purchase our first *colcha* some years later through Henrietta Harris, an antique dealer in Santa Fe. Its previous owner was the poet, Alice Corbin Henderson of Tesuque, New Mexico.

Some time after our dinner with the Gallups, we came to know Mary Cabot Wheelwright of the Boston Cabots. Mary had founded the Wheelwright Museum of American Indians in Santa Fe in 1937 with Hosteen Klah. Through her we gained an additional perspective about *colcha*s.

Mary was a patient of Sam's and we were guests of hers at Hacienda de Los Luceros on several occasions. The Hacienda is situated on the earliest documented Spanish Land Grant in the Southwest. It served as the county seat of Rio Arriba in the early New Mexico Territorial Period. The Hacienda is historically and architecturally unique, being the last remaining two-story adobe residence dating from the early Hispanic colonization of the United States. Its adobe walls are three feet thick. Mary lived there from 1923 until her death in 1957.

The first time we were invited to dinner at Hacienda de Los Luceros, Sam and I were ushered up a staircase to the second floor. There in the central hall, we were graciously greeted by Mary Wheelwright before entering the spacious Sala de recibo (living room). As I started to step forward into the Sala, I was astonished to see *colcha*s being used as rugs on the floor. I was afraid to walk on them and I said so to Mary. She turned to me and said, "My dear, do not be afraid to walk on them. I have many." Whereupon, she opened a beautiful, hand-carved wooden chest there in the hall to show me, saying, "When I first came here, the local Spanish ranchers came by often with *colcha*s to sell, and so I purchased a great number."

We moved on into the living room that covered the width of the Hacienda. Mary's concert grand piano was there and the magnificent fireplace could be seen as we were greeted by other guests. We also noticed the portal that encircled the second floor.

We had a delightful evening at Hacienda de Los Luceros, but as

I write, I cannot help but think of the one *colcha* we have which is being carefully preserved as a wall hanging!

I have learned something about *colcha* embroidery and the history of this craft in New Mexico since our purchase.

The word *colcha* is a Spanish term meaning "bed covering" or "coverlet." It refers to a form of embroidery indigenous to northern New Mexico and southern Colorado characterized by the use of wool embroidery in a self-couching stitch. This stitch consists of a long laid thread with small tying stitches set at regular intervals over the laid stitch. The same yarn is used for both the laid and the couching elements. The couching elements themselves can be set in varying patterns to add design and texture to the stitch and to the overall pattern of the embroidery.

The early *colcha* embroidery was wool-on-wool. The ground fabric was a *sabanilla*. *Sabanilla* means "small sheet," diminutive of *saban*. It can also mean "a piece of linen," "altar piece," and in some regions of Spain, a "headpiece worn by women." The *sabanilla* material was a white fabric of plain, balanced weave made of handspun wool. The typical loom width was about thirty inches, so that two to three panels of cloth were typically seamed as backing for the *colcha* embroidery. Selvedges were left intact while the ends were cut, turned and hemmed, then finished on all sides with simple woolen fringe. For the wool-on-wool pieces, the backing was fully covered with embroidery stitches creating the effect of another fabric entirely.

The earliest embroidered pieces appear to have been altar cloths, bedspreads and table covers. Designs included a wide range of geometric and floral patterns influenced not only by Mexican patterns, but also by European and Eastern motifs based on exposure to items brought in the colonial trade such as cotton chintz fabrics from India and other textile pieces from the Philippines and China.

Our *colcha* has two rows with four unusual diamond shapes in each row. Inside each diamond is a primitive floral pattern.

The period of the early wool-on-wool embroidery dates roughly from 1750 to 1825. A cotton ground came into use following this period, with the wool embroidery only partially covering the ground.

The early *colcha* works were a household art, and pieces still available are both rare and unusual. Yarns for the embroidery were all made of hand-carded wool, and they were dyed with local vegetable dyes and a few imported dyes. The dyes were set with mordanting following a preparatory washing of the wool itself. The mordant, either a chrome or aluminum alum, acted to combine with the dyestuff to form an insoluble compound or lake and produce a fixed color. [13]

6

THE TELEPHONE

Obtaining a telephone in Española proved to be an interesting experience. A man by the name of Frankenburger managed the local branch of the telephone company, which was housed in a small, run-down office in downtown Española. Sam approached him about a phone, telling him he was a physician and needed one for his practice. He was not the most hospitable person, and remarked in an off-hand manner, "Well, I don't see why you need a phone. All they seem to be good for is the women, who call up and gossip all day long."

I guess I was the one who convinced Mr. Frankenburger that a doctor really did need a phone. I told him that a life sometimes hung in the balance and saving it depended on a phone call to a doctor. He finally said, "Well, if you can find a phone, I will try and string some wire for you."

Roy Carpenter found a phone for us. Roy was an aspiring minister who preached in some of the rural churches in the area, and also worked as a handyman at McCurdy school. He was a robust fellow of great sincerity and affability, who liked to think of himself as a jack-of-all-trades. He had done the wiring at the clinic which was something to behold. When we went in the front door and turned on the light switch just inside, the kitchen lights went on. When we went back and turned on the kitchen light, the hall light by the front door went on. Somehow, good intentions aside, he had twisted the wiring around.

Roy was the one who thought he knew where he might find a phone. He showed up with the box-like apparatus housing an old crank-type phone with a large horn mouthpiece. It had come out of one of the barns where they raised hogs and other livestock at the school. We had this phone hooked up at the clinic in no time.

The telephone switchboard and exchange was located in the Granada

Hotel in downtown Española. Florence Holmquist, a short, rather plump woman who always seemed to overflow with energy, owned the hotel. She drove around town in a flashy, big Cadillac which she handled with great expertise and a good-natured show of self-importance. Her husband, Carl, was a slender, nice looking man of quiet disposition, who was responsible for the upkeep of the hotel.

Florence ran the switchboard while also managing the hotel. The switchboard was located off the lobby, and when Florence heard the switchboard buzzing, she dropped whatever else she was doing and answered the phone. She closed down the exchange at nine o'clock each night but when Dr. Sam arrived in Española, she offered to keep the switch board open until midnight. This was an act of great kindness. She was very helpful to us. If people needed to get in touch with Sam after midnight, they had to come by the clinic and knock on the door. Often times, Sam would still be up.

It was not too long before a man named Smith bought the Española branch of the Telephone Company. He built a small telephone office in Riverside near the Rio Grande bridge, and brought in a woman named Ramona Vigil to manage the switchboard. Ramona was wonderful.

We did not have phone numbers. We just cranked the phone to get in touch with Ramona, the telephone operator, who would make any connection we needed. She answered with "Operator," and we would then say, "Ramona, get me so and so," and she would immediately connect us. If we were going out for an evening or for a longer period of time, Ramona asked that we let her know where we were going, and she transferred calls around until she got in touch with us. We called Ramona when we got back from an absence, and she was more than happy to fill us in on all the news and tell us about anything that needed to be taken care of. She would say to Sam, "Doctor, Mrs. so-and-so is sick," or "so-and-so went into labor," or "things have been pretty quiet this evening. There is nothing to worry about."

Sam had a small desk for paper work along with the old crank-type telephone for calls in his little examining room at the clinic. He remembers the time he picked up his stethoscope when the phone rang, and without thinking laid the stethoscope on a patient's chest, saying, "Dr. Ziegler speaking. Can I help you?" The patient almost jumped right out of his chair. Sam apologized and then picked up the phone. This was not the only time he put his stethoscope against a patient's chest and said, "Hello, Dr. Ziegler speaking." Being so busy with patients and preoccupied with trying to take care of everything and everyone may serve as an explanation.

We were able to find another phone for our house when we eventually moved across the street from the clinic. This phone was again an old Alexander Bell crank phone with a large horn mouthpiece and a big crank handle. The phone box itself was mounted on an oak panel that looked like one of the panels used to mount trophy animal heads. It was a kind of monstrosity! I was ashamed of it, so Sam put it in the hall closet where we could hardly hear it ring. We finally moved it to a place where it was more serviceable, and it remained our phone for some time.

The telephone company picked up this phone some years later for use in an historical display. It was a museum piece. I wish we still had it. We did not appreciate its authenticity.

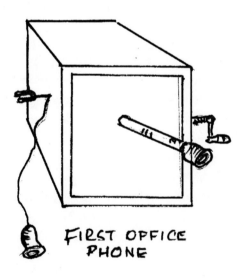

FIRST OFFICE
PHONE

Telephones were a luxury in Española in the 1940s. This is a sketch of the first telephone in Dr. Ziegler's office.

7

THE ESPAÑOLA UNITED BRETHREN CHURCH

We began attending the Española United Brethren Church shortly after our arrival. The church was housed in an old two story building near Hunter Motor Company in downtown Española. It sat on an unpaved side street now known as Railroad Avenue, along which the Chili Line had run. The sanctuary was on the second floor, with the first floor used for Sunday School classes and as a gathering place for dinners, banquets and other church social activities. The kitchen had a sink that drained poorly and a huge, black-iron coal-burning stove. The middle of the kitchen area was taken up with a large wooden work-table that allowed little room for the women to move about.

Shortly after we began attending the church, the ladies of the congregation became involved in a project to raise money for a new church. They were cooking and feeding every business organization in northern New Mexico. The women were busy and in demand because they had the reputation for being the best cooks in the area.

I began to help and came to know the women well. Their friendship was most welcome. I enjoyed one woman in particular. Her name was Susie Yates, the wife of Herb Yates, a local businessman. She was a jolly, good-natured person who was very warm spirited. She was also an excellent cook who loved food and had a wonderful time planning and supervising all the big dinners for the church.

Another woman who volunteered regularly was Charlene Hartell. Charlene joined right in with the effort and always seemed to make these times enjoyable. I came to recognize that she was an intelligent and resourceful woman. We have often "remembered," with some amusement, a near disaster that occurred one evening while we were getting ready to serve one of these dinners.

We had prepared a large baked ham. When it was done, one of the women went to remove it from the oven and place it on a carving platter set on the large wooden table that filled the center of the room. The narrow space between the table and the stove, the size of the ham and the intense heat from the oven all made it difficult for the woman to grasp the ham properly. It slipped out of her hands as she was moving it from the oven to the table, and slithered across the oil cloth that covered the table, landing with a great dull thud on the floor on the other side of the room.

All of us watched this accident unfold. We stood in a hushed silence as the ham hit the floor, trying to collect our wits and decide what to do. One woman who was quicker than the rest of us, was the first to the rescue. She marched over and artfully maneuvered the delinquent ham from the floor to the kitchen sink, where she proceeded to wash it clean. She then transferred it back to the table and patted if dry with a towel, remarking as she did with a sense of satisfaction, "There, that should do." She picked up a carving knife, and without wasting another moment, began to prepare the meat as if nothing had happened. The rest of us followed suit and went back into motion, glad someone had the presence of mind to handle the situation.

I had met Charlene in early 1947 when I began to explore Española. She had a dress shop on Oñate Street called The Hart Shop. I stopped in one day and introduced myself. Charlene immediately made me feel welcome and at ease. I liked her shop and thought her choice of name quite clever. I soon found a good looking pant suit which became my introduction to western wear. The suit had black slacks and a beige top with a black yolk of cactus designs embroidered on it. On the back was an embroidered steer head design. Our friends back in Ohio were not too sure of our move out West, so our first Christmas picture card was of our family in western attire, and I, of course, wore the western shirt from the Hart Shop.

Our minister, Rev. Albert L. Brandstetter, had come to the Valley in 1941. He originally served both the United Brethren Churches in Santa Cruz and Española, then became minister for the Española Church in 1946. Several of the United Brethren Churches in smaller outlying communities needed ministerial help at times, and our Rev. Brandstetter often helped there as well. He continued to serve as our minister until 1956. Rev. William Young, whose daughter had been in the McCurdy Pep Club with me, assumed duties for the Santa Cruz Church.

The Brandstetters opened their parsonage next to the church for Sunday School classes. Mrs. Brandstetter was a sweet woman who loved teaching the children. The Brandstetters also reached out to some of the smaller outlying communities, such as Velarde and Alcalde, that were in need of ministerial guidance and services. They were true missionaries. But I dare say, there were foreign missions that had better accommodations for their staff than were provided for the Brandstetters. The parsonage in which they lived was really quite dreadful!

One evening as we were coming out of church, Sammy and Norman heard a kitten crying. They looked and looked and finally saw that it was caught high in a tree at the front of the church. It was a little black kitten with one spot of white on its chin. We managed to get the kitten down from the tree, and the boys immediately wanted to adopt it. We tried to find an owner, but no one claimed it, so we kept the kitten. The boys named it Tar Baby and we gave it a good home. The little kitten grew into a beautiful long-haired mother cat, with fur similar to a Persian. She had many litters of kittens to the boys' delight. Tar Baby was very selective about her mates. She stayed with us for many years as a proud member of our household.

8

Our McCurdy House

As time passed, we found our living arrangements in the clinic more and more difficult. Trying to care for two small children in one room which served as our living, dining and sleeping quarters was too much. We had barely a semblance of family life with the constant interruptions to our routines and our privacy. Sam and I felt the increasing pressure. The growing numbers of patients simply added to the strain, making our situation unmanageable. We were near a crisis point, with me ready to leave if our situation did not change.

Paul McFarland had been aware of our difficulties and had discussed housing arrangements with the Church Board. He managed to convince the Board we needed a house in which we could live for at least five years. The house would be turned back to the Church afterwards, for use as a parsonage.

In the summer of 1947, Paul began construction on a house directly across the road from the clinic. He finished it within a short time, and we were able to move in the fall of that year. We stayed there for a year and a half.

The house was wonderful. It was a single story built on a square plan, with a separate living room and dining room, two bedrooms with a full bath between, and a nice kitchen. I remember when we moved in. I sat in the living room that first night and actually listened to the silence. It was so restful. We had been able to buy a Westinghouse automatic washing machine. I sat in front of that machine, motionless, the next day, watching it wash, rinse and spin out a full tub of laundry. The new machine was an absolutely unbelievable sight to me after what I had been through at the clinic, trying to get all the laundry done using those old machines and ringers. It was a miracle!

Shortly after our move into the new house, an incident occurred that almost ended Sam's surgical career. He was working in the living room down on his hands and knees waxing the oak flooring, when all of a sudden, he ran a large splinter about six inches long up into his left hand and wrist. The thought of this injury still sends chills down my spine. It pinned the tendons of his fourth and fifth fingers so he was unable to extend them at all. A tiny bit of the splinter, maybe a half inch, protruded out of his hand, and he could not pull it out. He was in considerable pain and feared the loss of his hand for surgery.

Bud Brashar, eldest son of Clarence Brashar, and his wife, Phyllis, happened to come by about this time. Bud immediately offered to help and assisted Sam across the road to the clinic, where Sam gave himself a shot of morphine to help control the pain. Bud took hold of the end of the splinter with a pair of strong forceps, and pulled out about one inch of it. The rest remained caught, having fish-hooked into the bones of his wrist.

Bud, Phyllis and I then put Sam into Bud's car and drove to St. Vincent Hospital in Santa Fe. We called Dr. Earl LeGrand Ward, who came in immediately and took Sam into surgery. Dr. Ward was finally able to remove all of the splinter. Sam bore a three inch scar that extended across his palm and wrist as a result of this near-tragic accident.

Our first formal callers were Major General Charles Corlett and his wife, Pauline. They came to visit us soon after we settled at McCurdy. They were very gracious people. They were so pleased that Sam had come to the Valley to establish his medical practice and would be involved with the building of the new hospital. They mentioned several times how important the new hospital was and how badly it was needed. Sam and I made every point of cultivating their friendship, and the Corletts helped us feel very much part of the social life in Española.

The General was quite a distinguished gentleman, very formal and military in his bearing, but he liked to be called "Pete" by his friends. He had many entertaining stories about his experiences growing up in the West and being in the military. He had served in both the First and Second World Wars in high commands, and during World War II he had worked closely with General Eisenhower. Pauline was a gracious woman who was proper according to protocol at all times. She had become knowledgeable about entertaining as a General's wife and gave beautiful dinner parties. It was always fun to go to Las Huertas ("The Gardens"), the Corlett's little ranch in Santa Cruz. I took a lot of pointers from Pauline.

I was interested to learn that the General's first wife was Amy Bond, daughter of Frank Bond of Española, whom he had married in 1917. Unfortunately, an early illness took Amy's life in 1926. A few years later, the General met and married Pauline Wherry, whom we knew in Española.

We attended the Ski High Stampede in Monte Vista, Colorado the summer of 1949 at the urging of General and Pauline Corlett, and Bruce and Estelle Hayter, who were all going. The Stampede was noted for its rodeo parade and its well-run rodeo with excellent bucking stock. We thought this a great suggestion and quickly made arrangements to go, all excited about the new adventure.

We followed the Corletts and the Hayters, convoy style, to Monte Vista the day before the activities were to begin. On arrival, we went to the home of General Corlett's brother, Claude Corlett, who was an attorney in Monte Vista. There we met Claude and his wife, Velma, and after a nice lunch with the Corletts, spent the afternoon shopping for proper rodeo attire including cowboy hats, boots, colorful western shirts and jeans. I am sure that when we appeared on the scene, we could easily be spotted as greenhorns, but that did not diminish our enthusiasm. The boys practiced walking bowlegged like they thought real cowboys walked, and we were on our way.

The parade the next morning began with beautiful floats and many horses and riders. The excitement of the morning came when Red Rider, the famous comic strip cowboy, and his Indian companion, Little Beaver, appeared walking along with their horses and occasionally stopping to shake hands with spectators and admirers along the way. Sammy and Norman were excited about meeting these characters, and they talked about them for months afterwards. Sam had his movie camera ready fortunately, and we have this important event recorded on film.

Sam was able to take me duck hunting near Monte Vista a few years later. The group we joined included Claude and General Corlett, Ted Van Solen, the well-known Santa Fe artist, and Dr. Mike Pijoan, who had joined Sam in practice a short time earlier. The men were nice to allow me to come. Going on a hunt was something I had always wanted to do. Sam took me to a shooting range in Española before we went, so I could practice with a shotgun. We then packed up our gear, prepared for the chilly fall weather, and were off. We stayed with Claude and Velma Corlett. Velma had a hearty, delicious breakfast ready for us at 4:00 a.m., and we then headed for the lake and our blind to wait for the ducks to fly in. The men set out decoys to entice them. It was exciting to wait for their arrival in the cold of the early morning. The sunrise was beautiful.

I was given the signal to shoot first when the ducks began to arrive. I took aim and shot first. In fact, I shot every shell that I had throughout the morning, but I never hit a duck. My only reward was a black and blue shoulder from the kick of the gun.

The men got their quotas, and Claude Corlett, who had lost his right arm in an accident as a child and shot perfectly well with his left, then turned to me after he winged a duck that we saw hit the water, and said, "Isabel, shoot that duck." I took aim again and hit the duck. Finally!

Claude commented afterward, "You aim perfectly, Isabel, but when the gun goes off and hits your shoulder from the kick, it moves just above the duck, so you have to aim low at the start."

How nice to tell me at the end of the hunt! It was a great experience regardless. I am sorry I did not have an opportunity to hunt again.

The Corletts gave us our first dog in Española in the fall of 1949. She was a beautiful Springer Spaniel with large brown and white spots and long, floppy ears. She had come from the dog the General kept with him when he was stationed in the Aleutian Islands. We called her Alaska ('Laska for short) for this reason. She ran out of the driveway into the street in front of a car one day in the summer of 1952, and was killed. The boys had been riding their bicycles down the driveway toward the street with her running ahead. I think she saved their lives. If she had not dashed out first, one of them might have been hit. We were saddened by her death, and buried her in the orchard by the house where she would remain close to us.

It was often late in the evening and dark outside when Sam finished his office hours at the clinic and returned home for the night. There were no street lights along the road nor any other lighting except the faint illumination from a house window here and there, and walking at night was often a little tricky. It was open range to make matters worse, with cows and horses wandering about at will on the roads. There were also no cattle guards along the roads to confine them. We chased them out of the yard by the house all the time, but it was a thankless task. They just came right back.

It was pitch black outside one night when Sam finished at the clinic. For some reason, he did not have a flashlight with him. The house was just across the road, and he probably did not think he would need it. He left the clinic and made his way slowly across the road. As he turned into the driveway and started up the short incline to the house, he walked right into the rear end of a horse. We do not know who was more surprised, the horse or Sam. They bolted in different directions as he gave a great shout which probably awakened the whole neighborhood. His pulse must have hit 120, and it took him several minutes to calm down. He had not seen the horse, nor had he heard it. It must have been coal black and just standing asleep at the side of the road. He was lucky it did not kick him, but it sure did scare him!

We slept in the front bedroom of the house which faced the road. One night, I kept saying, "There's someone outside the window." The window was on my side of the bed, and we had opened it, with just the screen latched shut. I kept poking Sam in the ribs, wanting him to do something. He listened and could not hear anything, and kept telling me there was no one outside. He just would not believe me, so I stuck my nose up to the screen to see what was there. Just as I peered out, there was loud "moooo" from a cow standing next to the screen. Talk about excitement! I tell you, I nearly jumped out of my skin. I flew back to the bed and threw the blankets over my head to hide. We burst out laughing and could hardly stop.

Gwen Pringle came to stay with us for a short time during the last months of her pregnancy. She and her husband, Dolph, had been classmates of mine at Otterbein College in Westerville, Ohio. Dolph had studied for the ministry and Gwen for a teaching position, and both had interests in the mission field. They decided northern New Mexico might be an interesting place to settle when they learned that Sam and I were here.

Dolph and Gwen actually arrived in Santa Cruz for a first visit on the very same day that Sam and I moved into McCurdy clinic. We heard their knock on the door that first evening as we were putting things away and trying to get straightened up. We were surprised to see them, and we were excited about their plans. Dolph was a nice looking, easy going man who blended well in most situations and made people feel at ease, and Gwen was always good natured. Sam and I knew they would do well in the mission field in New Mexico and we welcomed them.

The Pringles returned the following year. The United Brethren Church assigned Dolph to the Vallecitos area, where he took up residence. His ministerial work involved the three communities of Vallecitos, Petaca and La Madera. The roads in this area were narrow two-lane tracks often in disrepair, and many were not paved. Vallecitos was also some forty-five miles from Española. Dolph often had car trouble as he drove about the area, and he counted fifty-eight flat tires in two years.

When Gwen became pregnant with their second child, she and Dolph wanted Sam to deliver the baby. They asked if she could come from Vallecitos with their son, Billy, and live with us during her last month of pregnancy. We now had room to accommodate them both, and were glad to have her with us.

The last month passed quickly, with some adventures along the way. Billy was the same age as Sammy and Norman, and they played together in the field behind the house. One day Billy accidentally sat down in a patch of cactus. Poor little thing! Norman came running to the house calling that Billy had sat in some cactus and was hurt. We rushed out to help and found him walking very slowly back to the house with Sammy's assistance. He could hardly move his legs. We managed to get him across the street to the clinic, where Sam spent the next several hours pulling cactus needles out of his bottom and legs with a pair of tweezers. Believe me, he had a sore, red behind for some time.

Gwen's baby, Joe, was born at the clinic. I gave the anesthesia for the delivery. She had a difficult time with Joe because he weighed 10 lbs. Helping Gwen through her delivery was quite an experience for me.

Dolph and Gwen later settled at McCurdy. Dolph became the grade school principal while continuing his ministerial work. Gwen was the Home Economics teacher and took over my responsibilities with the Pep Club.

One of our babysitters while we lived at the house across from the clinic, was a young high school girl by the name of Jackie Gibson. Jackie was the daughter of Ova and Jack Gibson who lived in the Fairview area. She was an active, cheerful girl with dark, curly, short hair, who soon became a favorite person at the house.

Jackie loved to ride horses. She would come down to baby-sit and bring her horse with her. She had a big black Quarter horse, really a nice horse to see. She managed this horse beautifully, and he was very gentle. The boys were four and five years old, and she took them riding around the yard and down the street. There were several acres of open land by the house, so there was plenty of space to ride. The boys loved the horse. Jackie's guidance was the first riding instruction they received.

Dorothy Burnam brought an old white burro named Blanca down from Ghost Ranch to stay with us soon after Jackie began letting the boys ride. Blanca was thirty-five years old, very patient and perfect for the boys to sit on and plod around the yard. The boys had a wonderful time. Jackie helped with Blanca when she came to take care of the boys. I rode Blanca occasionally, but she was a little broad in the back for me from all our good feeding. Blanca liked to come up to the front porch and rest her haunches against the window sill while she relaxed. She made a very picturesque sight.

My relatives started coming out West once we were settled in the new house across from the clinic. My mother and father were able to come to New Mexico in 1948, shortly before Mother died in 1950. My sister, Martha, her husband, Harold Bell, and their two children, Larry and Linda, also came as did my sister, Paula, her husband, Arthur Williams, and their three sons, Lee, Denny and Leslie. I think Larry Bell fell in love with New Mexico from the time he came when he was three years old. He eventually returned and became a prominent surgeon in the Valley.

I remember sitting outside on the small patio behind the house with everyone there. I can see my mother now. She was frail even then. I knew that she sensed my discomfort in adjusting to New Mexico, and was aware of the trials we had been through over the last months. She felt strongly that Sam had undertaken a great responsibility and that I must be behind him one hundred percent. I felt I had been doing that, with a little grumbling on the side.

My relatives came each year and spent their whole vacations at our house. They fell in love with the area. We were able to see the points of local interest when they visited, and they could not say enough nice things about New Mexico. I learned more about the local area as I spent time taking them sightseeing. Pots of vegetable soup, beans and chili were always on the stove. We kept things simple, so we had lots of time to explore.

On an early trip to Truchas with my sister Martha, and her husband, Harold, I remember seeing a bucket brigade that was just beginning to break up. There had been a fire in an old barn along the road. Men and boys were still lined up with buckets in their hands which they passed from one to the other. We were amazed at the efficiency of the line and the great effort made to control the fire.

9

DR. SAM STARTS HIS PRACTICE

There were only seven doctors in the Española area in 1946 when Sam began his practice. The seven included four Doctors of Medicine (MDs) and three Doctors of Osteopathy (D.O.s). The group served a population of some 40,000 people in the northern part of the state. This area included not only Española and Santa Cruz with their combined population of about three thousand, but all of the small outlying villages of Alcalde, Velarde, Hernandez, Truchas, Chimayo, Petaca, Vallecitos and others, in addition to the local Indian pueblos of Santa Clara, San Juan and San Ildefonso.

Ernest Lee, MD was a general practitioner in his eighties and dying of prostate cancer. He passed away in October of 1946.

Orval Nesbit, MD was a general practitioner in his late fifties with a small country practice. He was a competent physician doing an occasional appendectomy, some hernia repairs, and very basic orthopaedic work setting fractures, in addition to sewing up lacerations along with his general practice. He used the facilities at the Fairview Clinic osteopathic hospital for his surgery. The Clinic was a fifteen-bed hospital located on the Taos Highway.

Dr. Nesbit had a massive coronary in May of 1947. He was so traumatized by his heart attack that he retired from practice shortly after his recovery and moved to Albuquerque.

A third doctor, Tobias Espinoza, MD, was a Hispanic gentleman in his late sixties. He appeared frail in stature and walked with a slight hesitating step, but he bore himself with dignity and was always refined in appearance. He dressed immaculately, sported a thin white beard and had a pleasant demeanor. Dr. Espinoza conducted his practice from his office on Oñate Street in downtown Española, not far from the Granada Hotel. His waiting room was full of older Hispanic patients who had been with him for many years. He was respected by his patients and much devoted to them.

Dr. Espinoza maintained an active interest in local medical affairs until his retirement. Whenever there were state or county medical functions, he would come in the accompaniment of his beautiful daughter, Felicitas. Dr. Espinoza came from a family of well-educated, professional people, much respected throughout the state of New Mexico.

Drs. Nora Hubbard, Fred Wise and Earl Lindsley were the three osteopathic physicians (D.O.s) in Española. Drs. Hubbard and Wise ran the Fairview Clinic on the Taos Highway. Dr. Lindsley had his own private practice. He was a good-looking man of medium height and fair complexion, who was always well dressed.

There were other physicians in Santa Fe at St. Vincent Hospital, in Taos at Holy Cross, and at Embudo Hospital north of Española on the Taos Highway, but these potential supports were some distance away and could not easily be counted on for assistance.

Sam began conducting tonsil and adenoid (T&A) clinics at the McCurdy Clinic with the help of Howard Seitz, MD from Santa Fe. Sam also held well-child clinics in Española, Santa Cruz and other small villages such as Truchas, Vallecitos, and La Madera, at the request of Dr. Marion Hotopp, Director of the Maternal and Child Health Division of the State Department of Public Health.

I accompanied Sam to many of these clinics to act as receptionist. The clinics were all-day affairs, and we packed a lunch and carried our own water. The boys always came along and amused themselves in the car or played around the area if the weather was nice.

One of the conditions that Sam found most worrisome among children was severe infantile diarrhea. Sewage disposal was primitive. Outhouses were widely prevalent along with open wells for drinking water, and irrigation ditches, the water from which was also used for drinking. Sam would comment that contaminated well and ditch water were prime avenues for the spread of disease, and he saw cases of typhoid fever and tuberculosis along with one rare case of tubercular meningitis.

While sources of drinking water were problematic, Sam said that the primary cause of the infantile diarrhea was not contaminated water, but flies. Native houses offered little protection to infants and younger children with their lack of screening on windows and doors. Diarrhea was particularly wide-spread during the summer months when fly season was at its height. Many of the cases we saw were distressing because the young children became dehydrated so quickly. These clinics were held before the Española hospital opened, and it was heart-breaking for him to watch a baby die in the arms of a nurse before the child could be properly cared for. Keeping fluids in these children was very difficult, and Sam did not yet have proper equipment to accomplish this.

Sam also did occasional school clinics in Nambé, Pojoaque and Española for the Public Health Department. In the Pojoaque area he noticed that children had fine teeth on one side of the river, while on the other side of the river, dental hygiene was quite poor. The Health Department initiated an investigation which revealed differences in fluoride content of the soil between one side of the river and the other. They began a push for the use of fluoride in the toothpaste and drinking water in Santa Fe and Rio Arriba counties. However, the Santa Cruz area was found to have a naturally high fluoride content in the soil.

While doing football team examinations for the Española and McCurdy Schools, Sam had an interesting experience. One after another of the boys on the McCurdy team came through the exam room weighing 120 lbs., 123 lbs., 118 lbs., with only one or two at 136 to 140 lbs. Having played high school football in Dayton, Ohio, Sam was expecting that there would be more "beef." He said to the coach, "I am done with the second team. You can send in the first string now." The coach laughed and told him, to his surprise, "You just examined the first team." There was much we had to learn about the cultural and physical differences between Hispanics, Anglos and Indians.

The people of Española and Santa Cruz welcomed a young, modern trained surgeon and obstetrician to the community and eagerly awaited the building of a hospital. Both Anglos and Hispanics quickly gained confidence in Sam, and I know he felt honored to be of service to them. The remoteness of many areas, however, and their isolation from good medical care had bred attitudes of mistrust among portions of the population. The older Hispanics, in particular, were suspicious. It was the younger people who developed confidence and began bringing the older people. Sam remembered a woman from Truchas, who came down to the clinic at McCurdy one day. She was thirty-five years old, and she said that this was her first trip out of her native village.

We were exposed to a good deal of traditional folk medicine during those first years of practice at McCurdy. Hispanic men would appear wearing blue tobacco stamps on their foreheads as a cure for headaches. Some people had copper wires tied around their wrists to help alleviate arthritic pains. For many people, the old methods had great psychological importance.

One case of Sam's typified the interaction between the old and the new. It involved a woman on whom he had performed surgery several years before. Sam said that when she came to his office one day, she was very weak and said she was bleeding from various parts of her body. He immediately hospitalized her for a work-up. Lab results showed a profound anemia and she was diagnosed with leukemia.

Sam treated the woman with blood transfusions, and when she was strong enough, he discharged her home with a very poor prognosis. However, people with her condition did experience short spontaneous remissions in rare cases. Several months later, she appeared at his office in the picture of health. According to Sam, she told him that after she had gotten home from her hospitalization, a *medica* had poulticed her whole body with turpentine and cow dung, a common local remedy. Coincidentally, she had gone into a period of remission and had gained weight and blossomed out. The woman attributed her health directly to the attentions of the *medica*. There was news several months later that she had passed away at home, her disease having run its usual course.

Local doctors dispensed their own medications prior to Sam's coming to Española. It was common practice for a doctor to have his satchel full of pills for all emergencies and situations, and to dispense at his office or while out on house calls. Sam changed this practice. He immediately began to write prescriptions for his patients, with the expectation that they would go to the drug store and buy their medications.

The local druggists could not believe their ears when told about this development. They did not believe there was a doctor who was actually going to write prescriptions. He became a very popular person with Angus Evans and Jennings Doak, the young pharmacist working for Angus.

Angus Evans had two drug stores, a smaller one called Evans Drug on Oñate Street in downtown Española, across from the Granada Hotel, and a second, larger store called Riverside Drug near the "Y" in Riverside, just across from the Livingston Motel. Angus spent most of his time in the smaller store. Jennings Doak ran the pharmacy in the Riverside store, while Reecie Evans managed the store, which handled a wide variety of merchandise including sporting goods.

Jennings Doak left Angus and built his own drug store nearer the Fairview area called Pueblo Drug several years after we arrived. He and his wife, Verina, operated the store as a general drug store with Jennings handling the pharmacy. The store had a full soda fountain, where we had many an old-fashioned coke. They were made with coke syrup poured into a glass and ice placed on top. The syrup was then fizzed from the fountain dispenser. Great cokes! Much more tasty than today's bottled and canned varieties.

Sam and I drove to Embudo Hospital in the November of 1947. Sam wanted to introduce himself to Dr. Sarah Bowen and her staff, and talk with her about obtaining admitting privileges at Embudo. Dr. Bowen said she would talk with the Board of Directors and let Sam know. She invited Sam to lunch not long thereafter and informed him that the Board had voted *not* to extend privileges to him because he was not Presbyterian.

The Presbyterian and United Brethren Churches had divided up territory in northern New Mexico at this time by "mutual agreement" and they guarded their respective areas with some tenacity. The Presbyterians were active in the villages of Dixon, Embudo, Pilar, Peñasco and Chamisal, while the United Brethren Church claimed Española and Santa Cruz as well as Vallecitos, Velarde and Alcalde. Taos and Santa Fe were within the Catholic realm with Holy Cross Hospital in Taos and St. Vincent Hospital in Santa Fe.

Sam did surgery at Embudo on several occasions when none of their regular surgeons were available or when they called to ask if he could help on a special case. He came to know Dr. Bowen well over time, and he grew to like her as a person and to respect her as a physician. He remembers very clearly what she said to him when they first met. "Oh, you're not going to like it around here," she remarked. "You're not going to have anything to do." That prediction was incorrect, of course, and stated, Sam thought, because of an initial jealously about territory. Dr. Bowen eventually began to send cases to Sam that were beyond her scope of practice and expertise.

Dr. Bowen and Sam had much in common by way of family background and general orientation toward service in the medical profession. She was born in China in 1902, the daughter of missionary parents. She had planned a return to China following her medical training and residency, only to be turned back by the Japanese invasion of Manchuria in 1931. The Presbyterian Board of National Missions agreed to send her to New Mexico shortly thereafter. She arrived in Dixon in 1931 and practiced in northern New Mexico for the next thirty years. The Embudo Hospital opened in 1940.

In May of 1947, Sam and I made arrangements to attend our first State Medical Society Meeting, in Roswell, New Mexico. Travel to Roswell marked our first trip of any consequence since our arrival. We looked forward to the drive down, to seeing the country along the way, and to becoming better acquainted with other physicians and their wives throughout the state. It turned out to be a welcome experience for both of us. A number of the doctors we met were relocating with their families after the war, and many were involved with rural medicine.

I was still of a mind that I could take or leave New Mexico without much of a second thought. Our introduction to the motel in Roswell did not help matters. A great big centipede about six inches long dropped right down in front of my face as we opened the door to go into our room. I screamed and almost jumped out of my skin. I did not feel this was a very reasonable way to be greeted by Roswell!!

This meeting was the beginning of many State Medical Society meetings which we faithfully attended. These included not only the annual meetings in May of each year, but the interim meetings in November. The meetings were held in different cities throughout the state, but often either in Albuquerque or Santa Fe because of their central locations. Santa Fe was always a place people enjoyed visiting.

We attended the annual meeting of the Southwestern Medical Society in El Paso, Texas in 1949. We ran into very heavy winds and blowing sand during our drive through the arid portion of south central New Mexico. We reached El Paso safely, but others arriving after us had much of the paint stripped from their cars by the blowing sands.

10

HELPING TO ORGANIZE A LIBRARY

The Española Woman's Club was formerly known as the Pricilla Club of Española. It was federated in 1915 as the "Española Woman's Club and Library Assn." The club developed the first library that same year. Many of the books in the initial collection were contributed by members or purchased for as little as $1.20 each.

The books were placed in the home of Mrs. Margareta Sargent, a daughter of Samuel McBride, the local station agent. She was paid $1 a month as librarian and issued the books out of her home while working as telephone operator. She also had the town's switchboard in her home. Books were originally loaned out at 5 cents each.[14]

I attended a meeting of the Española Woman's Club one afternoon in late 1946. The meeting was held in a large, one-room adobe building located on the "Y" in Española, just south of Bond Willard Mercantile. When I arrived, I found four women seated around a long wooden table in the center of a large room. They were all folding literature for a tuberculosis campaign. I was pleased to see the friendly face of Violet McCracken, wife of Dr. Glen McCracken, Superintendent of McCurdy School. Mrs. Diego Salazar, wife of the Mayor of Española, was sitting next to her. I did not know her, but was happy to meet her. She had a gentle reserve about her manner, and she welcomed me with a polite nod. She was dressed conservatively and wore her black hair in a bun at the back of her head like a number of the older Spanish women I had met in the Valley.

The third woman at the table was Verina Doak, acting president of the Woman's Club, and wife of Jennings Doak, the pharmacist at the local drug store. Sam had met and talked with her and her husband, and told me about them. I was happy finally to meet her. She seemed energetic about her work, and beckoned with an outstretched arm and a broad smile.

Rachel Lilystrand was the last woman there. She rose from her chair to greet me as a newcomer, and came over to give me a nice warm smile and to shake my hand. She immediately seemed someone whom I would want to know.

There were several bookshelves at one end of the room filled with a haphazard array of books. I asked if there were a library in Española. I was interested for the sake of our children's education, and for Sam and myself. Mention of the library stimulated animated conversation. I was pleased to learn that the Woman's Club had chosen to establish a library a number of years before, and this project entitled them to become federated. The club had not been able to do much because its funding came primarily from member dues. The only other income was from rental of the building space for local union meetings. Verina Doak confirmed the general state of affairs when she commented, "Yes, we have a library, but we are having difficulty getting it organized and running."

My questions about the library seemed perfectly innocent to me, and I was surprised when the Woman's Club asked me to serve as its second vice-president for the coming year. The second vice-president was in charge of organizing and running the library. The offer of a position pleased me. The position would give me an opportunity to become more involved with local people, and it would involve me doing something of benefit to the community. I was thankful I had some library experience from working in the Westerville, Ohio public library during high school. I at least knew something about the library filing system and the management of books.

I began to participate in the Woman's Club meetings to become better acquainted with local women as I organized myself about the library. I accepted the position of second vice-president with the proviso that I be allowed to organize the library according to State Library regulations and requirements. Irene Peck, Director of the New Mexico State Extension Library in Santa Fe, was my first contact. When I went to see her, she said to me, "Do you realize what you are trying to do? We have attempted to get a library working in the Valley for years without success." I smiled and replied, "If you will help me set it up according to regulations established by the State Library, I will do it."

Irene Peck sent Sophronia Dewey, field librarian for the Extension Library, to assist me. Sophronia was a rather picturesque young woman with curly black hair swept tightly back from her face into a bun. She dressed modestly in a simple skirt and blouse, and wore small, wire-framed glasses that perched on her nose, making it seem as if she were continually peering at you.

Following guidance from Sophronia, I arranged for the women in the club to come to the clubhouse and help catalogue the books. We set up an assembly line, each woman having specific tasks to do for each book as it came her way. I took many library cards and book jackets home because much needed to be done and the women met only once a week.

Most of the books were novels and biographical works, but there were also several old, valuable books on the history of New Mexico. These included the works of Governor L. Bradford Prince, William Keleher and Ralph Emerson Twitchell. These books were to be kept in the library for reference. I have no idea where they came from, but were probably local contributions. The books in all numbered several hundred and were in average condition, good enough for use by the public.

Members of the club decided that as long as we were setting up a library, we might as well refurbish the Woman's Club building at the same time. The only heat in the building came from an old coal and wood-burning stove. We replaced it with a little gas stove which heated the room better so we could move along with our project. We knew further renovations were also needed. We canvassed the businessmen in Española for equipment for a bathroom and a kitchenette along with other necessities. Cook's Española Mercantile, Bond Willard Mercantile and the M&S Oldsmobile Agency contributed all we needed. Rachel Lilystrand was especially helpful in contacting and talking with local businessmen. We had the hardwood floors in the building sanded. They turned out beautifully. We made draperies for the windows as well, and turned the drab, old room into a charming and comfortable reading room. There was an old piano which we even painted to match the walls. All the work was a lot of fun!

We all continued the work of cataloguing and caring for the books at the library in preparation for the official opening of the library. Gertrude Hampton had taken over responsibilities as chairperson of the library committee. She reported regularly on progress, with information about the growth in our number of books and notes about community interest. Other members of the library committee included Ruth Barbee, Alice Prather, Margaret Gallup, Rachel Lilystrand, Ruth Stark and myself.

While we were so involved with getting the library ready to open, the famous Freedom Train arrived in Santa Fe on February 15, 1948. Gertrude Hampton and I were asked to represent the Española Woman's Club and Library Association at the event. The seven-car streamliner carried a precious cargo of one hundred twenty-five priceless documents which marked the course of democracy through the ages. These documents dated back to the Magna Carta, one of the four copies of which was exhibited on the train. Attendance in Santa Fe was noted to have been larger than in Albuquerque. The arrival of the train was the climax to a week-long program of rededication to our American heritage observed by the City. We were given gifts from the Freedom Train that had been made in France, to present to our club in remembrance of this historic event.

The library officially opened on May 3, 1948. This was an important and fun day for all of us who had worked so hard getting the library organized. Special guests for the opening included Irene Peck and Sophronia Dewey along with Nellie Byrne, chairperson of the Federation of Women's Club Libraries, and Elizabeth Margulis, who had recently taken a position with the Extension Library in Santa Fe. Rachel Lilystrand organized an art exhibit for the occasion with works from the local artists Gustav Bauman, Louis Ewing and Norma Hall. The club also asked local Indian craftsmen and artists from the Pueblos to bring in pottery and jewelry to exhibit and sell.

I was pleased to report at our club meeting in July that the library now had 1,489 books, with 224 more being purchased to add to the collection. Margaret Gallup, Treasurer, reported at this meeting about the club's successful rummage sale to help defray expenses the club had incurred in its remodeling. We were all pleased with the news. Catherine Scheutzel offered to speak at the next meeting on "Navajo Customs and Legends," which sparked my interest. I looked forward to hearing her.

There was much excitement as the library gained recognition in the community. It was open Mondays 1-3 p.m., Wednesdays 7-9 p.m., Fridays 10 a.m. to 12 noon, and Saturdays 10 a.m. to 12 noon. Club members who were willing and able served as librarians. Marie Cravens was one dedicated helper, as were several others. We made a special effort to accommodate students because there was no library at school, and we opened it especially for them on Wednesday evenings. Later on, to encourage their coming, we occasionally made these Wednesday evenings into social events, with music and an opportunity for the students to dance under appropriate supervision.

Years later, at a local wedding reception in 1972, a nice young couple by the name of Mr. and Mrs. Phil Lucero, introduced themselves to Sam and me. Phil took the opportunity to say, "Mrs. Ziegler, I wouldn't be out here dancing if it were not for you and the social evenings at the library in Española for high school students. I want to thank you." He gave me a big smile. I had forgotten that I taught some of the young people to dance at the high school social gatherings.

Arrangements were made for a Saturday morning story telling hour for the younger children as interest in the library grew, and then I found myself accepting other responsibilities in the Woman's Club. At a meeting in August, the club discussed a complaint it had received about the overcrowding of children at the local El Ciné Theater, and about the noise and confusion created when the children threw popcorn and popcorn boxes during the showing of movies. There was concern about a potential fire hazard, and the Woman's Club was called upon to investigate. The president appointed Ruth Barbee and me to check into the situation. Ruth and I went to see for ourselves. I remember finding the theater full to overflowing. Children who could not find regular seats were sitting on the floor along each side of the central aisle. We spoke with those in charge. Our inquiries and comments about the potential fire hazard and overcrowding were well received, and Ruth and I were able to give a positive report to the club.

Catherine Scheutzel served as president of the Woman's Club and Library Association during 1949 and 1950. I was pleased to see her in this position. She was knowledgeable and educated, and showed good leadership and strength of character as she performed her role. It was during Catherine's tenure that disaster struck. The Woman's Club building was flooded in July 1950. The large irrigation ditch behind the building overflowed, filling the building with water and debris. Harold Scheutzel, Fire Chief of the Española Volunteer Fire Department, had to condemn the building as unsafe. He said the adobe walls were badly damaged and that it would be best to remove the books to a better location. Catherine quickly took charge of the situation. She called a number of us together to salvage things. We had to climb into the building through a window at the back to rescue the books and files, which was quite an adventure for us.

The City of Española allowed us to move the undamaged books into two rooms in the old fire house on Vigil Street. Harold Scheutzel helped to arrange for these rooms, which turned out to be very nice, and we continued with the library as best we could. We maintained hours much as before with club members serving as librarians. We also continued to encourage students to use the facility. Indeed, the flood provided a benefit in bringing needed attention to the library. Within the year and with community help and financial support, the Woman's Club was able to remodel the old firehouse building to suit the library's needs better.

It is interesting to note that from the humble beginnings of the library in 1948, the library is now in a city complex and has an inventory of 50,000 books and more. It also features the latest technology. This is a far cry from its meager start and illustrates what can be accomplished through people who are dedicated to a cause.

Each woman I met at the first Woman's Club meeting I attended left a strong impression on me. I can still see each one clearly in my mind, even today as I think back about that time. All were gracious, polite and friendly, but I am sure I would not have continued my involvement with the club if Rachel Lilystrand had not approached me.

I was pleased to learn at the first meeting I attended that Rachel had agreed to become program chairperson for the coming year. She seemed to be someone who would provide interesting and stimulating agendas from her comments during the meeting. I received a note in the mail from her about a week later, asking me to join her for lunch at the Granada Hotel in Española. She asked if I would like to serve on her Program Committee, and if so, wished to discuss some ideas with me. My comments at the meeting seem to have struck a chord with her for she wrote, "I think we think alike!" I was pleased to receive Rachel's note and readily agreed to the luncheon date.

Rachel was probably old enough to be my mother, but I never thought of her in that light. She was a tall, stately woman with a walk full of grace and poise. She had beautiful, dark red hair she wore piled up on the top of her head, and a face full of light red freckles. Her hazel colored eyes spoke of intelligence and curiosity about the world. I came to enjoy and respect Rachel as a person, and to value her as a friend.

I realized very quickly as Rachel and I began to talk at lunch that day at the Granada Hotel and after, that she was someone with a wealth of knowledge and understanding about New Mexico. Her background in the arts and experience as curator at the Philbrook Museum of Art in Tulsa, Oklahoma showed in her appreciation of local artists. She was acquainted with several and enjoyed talking about them and their work. Rachel knew Bertha Dutton, a well-known anthropologist from Santa Fe, to whom she introduced me, and I met Pansy Stockton, the Santa Fe artist, through her. Rachel had both of these women come and speak to the Woman's Club. Rachel had many Indian friends from San Ildefonso Pueblo whom she entertained at her home. Sam and I were often invited to these occasions and met the Governor and Mrs. Abel Sanchez of the pueblo. These were interesting and enjoyable evenings for us. These and other of Rachel's friends and acquaintances were well-versed in local history and art. I found myself inspired by them and eager to learn more about New Mexico and its people. This stimulation helped me to appreciate my new surroundings more and to grow in myself. Rachel also admired and talked with women who had braved difficult lives to establish themselves and their families in New Mexico. One was the writer, Agnes Morley Cleaveland from Magdalena, New Mexico whose book about ranching life in New Mexico, *No Life for a Lady*, Rachel recommended to me.

I was impressed with Rachel's former life in New York City, but that was really a world away from me. I was more taken with the way she approached and handled her life in Española, tactfully and with dignity. She provided an enthusiastic and cultured spirit, helping to uplift activities in which she participated. It was not long before I became involved in civic affairs in Española. A number of my activities originated from my first visit to the Woman's Club. Rachel was a guiding light for me in many ways, and I always turned to her for counsel. She helped me cope in those early days. She was a good listener, and we had enough interests in common to keep our friendship active and alive. I was able to talk with Rachel about living in a community so new and different for me, and about raising my children and seeing that they were properly educated. Rachel was knowledgeable about the area, and reassuring that matters would fall into place in their own time.

Rachel had found that life is beautiful without the great wealth to which she had been accustomed in New York City before the Crash of 1929, with its limousines and servants, and she shared that acceptance with me. She would call and say, "Let's go to Santa Fe. We'll just shop with our eyes." This we did, not only visiting the stores to look at clothes, but taking in the museums as well. Rachel would occasionally take a trip to Mexico by herself, and when she returned, she always had interesting things to say about her trip, food she had eaten, a scene she thought restful or beautiful and a painting she liked especially and brought back to show us. She was really a teacher for me in many ways as well as a friend, and I was willing and open to listening and learning.

I believe that I may have seemed like a daughter to Rachel. Sam and I probably filled a void in her life with her own children away and infrequent in their visits. When the children did come, we were invited to a "family" gathering, which was a real delight.

Rachel was a capable, self-sufficient woman, but we worried about her alone in that big, rambling, old adobe ranch house when her husband, Ted, was away on business. They called their place "Black Mesa Ranch." Sam and I drove out to check on her late one cold winter evening, knowing Ted was not home. Their house had no central heating. We found Rachel sitting in her kitchen huddled in front of the corner fireplace. She had a long log burning the end of which stuck out some three or four feet to the side of the room. She kept shoving it into the fireplace as it burned. She seemed to think there was no reason in the world why she should have to bother chopping the log into smaller pieces. She seemed content just to sit before the fire away from the late evening chill that pervaded the rest of the house. Sam and I brought more wood into the house and placed it where she could easily reach it. We offered to take her to our house for the night, but she said, "No," that Ted would be returning any time.

11

Out on the Town

Española and Santa Cruz did not have very much by way of amenities. There were no restaurants in Santa Cruz, and only two in Española outside of the Granada Hotel. The town of Española closed up at nine o'clock at night. People were pretty much left to their own resources for entertainment.

We were entertained a great deal when we first arrived. People could not do enough to welcome us and make us feel at home. Carl and Florence Holmquist, owners of the Granada Hotel, had a dinner party and dance for us. The party was wonderful! The hotel dining room was filled with people and we were the guests of honor. There was delicious food followed by music and dancing. Three fiddlers provided the music, playing what I knew as polka music, which the local people loved. I was amazed! I guess I had been expecting a big band, but the three fiddlers played and played and stamped their feet. People got up and danced and had a marvelous time. It was not long before someone had me on my feet dancing to these polkas with their own local beat. It was exciting!

The Lions Club also had their yearly social, one of which took place shortly after our arrival. We did a lot of dancing that night, too. Angus Evans, the local druggist, asked me to dance, and while we were on the dance floor, he remarked, "Most people think I look like Edward G. Robinson. What do you think?" I hardly knew Angus and was caught a little off balance by his question. I am sure I made an acceptable answer, and remember laughing with him.

It was through bridge luncheons that I was introduced to many of the women of the Valley. Sam and I were also invited out to dinner with local people at their homes. And if we wanted a night out for ourselves, there was El Nido in Tesuque. Charlie and Mimmie Besre were the owners, and were both outstanding cooks. The escargot was unmatched. Everyone from Taos, Española, Los Alamos and Santa Fe found their way there, some in ski clothes, others in denims or silks. It was good to see friends, and after dinner, to dance to music on the juke box. Charlie kept a small rug in the middle of the dance floor until 9:00 p.m. He then removed the rug and put some money in the juke box to start things off. It was time to dance! El Nido was the "ultimate" escape for relaxation.

We went to Santa Fe when we wanted to get dressed up and go out for the evening. We laughed about how we managed our first trips to town. We used to pack a lunch and plan a full day's outing when we lived at Ghost Ranch. We usually stopped at Camel Rock to eat our lunch and rest in the shade of a piñon tree before driving on into town. We were not used to long distances we had to travel nor to the difficulties we sometimes met on the way. It was over sixty miles from the ranch to Santa Fe. If it had rained, the arroyos were running full and would delay travel for several hours. We had to turn around on occasion and find a place to stay for the night. Now, of course, with our modern highways, we think nothing of zooming back and forth between Española and Santa Fe or even Albuquerque. But it was different then.

I sometimes went into Santa Fe on my own when I was getting to know northern New Mexico and wanted to do some exploring. One morning when I left for Santa Fe, it was a clear, sunny day, but by mid-afternoon, a storm had gathered over the Sangre de Cristo mountains. I could see thunder and lightning as I started back toward Española. The storm remained over the mountains to the east. There was no rain along the highway and the Jemez Mountains to the west were clear. When I reached Arroyo Seco just outside of Española, however, the arroyo was full with swirling, muddy, turbulent water. I had to pull over and stop. I saw small trees and debris of all kinds being swept along with the rush of the water. The arroyo was more than fifty feet across and filled up to the banks. The water must have been at least four to five feet deep. There was a police car with its flashing lights on the other side signaling danger. The fact that a storm in the mountains could send such a powerful rush of water down across the highway was new and frightening to me. I had some introduction to these arroyos at Ghost Ranch, and I had heard many tales about them running high with water. Seeing was believing!

La Fonda was the only place to eat in Santa Fe outside of a few small restaurants. A man by the name of Conrad was the chef, and he was exceptional. The hotel band led by Billy Pallou played wonderful music local people loved. It was at La Fonda that Sam and I learned to do the schottische and varsoviana and some of the other dances then in vogue. Milton and Hollis Scarborough took us there and introduced us to these dances and to hot New Mexican food.

I came to recognize a handsome Santo Domingo Indian called La Fonda Joe who often sat outside La Fonda Hotel on the northwest corner diagonally across from the plaza. He wore large earrings of plain, oval shaped turquoise that dangled from his earlobes on strings, and a very lovely long-strand turquoise heishi necklace. I tried on a number of occasions to get him to sell his necklace and earrings to me, but he always refused. I knew turquoise was the Gem of the State and had even heard it spoken of as a "piece of fallen sky." I was eager to own some.

One Sunday, he saw me as I was coming across the plaza to the hotel with several friends, and he came over and asked if I were still interested in buying his necklace. I said, "Yes, I would. Your necklace is beautiful. I would like to buy your earrings, too."

He immediately shook his head and remarked, "Necklace, OK. But earrings not for sale. They very old, and see, they no fade."

I bought the necklace and went on my way. I was entering the dining room a few minutes later when La Fonda Joe came up to me and pointed to his earrings, saying, "I sell to you." An Indian friend with him then took out a pocket knife and cut the strings tied through his earlobes so I could have the stones. His price: $14.00. What an experience! Only in Santa Fe! I later had the earrings set with silver posts.

I still have the necklace and one earring. The other I lost at a lawn party at Dr. Rudy Kieve's home in Santa Fe. I feel very badly about its disappearance. I have never been able to match the remaining one.

La Fonda had a charming outdoor patio restaurant where the people used to gather. You could always see someone you knew and local artists frequented the restaurant. Pansy Stockton in particular was one who made quite a showing. She was a large woman with lovely dark hair. She always wore a big brimmed hat, lots of purple clothing and loads of silver and turquoise jewelry. She had a very jolly laugh and really stood out in the crowd.

I had met Pansy Stockton through Rachel Lilystrand during one of our visits to Santa Fe. Later we asked her to speak to the Española Woman's Club. She brought a number of her "Sun paintings" to show us when she came to speak. These were paintings constructed out of materials that included sun dried flowers, chips of wood, leaves, bird feathers, cotton, and other natural material. She said that she laid these materials on the floor and arranged them with her toes. This manner of working provided her with the distance and perspective she needed to create.

Pansy accepted Sam's and my invitation to dinner at our home following her lecture. She brought several of her paintings with her when she came. We were able to look at her paintings up close and we purchased one called "Storm over Taos." It is most interesting and very beautiful.

A man came up to us in the lobby of La Fonda one day, saying, "Aren't you Dr. and Mrs. Ziegler?" He had been sitting in a chair not far from the entrance, seemingly waiting for us. We replied that we were the Zieglers and he extended a friendly handshake and introduced himself as Brian Boru Dunne, a columnist for *The New Mexican*. He looked at Sam and said with a smile, "I understand you are going to have a hospital built in Española, and you're going to be in charge of it, Dr. Ziegler. Is that correct?"

B. B. Dunne wore a flattop western hat with a broad brim and looked up at us from a stooped posture, his face lined and aged, his eyes alive with interest and his mouth pulled to the side in a half-smile. We had a pleasant conversation as he busily scribbled down notes all the while we talked. He wrote about Sam in his column a few days later:

> Arthur Pack drops into Santa Fe—to La Fonda—from time to time. He owns the Ghost Ranch near Abiquiu, 60 miles north of Santa Fe. . . Señor Pack is reported to be the New Mexico representative of the Charles E. Pack Foundation in New Jersey . . . that deals out "one hundred grand" ($100,000) from time to time. *First hundred grand check to that hospital in Española, where a talented medico is said to be curing the sick, teaching them how to stay well. . . Hats off to the Pack Family!*[15]

B. B. Dunne was one of the outstanding characters we met in those early days. His portrait hangs today above the chair where he always sat in the main lobby of La Fonda.

There was a woodcarver's shop which caught our eye as we drove through Tesuque on our way to Santa Fe. A life-sized Indian dressed in western clothes with two long braids of hair sat out in front of the shop. He looked so real I always had to look twice to be sure. We stopped in the shop out of interest one day, and to see about some furniture. We had no idea that the owner was Andy Anderson, a publicized woodcarver, recognized throughout the world. Sam saw immediately that Andy had exceptional talent. He was also a most engaging personality.

Andy's true desire had been to become an actor and get into the movies. He had gone to Hollywood earlier in his life, and sat outside studios waiting for interviews. He whittled characters of the movie stars who walked in and out while he waited. He soon became famous in Hollywood for his woodcarving, but never made it as an actor. Andy loved the wide open spaces, so he moved out of busy, crowded Hollywood and settled in Tesuque, New Mexico.

We saw a number of Andy's character woodcarvings, one of an Indian warrior and several of cowboys and horse wranglers. They were delightful. Their cartoon-like postures and antics brought immediate smiles to our faces.

We later came to an agreement with Andy about furniture he was to make for us. We wanted a kitchen table and four chairs, twin beds for the boys, and a chest of drawers for each. We also wanted a desk with two chairs, a floor lamp and a coffee table for us. Each piece of furniture was to include some local scene or character portrayal.

We have always loved the furniture Andy made for us. Our children have now taken most of these pieces for their own families. The furniture will always remind us of a wonderful character and acquaintance from our early days in New Mexico.

12

AT SWAN LAKE RANCH IN ALCALDE

We met Hamilton and Jean Garland in 1947. Hamilton was a tall, good looking man with the physique of an athlete. He moved with a slow, easy grace. A multi-millionaire who had inherited his money, he seemed unspoiled, and as far as we were concerned, he never flaunted his status or his wealth. Hamilton had met Jean in New York when she was the dancer, Jean Barry. Jean was a high-strung woman with a forceful personality who loved being the center of attention and possessed a personal magnetism and intelligence that drew people to her.

The Garlands lived at Swan Lake Ranch in Alcalde just north of Española. Hamilton's mother, Marie Garland, had originally owned the property. She came to New Mexico from New England to spend time at various guest ranches in the locality including San Gabriel in Alcalde, and eventually purchased the land and buildings north of San Juan Pueblo that became Swan Lake. Hamilton and Jean took over a major portion of the property. Marie allocated to herself a smaller section directly across the road with sufficient quarters to entertain which she often did, we were told, on a lavish and beautiful scale.

The ranch had a plentiful supply of water, being close to the Rio Grande. Huge cottonwood and lovely, tall poplar trees filled the grounds and provided wonderful shade. A high adobe wall lined the Alcalde Road that bordered the property along its eastern edge, and a huge gate opening onto a finely graveled parking area allowed admission to the interior. The residence itself was built around an open patio lined with shrubs that had a fragrance which reminded me of jasmine and stephanotis, with an open circular area for a fireplace. This area was delightful in the evening after dinner for coffee and casual conversation. All of the rooms in the house opened onto the inner patio. Many rooms also opened out onto the spacious landscaped grounds and lake, where Ham kept his black swans. The swans were beautiful, almost magical in this setting which provided an isolation from the world and a wonderfully restful sense of well-being.

Not long after our arrival in Española, we received an invitation from Ham and Jean to attend a dinner party for forty people at Swan Lake. We were delighted to be invited and pleased to have the opportunity to be with the Garlands and their guests. We found a large group of people already gathered when we arrived. The men were dressed in black ties and tuxedos, and the women in elegant, long formal gowns. The Garlands met us at the door and introduced us to the other guests. We were served a cocktail and then became involved in light conversation with those around us.

Though we were graciously introduced upon arrival, there were a number of people we did not meet before dinner. Among these were Mabel Dodge and her Taos Indian husband, Tony Luhan. I had read about the Taos Pueblo and seen it from a distance. While waiting for dinner to be announced, I noticed Jean Garland, Pauline Corlett, Mrs. Van Solen, wife of the noted artist, Ted Van Solen, and another woman from the Valley standing together in what appeared to be a huddle. They would talk and then look at me, and then go back to their discussion. I became curious and little self-conscious. I finally said to Sam, "Good heavens! Is my slip showing or something? Don't they like my dress?"

Jean came over to me shortly thereafter, and said with a glowing smile, "Isabel, we have decided that you are the one to sit next to Tony."

"Tony? Who is Tony?" I asked.

Jean answered straightforwardly, "Tony Luhan." I still did not know who Tony was, but Jean informed me that he was the Taos Indian married to Mabel Dodge Luhan.

I replied simply, "That's fine," not knowing any of these people, and smiled back at her.

Sam and I went into the dining room when it came time for dinner, and found our places. Jean's table was fabulous. It was set in the shape of a "U" to accommodate all the guests. She had used a lavender, purple, and white color scheme, with a huge white porcelain swan in the middle of the head table and smaller swans on each wing, all filled with beautiful flowers. The crystal, china, and linen were selected with an eye to color, so that everything blended with great elegance. I learned that Jean had numerous matched settings, each with a different color theme, which allowed her considerable variation in her arrangements.

It was not long before Tony Luhan came in. He was a handsome man with his dark hair in two, long braids that hung over his shoulders. He wore his formal Indian dress of white leather leggings and beaded moccasins, and a white leather beaded vest with silver conchos over a white shirt. I called to him and said, "Tony, your place is over here." He smiled and came around the table to sit beside me.

I found myself almost immediately comfortable in his presence and we had a most interesting conversation that evening. At times, I found myself in awe as Tony discussed his belief that the earth would be destroyed by fire. He spoke about Blue Lake, the sacred lake of the Taos Indians, which lies in the mountains above Taos. He invited me to go there with him. I knew that outsiders were permitted to visit Blue Lake only by invitation and that they had to be accompanied by a Taos Indian. Travel to the lake was by horseback. I told him that I felt privileged to be invited, but did not see how it was possible. "You know, Tony," I said, "I have two little boys."

"Well," he answered with a light laugh. "You can bring them along with you."

He never did mention Sam's coming, so I politely told him, "Maybe some other time." I have always wished I had been brave enough to accept his invitation.

I did not know about Mabel Dodge, Tony's wife. I found out that she was not only a very wealthy woman, but a very jealous one. She would have nothing to do with me as the evening wore on. She ignored me completely. People said afterwards that she reacted that way because Tony had such a nice time talking with me at dinner. I was both pleased and disappointed.

Jean asked us to linger for awhile after dinner and coffee. We went to the open patio and sat around a wood-burning fire. Other guests there were Bruce and Estelle Hayter, Margaret Schmidt, and the Mayers from Santa Fe. Bruce Hayter was an inventor associated with the Breese Burner, a special pot-type gas-burner stove with an integral water heating device. His wife, Estelle, was a charming woman. We came to know them and were entertained wonderfully at their home, Rancho Cottonwood, on a number of occasions. Margaret Schmidt was a delightful, plump, bosomy woman whose deceased husband had been an artist. She was much involved in social affairs in Santa Fe. Walter Mayer was a wealthy cattleman with ranches in Oklahoma and elsewhere, and Peaches, his wife, was a dynamic personality of Santa Fe.

Mabel Dodge was also present along with Frieda Lawrence, the wife of D. H. Lawrence. Mabel contributed nothing toward the conversation, but Frieda was most engaging. Frieda struck me as a very different person, certainly someone outside the scope of my general frame of reference. She was dressed in a simple Navajo skirt and blouse, clothing that contrasted sharply with the elegant dress of the others. I sensed that generally accepted social conventions were unimportant to her, and that she was not given to the light chit-chat that occurred at the average dinner party. I was glad to have met her as the evening progressed because she was witty and entertaining, and very pleasant to be around.

How I wish now I had known more about these people in those early days!

The Garlands took over management of Swan Lake Ranch in the fall of 1948, about a year after we attended the dinner party there. It was really Jean who built up the restaurant, making it into a wonderful show place for entertaining in the Valley. Managing the restaurant provided her with a "stage" for entertaining. Her need to be before the public was a driving force in her personality. She loved being seen, and the restaurant constantly brought people before her. It also allowed her to show off her culinary artistry, for Jean could cook and entertain on a grand scale. She had gorgeous buffets. We often went out because reservations were easy to make and Swan Lake was close to Española. The hospital could reach Sam easily by phone, and the trip back was only a matter of minutes for him. The food and the décor were as nice as that in the best and most expensive New York City restaurants.

Jean opened the library after dinner for her guests. The library was a beautiful wood paneled room that served as a lounge. Hamilton had commissioned a full-length portrait of Jean some years before. The portrait hung in the library, and was a fitting tribute to her grace and elegance. When the guests were seated there, Jean would often begin to dance. She was a beautiful dancer. It seemed strange to me to see her perform after a sedate quiet dinner, but she was Jean Barry.

Jean was anxious to do something for our boys, whom she had met and seemed to like. She had no children of her own and was not quite sure how to proceed. She invited us for dinner one evening. It was cocktail hour when we arrived, and Jean was bound and determined that the boys should be included in everything, even though they were only seven and eight years old. She made a point of offering them fine champagne in champagne glasses. She had not given thought to the fact that the boys would not be drinking any of the champagne. She was not accustomed to the Roy Rogers and Shirley Temple drinks. She just wanted to do something nice for us. We had an abbreviated cocktail hour, then proceeded to the dining room where we were served a sumptuous dinner of filet mignons. The boys acted like real gentlemen and made a nice impression on Jean.

Hamilton seemed as happy out in the fields with his tractors as he was behind his bar serving the restaurant patrons or personal guests, or in his Corvette running errands. He obtained his enjoyment in simple ways. A large apartment complex occupied part of the grounds, and it was here that he constructed an O-gauge railroad which ran through its many rooms. He landscaped the whole railroad with towns, mountains, lakes, bridges and tunnels, spending many hours building this quite remarkable model. He put in a master control system so he could run several trains at the same time. Ham laid additional tracks outside around the lake for a larger-sized train.

There is a club in Santa Fe called the Quien Sabe Club. It is made up of a group of well-to-do writers, artists, poets and musicians. Club members meet once a month for lunch at each other's homes, and the host for the occasion is responsible for preparing a sumptuous repast.

Hamilton Garland was a member of the club. He always invited Sam out of friendship whenever it was his turn to host the gathering at Swan Lake. Sam met a number of local artists and writers through Ham, including the poet, Witter Bynner, and the artists, Ted Van Solen, Will Schuster, and Randall Davey.

We developed a friendship with Randall Davey in the mid-1950s. Randall took quite a liking to our daughter, Julie, then about six years old. He thought she was a good candidate for a portrait. We were on the verge of finalizing times for sittings when Randall was unexpectedly killed in an automobile accident. He had left for California in his Jaguar to complete a commissioned work. His car went out of control while he was driving across Frenchman's Flats in Utah at a high rate of speed, and he crashed.

J. B. French was one of the gourmet chefs Jean hired to work at the Swan Lake Ranch. J. B. was from New York City, and was both an excellent chef and a man of some refinement. His father was a prominent business-man in the City and his mother an accomplished pianist who accompanied many of the Metropolitan Opera stars. J. B. told us his father had wanted him to join the family business. "But I am the black sheep of the family. I just wanted to be a great chef," he said with a laugh.

Sam and I got to know J. B. well from our visits to Swan Lake. He called one day to invite us to a dinner party he was hosting at the Cygnet Club, a private dining room at Swan Lake. We were pleased to be included and excited to have the opportunity to meet George Balanchine, the famed choreographer. There were twelve guests from Santa Fe, Taos and Española at the dinner. We had a delicious meal with lively conversation on all sides. Jean, in her filmy chiffon pant suit suitable for dancing, came over to the table after we had all finished eating, and stood before Balanchine, who nodded toward her in recognition. She then extended her hand to him and pulled him to his feet to dance. And dance they did, beautifully and grace-fully. We were all spellbound. The dancing was wonderful.

Several women from Española and I took cooking lessons from J. B. French at Swan Lake. I still have recipes from those classes. J. B. would say with a wry smile at the end of a lesson, "Now, you must know that the real secret to a good cook is one who seasons with a bit of wine, and always remembers to save some for himself."

One evening as we were finishing dinner at Swan Lake, Jean said to us, "When you are finished, go to the library. I have someone special for you to meet." Jean introduced Greer Garson and Buddy Fogelson, her husband, who knew Jean in Hollywood and had come to Swan Lake Ranch to spend their honeymoon. Jean put some good music on the record player, and we all talked and danced and had a pleasant time together. Greer Garson was just as lovely in person as on stage.

Jean could read your personality by numbers. She would ask the date and time of your birth, and with these numbers, could analyze you. She did this at a party one evening. She analyzed almost everyone, and did them right down the line, but when she came to me, she missed badly. I said to her, "Jean, you missed me by a mile."

She looked straight at me with a perturbed pout on her lips and replied, "Now, just a moment. Give me those numbers again."

I did, and after some thought, she presented a second analysis. This time she said, "When you were born, you were nine days late in arriving." I had been nine days late. Her remark was exactly right. My mother had told me I had been late. How in the world would Jean know that? What a difference those nine days made in how she read my personality. This time she was correct. She said I was a determined individual who was creative in a number of different ways, and that I had a warm personality and a good ability to organize.

Jean eventually became restless in the Alcalde area. She and Ham sold the ranch in the early 1970s to Delancy Street, a drug and alcohol rehabilitation group centered in Los Angeles, California. It took thirteen full-sized moving vans to carry all of their possessions. They moved to Chino Canyon in Palm Springs, California where they took over a mansion which was not quite big enough for all of their belongings. Jean bought another house nearby to accommodate everything. They also had condominiums in Las Vegas and in Honolulu.

We will always remember Hamilton and Jean for the grace and elegance they brought to the Valley. We are glad to have been part of their lives and to have shared their friendship.

Gathered for this occasion were (left to right) Catherine Scheutzel, Sam Ziegler, Jean Garland, Isabel Ziegler, Harold Scheutzel and Martha Bell. Photo from 1950.

Swan Lake Ranch in Alcalde, the home of Hamilton and Jean Garland provided for many social events. Hamilton Garland served as bartender.

13

I Especially Noticed John's Hands

John Marsh was a tall, handsome man standing over 6'1", almost raw-boned in physique, his face angular and striking. He had a full head of wavy, black hair, prominent eyebrows and a thin mustache. His nose was long and straight, and his mouth full and expressive. I especially noticed John's hands. They were large, with long sensitive fingers he moved with great animation when he spoke. He was exciting and dramatic in all he did. He was also forever playful. His voice carried a spark that matched the amused turn of his mouth.

John's wife, Mary, was a petite woman, shorter than John by almost a foot. She had an embracing smile and warm laughter, and always seemed full of good will. She was very much alive to everything around her, and spoke with great sensitivity about people and things of the world. Her enthusiasm for life matched John's. They complemented each other's zest for living well.

We first met John in the fall of 1947 when he came into the clinic one evening with a badly cut lower lip. As Sam told the story, John arrived in the accompaniment of one of his friends, Webster Aiken, head of the Music Department at Southern Methodist University, who had come to town on a visit. During the course of their "celebrating" Webster's arrival, John had tripped at home and fallen, hitting his lower lip on the edge of a chair and cutting it deeply. Webster immediately drove John to the clinic for medical attention.

Sam had a difficult time sewing up John's lip and he learned a good deal about John in the process. John Marsh was a man who had a mind of his own. He kept trying to tell Sam what to do as Sam was trying to work, moving his hands about, stammering and arguing. Sam kept telling him he already knew what to do, and that John should just be quiet and let him work. They apparently went round and round for some time. Sam finally got John's lip sewed up, and it appeared that it would heal nicely with some very basic care. Sam had a few moments to talk with John and Webster afterwards as they introduced themselves to each other. John immediately impressed Sam as someone well worth knowing. John's spirits also seemed to pick up as they talked, and Sam certainly felt better for him.

Not long after, Sam was called to the Marsh's home in Cuartales, an area several miles east of Santa Cruz on the road to Chimayo, to take care of Mary. John phoned to say that Mary had been injured while working in the kitchen. Sam readily agreed to come out to their house, and I went along with him on the call. We learned upon arrival that Mary had been lighting a kerosene stove, and for some reason, there was a flash explosion that burned her hands and face. Fortunately, none of the burns were serious, and she recovered nicely.

This occasion marked the beginning of a wonderful friendship that Sam and I always cherished. John and Mary played important parts in our lives during the more than thirty years that followed.

John Marsh was a concert pianist. He had started on concert tour at the age of twenty-five. Three years later, he suddenly developed meningitis and was taken seriously ill. He appeared to recover following a course of treatment, and then began the long hours of practice necessary for his return to the concert stage. Shortly after beginning his first return performance, however, he walked off the stage, and at age twenty-eight, vowed never again to play the piano. It was quickly apparent to him that his hand/finger coordination had suffered considerably from his illness and was not what it should be for a world class pianist. To my knowledge, he never played the piano in public again.

John then took a position in the northwest as Program Director for a large radio station. He met Mary Lincoln Landis while there. Mary's father was United States Congressman Landis from Indiana. The "Lincoln" in Mary's name came from the fact that she was born on February 12th, Lincoln's birthday. Her uncle was Kenesaw Mountain Landis, the first Commissioner of Baseball.

John taught piano to a few people in the Española Valley. Patty McCracken was one of his students. She became quite an accomplished pianist and musician by the time she finished high school.

The Marsh's home in Cuartales was a beautiful, old adobe set back some one hundred yards from the road and screened off from the world with a seven foot high coyote fence that ran the length of the property along the road.

The house was 3,500 sq. feet, built in the Spanish "U" with flat-roofed Pueblo style architecture and corner fireplaces in all rooms. The central part of the house dated from the 18th century. The ceilings were made either of large, dark-stained wooden beams or of pine vigas with aspen or split cedar latillas.

John was a real perfectionist. When he and Mary purchased the property, the house was in need of repairs. John and his workmen labored to refurbish the house in every detail, always being faithful to the original construction. The men took up the latillas in all of the rooms and washed them with lye, then replaced them with precision. The outside of the house was replastered with smooth adobe plaster. John would not permit hard plaster anywhere.

A beautiful Steinway Concert Grand piano stood at one end of the central living room. There was a small library off the west end of the living room. John laid a beautiful flagstone floor in the library himself, and polished it to a high luster. Bookshelves filled with books lined the walls, and in one corner was a small adobe fireplace. The room was furnished with a couch and several chairs. We often met in the library in the fall and winter evenings when John and Mary would call and ask us to come over and talk before dinner.

The house was situated on a number of acres of land extending down from the Chimayo road to the Santa Cruz River. They were filled with fruit orchards and alfalfa fields. John had designed a wonderful rose garden on the south side of the house, which he tended with great affection. Alongside it was a small pond with goldfish and water lilies.

The Marsh's home was the scene of magnificent dinner parties. John was an excellent cook, and he and Mary entertained on a lavish scale with people seated at tables throughout the living room. Mary used to say with a smile that she washed dishes as fast as John dirtied them, and he used every dish and pan in the house to prepare for these parties.

The Christmas season was an especially happy time at the Marsh's home. John's birthday was on the 26th of December, and he would say with special emphasis in his voice and a wink of his eye that he was born *the day after* Jesus Christ, making December 26ᵗʰ an additional day for celebration. John was not a particularly religious man in a formal sense, but he was a fair and decent man with a profound spiritual sense of beauty, love and companionship among peoples. Christmas held a special fascination for him because it was a time of festive decoration. It was a time when he became perhaps his most creative. John placed Christmas trees in every room of their home, each tree decorated with a different theme. He decorated the dining room table with a fairy land of gingerbread houses with white icing, and there was a miniature railroad train and track on the table, built around a station house and pastoral scene with houses and figures of people.

John always had an enormous tree in the living room that reached to the ceiling. The tree usually stood to the right of the fireplace, and guests could walk around it to see its beauty. Many of the ornaments he used for the tree were medium to large glass balls John had decorated himself with onyx and long glass bugle beads. The onyx and bugle beads had originally adorned the elegant silk and chiffon dresses Mary's mother had worn while living in Washington, D. C. as wife of Congressman Landis. John did festive baking at Christmas, too. He filled Christmas baskets with goodies ready to be served and enjoyed, placing them about the dining room.

I remember one occasion with great amusement. John had called me around 5:30 p.m., asking in a very excited voice, "What time will Sam be home? You have got to get over here as fast as you can. We have something to tell you that you won't believe!" Both John and Mary seemed to be in hysterics as I listened to John on the phone. They could not stop laughing about something. I called Sam at his office to relay the message. He picked me up soon thereafter and we drove to John and Mary's, filled with great anticipation.

When we arrived, John and Mary ushered us into the library and proceeded to tell us what had happened. They had been sitting there earlier talking, when Mary, who was seated on the couch facing the bookshelves, looked up and remarked to John, "John, dear, I don't recall our having an owl bookend."

John responded hesitantly in a puzzled voice, "Well, we don't have an owl bookend, do we?"

Mary then pointed up and said, "I certainly see one up there at the end of that bookshelf."

A real owl sitting on the bookshelf turned its head toward John just as Mary spoke, and gave a deep wink with one eye. John and Mary both jumped up with a shout of surprise and near pandemonium broke loose as the owl flew off from the bookshelf and began to circle around the room. John laughed almost uncontrollably as he told the story. He said that when the owl winked at him, he had not known for a moment where he was.

During all the commotion, the owl managed to find its way back up the chimney from whence it had come. It was no longer to be found by the time Sam and I arrived. John and Mary were still in stitches, however, and we could not help but join in their laughter about what had happened.

Mary brought an antique four-poster bed of her family's out of storage when she and John decided to sell their property in Cuartales and travel around the world. She had slept in this bed as a child. It dated from 1875. She said that she wanted our daughter, Julie, who was just ten, to have this bed.

John and Mary were getting rid of much of their furniture at this time. I had noticed a tall secretary in one of the guest bedrooms. John said that he was waiting for the Salvation Army to come and pick it up. I told John it was a beautiful secretary and asked him why he was giving it away. "Because I don't like it," he replied. "Never have. My great-grandfather made it, and it had the original ebony knobs on it." I liked the piece and told John so. He laughed and told me that if I liked the secretary, I could have it. So we took it home.

The secretary was covered with black paint. We managed to take this paint off and refinish the wood. The same was true for the antique bed that Mary had given Julie. After removing all of the old paint, we could see that the bed was made of a number of different woods including bird's eye maple, mahogany, black walnut and pine. The mattress was suspended from rope looped around knobs set along the bottom of the side rails to form a bedding. We had to have a special mattress and box springs made to fit it.

John and Mary left for Europe. They loved traveling, but they were searching for a place to settle. They thought they would make Rome their new home when they arrived in Italy, but they went on to Florence for a visit and while there, Mary became ill. They had an extended stay in the city during Mary's recovery, and they both fell in love with Florence and decided to settle there.

They kept writing to us once they were settled, saying, "You must come to visit. You must come to Florence. You must come and stay with us." Sam finally said he felt it was time for us to take a trip. We made our first trip to Europe in June of 1960, taking Julie with us.

Our visit to Florence was very special. Julie, at ten years, was the perfect age to travel. She was interested in seeing and learning about this new city and country. John and Mary were very well informed about places to go and things to see. They were avid readers about the Renaissance and about the history of Florence and Italy, and had spent much time on their own searching out what they had read about. They had an itinerary prepared for each day we were there. We would meet for lunch at Harry's Bar on Lungarno Street by the Arno River, just near the Ponte Vecchio Bridge. They were well acquainted with the Mariottis who were the owners, and the food was delicious. We had such a fun time in Florence with John and Mary that they decided to join us on our travels to Venice and then on to Rome. Their knowledge and guidance made our visit to Italy a truly exciting adventure.

Typical of our experience was our arrival in Venice. When we reached our hotel early one afternoon, John said we were to meet later to do some more exploring, then added in his usual dramatic fashion, "You cannot go to San Marco Square until I say you can!" We met later in the hotel cafeteria for some refreshments, and then when the time was just right, proceeded on to the Square, which was just nearby. It was exactly 4:30 in the afternoon as we entered. The sun was just beginning to shine on the gold domes of the cathedral and buildings surrounding the square. The light and color were absolutely breathtaking, a truly magical moment that only John could have orchestrated.

John and Mary treated us in very special ways, and in doing so, opened up new worlds to us. I think Sam and I filled a void in their lives with our enjoyment of them as people and our eagerness to share in their adventures and their lives. We became part of their family, almost like the children they never had. They were so well read and literate, so wide awake to the world and its beauty. It was a wonderful experience to know them. They were exceptional people whom we loved dearly. I shall always miss their companionship.

John and Mary Marsh, 1961, longtime friends of the Ziegler family.

14

EARLY FRIENDSHIPS

Clarence Brashar, manager of the Española State Bank, was our first official contact when we arrived in Española in 1946. He was closely involved with the development of the hospital, and he and his wife, Gertrude, became good friends who helped to introduce us to the area and to local people.

Clarence's father had owned a farm in Rock Island, Iowa. Clarence learned that the farm was sold when he returned from the war, and he then came to the Española Valley to visit his uncle, Mr. Rueth, who ran a mercantile store at San Juan Pueblo. A man named Sam Eldodt had originally established the store under the name San Juan Mercantile. Sam Eldodt was a Jewish businessman who emigrated from Germany around the turn of the century. He joined with Mr. Rueth at some time, and together they built up a flourishing business. They changed the name of the store to Eldodt and Rueth General Merchandise. Rueth and a cousin by the name of Kramer took over the store following Sam Eldodt's death, and renamed it the Rueth-Kramer Mercantile.

We did not know the Kramers well. I remember Mrs. Kramer as a plump, jolly woman with a wealth of anecdotal material about local people and their doings which she loved to relate. She told an amusing story about local merchants which I have not forgotten. She said, by way of introduction to her story, that to show respect when someone of importance in the town died, all of the merchants along the main street were expected to raise and lower the blinds in their store windows as the horse-drawn hearse passed by. There was a wooden bridge across the Rio Grande into Española in those early days. On one particular occasion as the hearse crossed the bridge, one of the horses stepped on a wooden plank that came loose and flipped up, hitting the horse in the leg and startling it. The horse reared and then bolted.

The driver lost control of the team as the horses took off clattering through town. Merchants did not know what to do, the timing for their ritual having been entirely disrupted. All the blinds in town were going up and down in wild abandon as the horses ran by, or so the story goes. Early Española to be sure!

Gertrude Brashar recalls that there were plans to remove the narrow gauge railroad tracks that ran through the center of Española, and a last train ride was scheduled from Española to Santa Fe around the time of our arrival in 1946. Gertrude insisted that her father, Mr. Frankenburger, be on the train for this memorable occasion. Clarence was able to convince her father to go on the train, even though he loudly complained and thought it ridiculous to spend so much time on the train for such a short trip. It took three hours to go from Española to Santa Fe by train in those days, a distance of only twenty-five miles. I am not sure it was much faster by car!

Caroline Dozier, our housekeeper from Santa Clara Pueblo, told me about her family traveling to Santa Fe by wagon when she was a child in the 1920s. It took them almost a week. The roads were very bad, and if it had rained, they often got bogged down. They camped by the side of the road at night, she said.

Clarence and Gertrude lived for a number of years on the Frankenburger ranch, located along the southern side of what became Fairview Lane, and situated near the juncture of this road with McCurdy School Road. The Mormons settled this land in the 1860s and planted the large English Elm trees that still line the northern side of the street. They also planted many of the orchards in this area. There was a Mormon church and a school in which John Holterman, a neighbor of ours, taught for many years on land now owned by former Mayor Richard Lucero. These buildings were eventually torn down. Some years later, a new Mormon Church was built on the corner lot next door to the original property.

Clarence and Gertrude made arrangements in 1925 to purchase the land and a house directly across the road from the Frankenburger ranch house. Information about this house is of interest because it is the one Sam and I bought and in which we lived for over thirty years. The original house was a two-room log cabin. The Brashars added a living room and a kitchen using adobe bricks for these rooms and other construction in the house. The bricks came from a church in Santa Cruz, and Gertrude said that adobe window sills they placed in the living room each weighed up to one hundred and fifty pounds. They were as hard as stone. Other adobe bricks came from the Mormon church when it was dismantled, and these were used for the little fruit cellar built alongside the house to the west.

The Brashars used to have some pretty good parties at their house. They brought a goat inside on one occasion, Clarence remembered. They turned it upside down to have a milking contest to see who could squirt milk up to the ceiling. "Yes, I remember that. Pretty little spots all over," Gertrude said with a smile as she listened to Clarence talk.

Mr. Rueth died in 1947. Clarence and Gertrude then moved to his house in San Juan Pueblo, and sold their home on Fairview Lane to Rev. Paul McFarland.

Rev. Paul McFarland and his wife, Jessie, were living at McCurdy Mission Clinic when we first arrived. Paul was working as the maintenance foreman at the time. He also performed ministerial services in some of the outlying communities. Paul, or "Mac" as he liked to be called, was a tall nice looking man. He had a heavy set build and a very jolly, outgoing personality with a contagious laugh. He was wonderful to be around, and worked especially well with the local people. Jessie was a pleasant woman who was a full head shorter than Mac. She had a quiet smile and a warm, friendly personality like Mac. She was ready to meet the challenges that presented themselves in the mission field, and was most interested in the activities and progress with the hospital. She made a very good partner for Mac.

The McFarlands settled into the Brashar's house in August of 1947. Mac was soon remodeling, and Jessie, who had a real "green thumb" and loved to garden, was responsible for the lovely rock garden in the backyard, filled with a myriad of beautiful flowers.

Mac was chosen to be the administrator for the new hospital in early 1948. He and Jessie then moved into a new home the Board of Missions built for them near the hospital. Mac and Jessie returned to the Midwest in 1952.

We also met Harold Scheutzel, his wife, Catherine, and their daughter, Carol Ann, shortly after we arrived in Española and soon became friends. Harold was General Manager of Bond Willard Mercantile. He was a handsome, solidly built man with light brown hair and a round, ruddy face. He always seemed cheerful and outgoing, and was helpful in most any situation. Baseball was one of his interests. He had played baseball in college, and was picked up by the St. Louis Cardinal's farm team for a time after he finished college. He and Sam took to each other immediately for Sam had also been an athlete in college. I remember Harold saying with a big smile as soon as he heard the name Ziegler, "Here's another Dutchman!"

Catherine was a teacher by training. She was interested in seeing that all of our children received the best education available from the local school system. She was certain, for example, that the children were not being taught proper phonics. I appreciated Catherine's advice, and in response to urging, I found myself teaching phonics at home to supplement what the boys were learning at school.

Harold left Bond Willard Mercantile in the late 1950s, and took a position with the Española State Bank, later First National Bank of Rio Arriba, where he eventually became a vice-president. He seemed to fit in well, and was liked by the bank customers. His cheerful and friendly attitude stood him in good stead. They first lived in the Morris apartments on Oñate Street just across from Sam's office in downtown Española, but later moved to a new home on Monta Vista Street in what became known as the Denton Addition. There it was much easier for the boys and Carol Ann to play together.

Carol Ann was a bit of a tom-boy and could easily keep pace with our boys. Catherine reminded me that when Sammy and Norman had chicken pox while we were living at McCurdy Clinic, Sammy told everyone that he had gotten the pox from the McCracken's chickens. He seemed very proud of this fact. All the children had mumps at the same time, and may indeed have gotten it from or given it to each other.

Sam remembered one funny story about the kids. He had begun taking care of Carol Ann, and it was time for all of the children's immunizations. A shipment of the vaccines had just arrived. The children were brought to the clinic the same day and all knew very well why they were there. It now became a matter of who would lead things off. Norman agreed to go first and he took his injection like a man, with hardly a flinch. Carol Ann came next and let it be known that she was not happy about having to get a shot. In fact, she screamed "bloody murder." Sammy, who had witnessed the other two getting their shots and heard Carol Ann's commentary, was not at all sure he wanted to subject himself to the torture. He proceeded to run around the table three or four times before he could be caught and settled down. He did not enjoy getting his shot, but the adults present found themselves having great difficulty containing their laughter.

15

BUILDING A HOSPITAL

Sam and I worked closely with Arthur Pack on plans for the new hospital as soon as we were settled at McCurdy. Arthur believed that most of the demand would be for obstetrical beds, and thought the hospital should consist of two wings, an obstetrical wing and a general medical/surgical wing, each with sixteen beds. "One of the big products here in northern New Mexico is babies," he insisted. "Half of the beds in this 32-bed hospital are going to be obstetrical, and half will be general."

Arthur asked an architectural firm from Princeton, New Jersey to do an initial plan for the hospital. He was familiar with the firm and felt they would do a competent job. The architects unfortunately had no idea what medical practice would be like in northern New Mexico. They submitted a design for a building that was as long as a football field. It was obvious that we needed something very different because managing patient care in the beginning was going to be a one-man operation. Sam and I sent away to the American Hospital Association, the American Medical Association and several large hospital supply companies for prize winning small hospital plans so we could pull together a more functional concept. Sam also went on a hospital tour in September of 1947 in southern New Mexico and El Paso, Texas with E.W. Bell of Albuquerque, representative of the American Hospital Corporation for our district. We hoped to learn what we could from other hospitals, and profit from their successes while being more aware of "mistakes" that we should not repeat. We then came up with what we felt was a core concept for the new facility after several months of intensive study. Our design placed surgery, labor and delivery and the emergency room together in one working complex. The wards, offices, lab and the kitchen were extensions off this main core.

Arthur was friends with the architect John Gaw Meem, whom many consider the real force behind Santa Fe as we know it today, with its pueblo architecture nestled among the rolling hills along the base of the Sangre de Cristo mountains. Arthur gave our plans to John Gaw Meem to study and revise. Meem's design incorporated our central complex and provided for central heating throughout the hospital. Arthur had originally argued that the weather in New Mexico was such that only space heaters would be needed in the patient rooms. I really hit the ceiling when hearing that idea. Sam and I both said that regular central heating must be part of the design. Arthur relented after some gentle persuasion.

The final design had a surgical suite with an adjoining obstetrical suite and emergency room. This arrangement was wonderful because Sam could move back and forth between these areas. He could be operating in the main operating room, see a patient being brought into the emergency room or labor and delivery, and communicate through the doors with the nurses about what needed to be done. On many occasions, he had to do just that.

The new hospital was to be built on twelve acres of land located just northwest of town off the Chama Highway. Frank Bond & Son of Bond Willard Mercantile donated the land. It was an ideal location with a beautiful view across the Rio Grande Valley onto the Sangre de Cristo mountains. Mac McFarland, the maintenance foreman at McCurdy School, had construction experience, and Arthur felt he could handle the job of construction boss and engineer. Arthur chose the well-respected local carpenter, Ted Peabody, to be chief carpenter and superintendent of operations. Ted was knowledgeable about all phases of construction, and was able to use local labor for everything except electrical and plumbing work, which gave a real boost to the local economy. Actual dirt moving began in early 1947 with basement excavation. Work progressed well, and by late 1947, the hospital structure was largely complete and many of the supplies and equipment for the interior were beginning to arrive.

The supplies were placed outside under large tarps because there were no storage buildings. We had a near disaster one day. A clean-up man working in the area gathered up the old scraps of lumber and empty cement bags, and built a fire to burn the refuse. A brisk wind came up, and in spite of his precautions, some coals from the fire blew into the storage area and started a great fire. The fire destroyed much of the waiting room furniture and equipment along with some bedding and mattresses. It also damaged equipment we had ordered for the surgical suite and delivery room. I will not forget how disappointed Sam was to learn that the large operating room overhead light had been burned. The damage turned out to be superficial. The light still worked and the hospital used it for many years thereafter. But the burn scars to what had been a beautiful shiny exterior were a reminder of a near catastrophe that almost kept the hospital from opening.

Sam and I were busy working on staffing while Mac and Ted managed the construction. We sent the first list of required staff to the Board of Home Missions in mid-1947. I believe they almost had a stroke when they saw it. Their original ideas about scale had been very unrealistic. They could not believe the size of the staff we projected. Our estimates seem quite modest on reflection. They came to a total of 36 people and included:

4: *Business Office.* Hospital administrator, secretary, receptionist and bookkeeper (admissions were initially to be handled by the front office staff.)

10: *Nursing Service.* Nursing supervisor with nursing staff sufficient to cover three shifts a day, seven days a week for surgical, emergency department, labor and delivery, and patient ward areas; we felt we would need a minimum of ten nurses to begin.

9: *Nurse's aides.*

4: *Dietary.* Dietician, cooks (2), and sanitation; in the early days, the patients were served from heated "food trucks," while staff served themselves in the kitchen and ate in the staff dining room.

2: *Laboratory and x-ray personnel.*

4: *Housekeeping.*

3: *Grounds keeper and engineering,* including an engineer for maintenance of the boilers.

Key personnel began to assume their positions by early spring of 1948. Mac McFarland, who had done such a fine job with construction, was chosen as the first hospital business manager and administrator. Ruth Specht was the first nursing supervisor. She was a tall, good-looking redhead from Hutchinson, Kansas with extensive nursing experience. She took an active part in the nursing on the wards, and showed a real concern for the patients.

She was not one to sit behind a desk! She supervised by example more than anything else. Her quiet strength and presence were greatly admired.

Local papers spoke of the new hospital with anticipation and excitement. *The Santa Fe New Mexican* wrote:

Tomorrow Is The "Big Day" for Española

> With the dedication of Española hospital tomorrow at 2:30 p.m., that community will be assured within a few weeks of facilities of the most modern kind.
>
> A. N. Pack of Ghost Ranch, Abiquiu, who with Mrs. Pack, was almost entirely responsible for the construction of the institution by reason of a $370,000 contribution, will be one of the principal speakers tomorrow. He is chairman of the board of directors...
>
> At first only 30 [sic] beds will be available but later there will be 100; all equipment has been acquired on the scale of the latter basis. Twenty bassinets are included in an isolation nursery; this equipment is of a new, clear, plastic type which permits the nurse to see each baby from every part of the room.
>
> The two operating rooms have been termed some of the best in the Southwest. The hospital will be able to give all types of anesthesia. Special materials used for the floor and walls are designed to eliminate danger from static electricity . . . .[16]

The building that had been in progress for so many months suddenly appeared almost ready to accept its first patients on Hospital Dedication Day, Sunday, May 9, 1948. Local dignitaries and important members of the United Brethren Church who had been involved with the planning and implementation of the project gathered at the new hospital to speak in its behalf.

Among those present were Mayor Diego Salazar and members of the Hospital Board including:

Rev. Glenn F. McCracken, Superintendent of McCurdy School
J. M. Scarborough, local attorney
C. H. Yates, local businessman

C. E. Medina, teacher from McCurdy School
C. K. Brashar, local banker
Major General Charles H. Corlett, ret. Army
Rev. Paul W. McFarland, Hospital Administrator
Rev. Dr. A. D. Smith, Hospital Chaplain.

Many fine words were expressed about the hospital and its importance to the community of Española and northern New Mexico.

The first patients were admitted on May 21, 1948, and on May 28th, the first baby was delivered there.

Nurses who came to Española were sponsored by individual United Brethren churches throughout the eastern part of the United States and Canada, where the church was quite strong. They received room and board plus a token salary of $2,000 a year. They brought with them a real Christian outlook with a deep desire to serve their Lord in their own quiet way, and it showed through the wonderful care that patients received. Several cooks were brought in from Wisconsin and they created delicious hospital food. Other support staff also went out of their way to help. The hospital would not have been as successful as it was without these dedicated people. Among the early staff of nurses and other personnel were:

Ruth Specht, RN, Nursing Supervisor
Judy Baca, RN
Beverly Bardens, RN
Bev Burrows, RN She was quite a cake maker and decorator. She made wonderful cakes for our daughter, Julie's, birthdays. She also made a beautiful cake to celebrate Dr. Ziegler's delivery of his 2,000[th] baby at the hospital.
Margaret Craven, RN
Ruth Dunne, RN
Verla Flading, RN. She was the first Operating Room Supervisor.
Iva Hildinger, RN
Lola Himmel, RN
Mary Ellen Hughes, RN
Carol Hutchinson, RN
Barbara Martin, RN. She was from Canada. Her mother and father were both deaf. Barbara was a great help with deaf patients because

of her fine facility with sign language.

Carol Miller, RN. She became the first nurse anesthetist.

Sue Woodward Sais, RN

Kay Sanchez, RN. She followed Verla Flading as Operating Room Supervisor.

Carol Streblow, RN

Dorothy Vogel, RN

Mary Alire, Nurse's Aide

Adelle Davis, Business Office

Gertrude Bauer, Business Office

Virginia Bushong, Business Office

Lois Coover, Business Office/Administration

Fran Donica, Medical Records

Ruth Ritter, Dietician

Wayne Wanless, Engineer

Lloyd Bardens, Engineer

The hospital's reputation for excellent care spread quickly to the surrounding communities and beyond. This reputation reflected not only good care from physicians, but nursing care unequaled anywhere in the state. Patients came from local communities in northern New Mexico, and from Santa Fe, Albuquerque and southern Colorado. On rare occasions we had patients from as far away as Los Angles, Denver, and Kansas City.

I shall never forget a special patient at the hospital. It was the famous movie actress, Greta Garbo. Miss Garbo had come to Santa Fe to visit her brother. She developed a medical problem while in Santa Fe. Her brother did not want her admitted to St. Vincent because of concerns about publicity, so he asked if she could be taken care of in Española. Sam admitted her to the hospital under the now famous alias, "Mabel Smith."

Greta Garbo had always been so intriguing to me. She was such a beautiful actress. I begged Sam for a chance to have at least a peek at her! He finally relented. He had me dress as a nurse and let me go in the room while he was with her. Greta Garbo was truly beautiful! We did not speak at all, and she was quiet while I was there. I was grateful for the chance to see her. Her features were very fine and delicate, and she had lovely, long eyelashes.

Sam had to be careful about traffic into Miss Garbo's room. There might have been a constant parade of the curious if word had gotten around.

The only personnel allowed into the room, other than physicians, were the nurse in charge on the ward, an aide who cleaned the room and helped with bathing and food service workers.

Greta Garbo was a quiet, withdrawn patient while at the hospital. She was uncomplaining and seemingly grateful for the care and the consideration shown her even though some of the procedures to which she was subjected were uncomfortable. We were careful not to seem overly solicitous, and requests for autographs were strictly forbidden!

Sam was quite busy with deliveries during the early years. There were some periods when he delivered over fifty babies a month. There was one very unusual four-day stretch in 1950 when he delivered five sets of twins. Talk about a crew of nurses going out of their minds making sure they kept these ten babies straight! The babies were all Hispanic and two sets had the same last name. Occasions like this one happen once in a lifetime. Sam said that the incidence of twins is only 1:16,000 deliveries, and here there were five sets in four days with no other deliveries during the same time! Sam had only been aware that three of these mothers carried twins and knew that their terms were close together.

There were also a large number of deliveries at Christmas time that year. Late Christmas eve the phone rang with the labor room calling to say one of Sam's patients was there and in active labor. He bid goodnight to the family and went to the hospital. The patient delivered a lovely girl shortly after midnight and everyone seemed delighted to have such a beautiful present early on Christmas Day.

While Sam was changing from his scrub suit to get ready to come home, a labor room nurse knocked on the dressing room door and said another of his patients had arrived and was in active labor. Three more delivered by 5:30 a.m.

Tired and feeling a bit disgruntled about being up all night, Sam finally did come home. He left the hospital as the hospital staff gathered that Christmas morning for a candle-light procession through the halls softly singing Christmas carols. The children were very excited to have him home, of course, and he finally had some time to relax and enjoy his own family. I know that after he had time to reflect, he appreciated better the fact that five families had been blest with the most wonderful gift of all for Christmas, a squalling healthy newborn. What greater joy could there be?

Frank and Inez Willard opened their home and their hearts to Sam. They followed Sam's activities closely, particularly after the hospital just opened. There were times when he would be physically exhausted from work, but could not go home to rest because of distance and pending deliveries. The Willards encouraged him to come to their home to rest. They lived close to the hospital, and Sam could sleep there for three or four hours completely undisturbed and quickly return to the hospital, if necessary.

Sam and I took an occasional break to go shopping in Santa Fe. If Sam had to rush back for a delivery or for surgery, the state patrolman would overlook his speeding as he traveled to the hospital. They knew his car and let him go by. Sam was rushing back for a delivery one time after we had purchased a new car, and State Patrolman Maddison, whom we knew well, pulled us over. He walked up to the car and saw Sam, and exclaimed, "My God, man! Tell me when you buy a new car!" He sent us quickly on our way.

A new patrolman was assigned to the highway between Española and Santa Fe on another occasion. I was driving back to Española in my car with Sam following behind me. We were both traveling at a pretty good pace. The patrolman pulled me over, and when he did, Sam stopped behind me. The patrolman asked for my license, and I handed it to him. He looked at it and said, "Who is in the car behind you?"

"My husband, Dr. Ziegler," I replied as nicely as I could.

He then said, "One moment, please." He left me to go and talk with Sam, returning after a few moments to my car handing me my license with the words, "Better be a little lighter on the gas pedal next time."

Sam told me when we got home that the patrolman had walked right up to his car and said, "Doc, I've been trying to get an appointment with you for over a month. Any chance I could get in to see you?"

Sam said with a laugh, "I gave that patrolman an appointment right away! No questions asked!"

There were times when Sam needed to get away from the telephone and the pressures of his work. Arthur Pack said, "Now, don't hesitate to come up to Ghost Ranch anytime you feel the need to get away. You can come any time, and they can't reach you here because we don't have a telephone." Getting away to the ranch worked fine until the nurses at the hospital discovered that they could send the state police to find Sam. That was the end of that hideaway.

We tried a break at Bishop's Lodge one weekend. Sam realized that he could not go far because he had a number of women ready to deliver. He called Bishop's Lodge and spoke with Mr. Vance, the manager, to make arrangements for our stay. We had a nice time at the Lodge and enjoyed the change of pace. I did not have to cook, and the children had lots of wide open lawn space to run and play. They made sure to go down to the corral to see the horses and the wranglers. As luck would have it, Sam was called back to the hospital, not for one but for *thirteen* deliveries. We finally said, "Forget it! We might as well go back home."

Sam was on call for the emergency room at all times in the early days. He would often get home from taking care of one patient only to be called back to take care of another, especially on Friday and Saturday nights. He finally took to riding around on weekends with a captain in the State Patrol by the name of Ben Martinez. This arrangement worked out well for all concerned. Sam was in a good position to provide medical service on the spot, if needed, which happened quite often on the weekends. The State Patrol also knew whenever he was needed at the hospital. They monitored all radio calls and had a short-wave radio to link-up with the emergency room. If a case came in while Sam was riding around, they could easily drive him back in a patrol car.

Ben Martinez was a big man built like a defensive lineman, with huge biceps, a great chest and a rough exterior. Sam found him to be a gentle, soft-spoken man in his dealings with others, however, and he learned quickly that he was very good at what he did. He had a tough job keeping order in the small towns in northern New Mexico, which were pretty wild settlements in those days. Ben and Sam became good friends over the year he rode with him, and he gained a great deal of respect for the way he handled himself.

Saturday night dances were popular but troublesome events in the mountain villages around Española. Boys from one village often crashed a dance in another to try and break it up. Local rivalries were very intense. Serious injuries often resulted from the fighting which broke out, making for some busy nights in the emergency room. What took place in one village on one weekend would recur in another the following weekend, as the boys from the first village sought to pay a return compliment. It took Sam some time to become accustomed to these local rivalries and the damage they wrought. He never saw much sense in them. He said that Ben just smiled and wrinkled his brow when he mentioned them to him. "Part of living in northern New Mexico," he said.

The Española Hospital, in 1948. Built as a 30-bed facility, by 1967 it had been enlarged to 70 beds. Dr. Ziegler was its first physician.

16

Settling in our Fairview Home

Rev. Paul McFarland offered to sell us his house one morning in February of 1949. I remember the day very clearly. We had just returned from a short vacation in Tucson, Arizona.

Paul McFarland's offer came as a surprise. He had picked up Sam on his way to the hospital that morning because I needed our car for errands. Paul and Sam talked about our living situation at McCurdy during the ride, and all of a sudden, Paul said, "Well, you know, if I had the right offer, I might just sell my house."

When Sam heard these words, he replied to Paul, "Well, if we can come to some sort of agreement, I might just buy your house." They made a deal between them, and that is how we came to own the house on Fairview Lane.[17]

After Sam and Paul had come to terms, Arthur Pack stepped in and settled issues with the bank, and Sam then worked our financing with both Clarence Brashar and Paul. Sam and I would never have been able to manage without Arthur's help. Arthur was very good to us, both with regard to the size of the down payment and the monthly payments. Sam kept an account book of payments for the first several years, with monies owed both to Arthur and to Paul. In March of 1952, he financed the balance through the Española State Bank and dealt with the bank regarding the mortgage from then on. Milton Scarborough, attorney, was involved in drawing up the original papers for the purchase of the house. It was a great day when we signed those papers and were able to move in.

Word spread quickly at McCurdy and around town that we were going to purchase a home of our own. Our good friends, Harold and Catherine Scheutzel, offered to help us move our few belongings, and before we knew it we were "settled" in our new home. I could go through a gate into the front yard and somehow, all at once, the world became ours.

The house consisted of six rooms. The front door opened immediately into the living room, its long side running parallel with the road. It was a lovely, warm room with thick adobe walls and heavy, dark stained vigas. A fireplace hugged the southeast corner. Off the living room to the west was the small master bedroom. It had a fireplace in the southwest corner. The room was well lighted with large windows on the south and west walls, but it had only a small closet at the west end. A doorway on the north wall at its eastern edge opened into a small hallway leading to the bathroom.

The hallway opened at its other end onto the dining room, a room about the size of the master bedroom. A door in the middle of its west wall went out onto a small, closed courtyard. On its east side was another room of equal size which we used as a bedroom for the boys. At the north end of the dining room, a door led into the kitchen.

Off the kitchen to the east was a small frame sewing room with windows all along its two open sides, giving it a cheery, warm feeling as the wonderful New Mexico sunshine flooded in. We used this room a great deal for busy work and we also had an extra bed there.

The property itself was a little more than three-quarters of an acre. East of the house was an orchard filled with apple, pear and cherry trees. Along its eastern edge ran an irrigation ditch that was fed from the old community ditch running alongside McCurdy Road. Out back in the northwest corner was an old two-story cow barn that then housed over a hundred laying hens. Stretching east from this old barn was open space filled mostly with weeds.

Life really began to have meaning for me when we started living here. I think the thing I needed more than anything else was to have a place I felt was ours, where I could decorate a window or move some furniture or do something creative if I wanted, and not have to worry that it might be questioned. I know my own life began to change for the better when we moved into the house.

We came to know Hollis and Milton Scarborough at this time, and they made every effort to see we felt welcome in Española. Hollis, in particular, made a point of coming to the house in the morning at coffee time. She would call from the door when she arrived, "Coffee time!" It was then that I really started liking coffee and enjoying the chance to sit down and chat. Hollis knew a great deal about farming and gardening. She showed me how to cut wild asparagus where it grew along the irrigation ditch, cutting beneath the soil so that new shoots would continue to grow. We would walk in the orchard, and as we walked, she talked about the beauty of the trees when they were in bloom in the spring, and of the Española Valley. Hollis helped me to feel at home.

We knew very little about the history of our home or its construction when we bought the house from the McFarlands. The McFarlands did not give us any information, and indeed they may not have known. We thought the house was made completely of adobes, and were in for a rude surprise when we had some minor alterations done. We asked Ted Peabody, the carpenter who helped build the hospital, to come by and do some minor renovation.

When Sam came home from the office late one evening, Ted was still at the house. He was sweating and cursing under his breath. He said, "Doc, I've never in my life sawed through such hard logs!" We were surprised to learn that not one, but two rooms, the bedroom and the dining room, were both made of logs. We "discovered" the original two-room log cabin that had been built by the Mormon Bishop for his son and daughter-in-law as a wedding present in the 1860s.

A number of very special people touched our lives while we lived in our Fairview house. One was Dora Giron, a young Hispanic girl from Vallecitos. We had come to know Dora at McCurdy when she babysat for the boys on occasion. She was from a well-respected Protestant family, and wanted to continue her education at McCurdy, but she needed some financial help. We arranged for her to live with us beginning in the fall of 1949 when she was fifteen years old, and to help with household chores and babysitting after school in return for room and board. She stayed for two years and was a most welcome addition to the household.

Dora was a lovely girl with long dark hair and large brown eyes. She had a beautiful smile and a jolly personality, and was always very neat in her appearance. She had a ready intelligence and an eagerness to learn, and she followed instructions well. She was able to fit nicely into our household within a short time.

Dora helped me start a garden. Much of the area out in back and through the orchard was full of weeds and old grass, having been left unattended for some time. I chose a plot to the northwest of the house for planting vegetables and sweet corn. Sam was taken with the idea right away. I asked Dora if she knew how to garden and irrigate. "Oh yes," she said with a big smile. So we prepared a garden plot and planted corn, zucchini and tomatoes. Dora showed me how to irrigate the rows of seeds, and how to fertilize. We had great stands of tomatoes, corn and squash before long.

There was a big old iron gate on the driveway to keep out the horses and cows that roamed freely up and down the roads. When Sam went to the hospital in the middle of the night, he sometimes forgot to close it, and one night, just when everything in the garden was coming along so beautifully, a big Roan horse found his way in. He ate up the corn and trampled all over the vegetables. I discovered his rambling the next morning and called Sam at the hospital to tell him what had happened. He exclaimed when he heard me crying, "Get the hell out of that garden and go to the grocery store!"

That incident ended Dora's and my gardening for that year. We had to make the best of our losses and salvage what we could from the remains of the garden. Dorothy Burnham of Ghost Ranch came to work for us as a gardener the next year. She had a lot of experience, and under her tutelage, we tried gardening again, this time out back in a protected area safe from the horses and cows that roamed the streets.

Dora went home to Vallecitos to visit her family on occasional weekends and holidays. She always came out of her house carrying a huge white flour tortilla hot off of the stove when we arrived to pick her up. She would sit in the car with us and divide the tortilla so that we could all enjoy some as we drove back to Española. I asked Dora if she could tell me her mother's recipes for tortillas, beans and chili. She said she did not have real recipes, but that she would make them and I could write down what she did as she cooked. I did write down these recipes, and to this day, they never seem to fail. Our sons' first requests for food when they return home are always for Dora's beans and chili and tortillas.

We wanted to share our home with others when we began to feel settled. Our house was small, and entertaining to any degree meant moving tables and furniture around to accommodate guests, but Sam was a good sport about these reorganizations, and I learned how to prepare table settings that could be arranged quickly once the tables were in position. We decided that people would have to accept us as we were, so we invited people to our house and moved furniture. We always had a lot of fun.

We were aware of and appreciated the hospital staff's dedicated service to the needs of the new hospital and local people. Their efforts were apparent from the beginning, and Sam and I both wished to show our gratitude for their efforts. We planned and served a buffet dinner for all of the hospital staff at Thanksgiving in 1949. A patient of Sam's had given him a big Tom turkey some eight or nine months before. We kept the turkey out on the second floor of the Barn, and fattened him on cracked corn. He was a real beauty and dressed out at 25 lbs. We had a struggle just getting him into the oven. The turkey along with ham and other food kept all of our guests well fed. There were about fifty people, a large number for us. They arrived in small groups because of their shifts at the hospital, and our buffet style dinner worked out very well.

The Holiday Season was a festive time for entertaining. We learned that although our house was small, getting friends of interest together for some tasty food and good conversation was what counted.

Sam and I were aware of the need to find some activity that the boys would enjoy as they grew up, and we finally settled on horseback riding. We contacted Herman Hall, the foreman at Ghost Ranch for advice. Herman picked out two cowponies he felt would be good horses for Norman and Sammy, and brought them down from the ranch. The boys were now old enough to take care of their own horses. We converted a back portion of the yard east of the Barn into a stable area. It was not long before Sam had a carpenter at work building stables and a feed bin to accommodate our newest arrivals.

The two horses that came were a ten year-old, mousy-gray gelding with a knobby head and a high, wide backbone, and a younger, more spirited filly with a smooth black coat. Sammy adopted the black filly immediately and called her Midnight. He was practicing roping and putting the horse through all of her paces within no time. Norman seemed to take to the other horse who was a bit more his speed. He called him Mouse. No other name would fit. He discovered that bareback riding was a bit uncomfortable because of Mouse's backbone. He walked kind of weird after he had been out riding for a couple of hours without a saddle. But Mouse turned out to be a very smart well-trained horse that responded quickly to commands and could outrun most of the other horses around. "He's a real cowpony!" Norman exclaimed with a smile. The boys learned to feed and water the horses, and groom them. They found out they had to be up early in the morning to get all this work done and still have time to fix their lunches for school. They managed well!

We found out in no time that the boys loved to race the horses. The foothills to the east of the house were wide open spaces, with lots of room for riding and exploring and "racing." Their friends, Royce and Coy Washburn and Chuck Denton, all had horses and were good riders, and the five of them began to spend a lot of time together riding.

My mother and father moved to Fresno, California in 1944 and loved the beautiful sunshine and weather to grow flowers such as camellias. There were five wonderful years, then Mother became ill in 1949 and was unable to recover. Before she died, I was able to visit and be with her. I was pregnant then. She knew right away so we talked about names for the baby. I said, "if it is a girl, I would like to name her Gayle, after you."

Mother felt that Julia was a beautiful name, so we decided Julia Gayle would be great. That is how we decided on the name for our daughter.

Mother died September 30, 1950 and my daughter, Julia Gayle, was born November 15th of that year.

Harold Scheutzel, the Fire Chief of the Española Volunteer Fire Department, drove the fire truck through town with the siren blaring to celebrate the occasion. He told Sam that if we had a girl, he was going to do just that. I think Harold woke up everyone.

I opened my eyes the morning after Julia's arrival to find a beautiful basket of flowers on the table by my bed. Draped over the basket was a sterling silver necklace with a large, turquoise stone of Lone Mountain spider web. Sam had designed the necklace and had an Indian silversmith from Packer's Trading Post in Santa Fe make it for me. It was beautiful! I felt very special! Again, that extra touch of Sam's.

We had much more room for all of my relatives and other friends to visit on Fairview Lane than we had in our house across from McCurdy clinic. There were as many as fourteen with us at times. The best way I could feed all of the guests was to keep big pots of vegetable soup and beans and chili cooking on the stove. We were able to sightsee and enjoy ourselves without worrying about food. All the boys could stay in the Barn which we had remodeled for Sammy and Norman. Things worked out well because they were family, and we made the best of our times together.

I remember the occasion my sister, Paula, her husband, Arthur Williams, and their three sons, Lee, Denny and Leslie, were all here. The boys loved to ride and they spent a good part of each day with the horses. We tried to keep them busy with other activities when they were not riding. One afternoon we gave them shovels and sent them to the orchard to dig. They had excavated a large hole within a short time, and then started making tunnels. We were all quietly involved with our own tasks, when all of a sudden, Norman came rushing into the house waving his arms and shouting, "Sammy's caught in a tunnel!" I immediately had visions of Sammy being smothered, and rushed out of the house to see what had happened.

Sammy had backed into the tunnel he had been digging and become wedged in so tightly he could not move his legs, which were pinned under him. Why he had backed in I still do not know, but we counted our lucky stars that day. We had the boys dig dirt away from the sides little by little in order to free him. He emerged smiling after about twenty minutes. He was a bit scared but not much worse for the wear.

Years later when I attended my sister, Paula's, funeral in Buena Vista, CO, Denny Williams, her second son, remarked to me what great fun they always had in New Mexico when they came to visit during the summer. "You will never know how wonderful those visits were," he said, "how much they meant to me and my brothers. We looked forward to coming out west from Ohio all year long, where we could ride horses, go to the rodeo, visit Bandelier and Taos and the Pueblos, and go on picnics." We liked to do all of these things, too, and we made them possible for all of my relatives. It was nice to hear one of my nephews say how much they had enjoyed what we had done for them.

Not long after we were settled in our new home, Roy and Elberta Honstein moved from their house in Totavi to their new home on McCurdy Road just adjacent to our property. I first met them one evening in early 1947 while Sam and I were having dinner at the Granada Hotel in Española. Sam had met them earlier in the course of his work and had been impressed by them. When he noticed them sitting across the dining room from us, he immediately pointed them out to me, saying, "I see Roy and Elberta

Honstein. I want you to meet them. They seem like a very nice couple." We went over to say hello after finishing our dinner and had an enjoyable visit.

Our relationship with the Honsteins developed from that time. Elberta or "Bertie" has become a close friend. I talk with her almost as much as I would a sister and we find time for fun together. When we first met, Roy held the Northern New Mexico Chevron Gas Distributorship and was active in business affairs in the community. He also refereed high school sporting events, and was a member of the Española Chamber of Commerce and City Council. Roy found time for neighborly acts. We would hear a strange motor in the driveway following a heavy snowfall, and would look out to see Roy on his small snowplow clearing the driveway. He would always wave a friendly good-bye as he left. Following his untimely death, Elberta has continued to manage the gas distributorship.

Roy and Elberta developed the Roy-El Morgan Horse Ranch once they had settled on their new property. Having their ranch so close has enabled us to see their beautiful mares and foals in the paddocks and pastures right next door. Sam and I were great supporters of theirs at the national horse shows, "hooting" along with all the others. Their daughter, Debbie, was much involved with the training and riding of their horses. She became an excellent horsewoman, and also served as a qualified judge at the National Morgan Horse Shows in Oklahoma City.

Roy and Elberta named one beautiful filly Roy-El's "Isabell" after me. I was very honored indeed. I can see her now from my office window that looks out over their paddocks. She is a young and spirited mare with a shining black coat. I love to watch her prance with head held high.

Beverly Burroughs, one of the mission nurses at the Española Hospital, brought a special birthday cake to Julie when she was a year old. Beverly loved to make and decorate cakes, and had a real talent for this craft. The cake she made was shaped like a baby's cradle and held two small baby dolls inside. It was perfect in every detail. Little did any of us know that one day Julie would have twins of her own.

We planned a special party for Julie when she was ten years old. Beverly remembered Julie's birthday and told us she wanted to bake and decorate another cake for her. She made a cake of Cinderella and her carriage this time. It was perfect in every detail, with doors and windows, a seat for the coachman, and bric-a-bac decoration on the carriage wheels and doors. It was hard to imagine how we were going to cut it and eat it.

Our cat, Tar Baby, remained with us for many years, never intrusive, but very much a part of the family. We were not particularly interested in increasing our feline numbers at the house, but Tar Baby seemed selective in her mates. Her kittens were always beautiful long haired, jet black Persian types, just like she was, and there was never any difficulty in finding families who would take a kitten.

Tar Baby had a special box in the cupboard behind the kitchen door in the back room which she preferred for her deliveries. One morning while we were having breakfast, we could tell that she was about ready to deliver. The boys kept running from the table to check on her, and the doctor in the family said, "Will you please leave the cat alone!" He then left for the hospital. The phone rang about an hour later. It was the doctor calling to ask, "How is the mother cat doing?"

The anthropologist and writer, Alice Marriott, came to northern New Mexico in 1945 to begin work on a book about her friend, Maria Martinez, the potter from San Ildefonso Pueblo. A grant from the Rockefeller Foundation and then a Guggenheim Fellowship sponsored this effort. She took up residence near Nambé Pueblo with her friend, the illustrator Margaret Lafranc, while she pursued her research about Maria's life and her work with pottery. Sam met her when she came to see him on several occasions during 1947 for minor complaints. It was Alice's concern for Maria Martinez that really brought us together and provided the opportunity for our friendship to develop.

Maria had a medical problem that brought on occasional bouts of fever and malaise which were of concern not only regarding Maria's general health, but because they disabled her for short periods of time. Alice took care to see that Maria had regular check-ups with Sam, and provided great support for her. Sam finally performed surgery on Maria in the early 1950s to correct her condition. She recovered nicely from this procedure and seemed largely symptom-free afterwards.

We invited Alice to dinner on several occasions when we moved into our home on Fairview Lane. She was always a welcome guest. We had a wonderful gathering one evening with Alice, the artists, Arthur and Norma Hall from Rancho del Rio in Alcalde, John Bonnel, owner of the White

Hogan, an Indian jewelry store in Scottsdale, Arizona and several physicians and their wives including Dr. and Mrs. Al Egenhoffer from Santa Fe, and Dr. and Mrs. Michael Pijoan from Española. Dr. Pijoan was Sam's new associate in practice.

Alice spoke with great interest and excitement about her work on this and other occasions. She was a sensitive individual who loved to talk about her experiences and did so in a most literate and engaging way. She had the true gift of a storyteller. Her voice seemed small and quiet when she began, but it rose gradually in pitch as she proceeded with her task and turned toward the heart of her tale. Her voice was always filled with warmth and good humor.

Alice told about her experiences with the Kiowa Indians of Oklahoma among whom she had spent many of her earlier years, and about her book *The Ten Grandmothers*. She also spoke of her friendship with Maria Martinez of San Ildefonso and about Maria's work as a potter. We were curious to learn that Alice had first met Maria in 1941 at the World's Fair in San Francisco. There was an American Indian Art Exhibit at the Fair with live arts and crafts demonstrations. Alice worked for the Indian Arts and Crafts Board at the time, and was responsible for helping the Indians who demonstrated their crafts, of whom Maria was one, make the necessary local adjustments to being at the Fair.

We completely lost track of Alice for many years after the mid-1950s when she returned to Oklahoma City to continue her free-lance writing and research. We received a call in 1986 from our good friends, Ike and Debbie Wyant of Santa Fe, asking us to dinner and telling us that Alice was visiting them with her friend and associate, Carol Rachlin. We were delighted to renew our friendship with Alice and to meet her friend, Carol, whom we found a most enjoyable person. Carol is also an anthropologist who had joined Alice in her work in 1968. Over the next years, they collaborated on eight different books about American Indian culture and mythology. Carol was writer-in-residence with Alice at the University of Central Oklahoma between the years 1968-1982.

We kept up a regular correspondence with Alice and Carol after renewing our acquaintance. We always looked forward to seeing them on their annual visits with the Wyants. We were able to see them in Oklahoma City on one occasion, when we attended the National Morgan Horse Show with Roy and Elberta Honstein. Alice passed away in March of 1992. Sam and I maintained our contact with Carol Rachlin since Alice's death. Carol remains an avid correspondent. I still welcome her letters and her continuing friendship.

The road in front of our house remained unpaved and without an official name until 1950. Local people referred to it as Fairview Lane, but we learned that before the turn of the century, the Mormons had called it La Joya (The Jewel). We liked the name La Joya. Sam tried unsuccessfully several times to have the City Council consider this name. Then Bill Laws, owner of the grocery store on the corner at the intersection of this road with Taos Highway 285, submitted an official request to the City Council to have the street named "Fairview Lane." Bill Murphy, our neighbor several houses removed, attended the Council meeting at which this request was brought up for discussion and vote. Murphy argued that the name had to be Fairview Lane because he had a large stock of his business stationery already printed with that name and could not change his stationery without incurring considerable expense. The official request from Bill Laws and Murphy's plea had a decisive effect on the Council's decision. The vote for Fairview Lane passed with only one dissent, that of Sam's.

Our road was now officially "Fairview Lane."

We gave our home on Fairview Lane several names after we moved in. The one we finally selected was "The Rocking Z." This name seemed most appropriate because our family appeared to be in constant motion. No single member was ever quiet or still for very long, each off on a new adventure of one kind or other. Somehow in the midst of it all, we have managed to maintain a real sense of family, of caring and loving and being there for each other.

17

GEORGIA O'KEEFFE

Georgia O'Keeffe came to see Sam in 1949 about some problem. He remembers having to put her straight immediately about who was in charge in his office. She had started to tell him how to treat her medically as soon as she sat down and they began talking. Quite frankly, he was somewhat awed by her presence. The renowned artist herself sat before him. But Sam took a deep breath and said, "Georgia, I have no intention of telling you how to paint. I do not expect you to tell me how to practice medicine." He was her primary physician from that time forward, and she came to consider Sam a true and close friend. He never knew whether she followed his instructions completely on that first occasion, but in the years to come, she always respected his advice and was rigorous in following his orders.

Sam and I became close friends of Georgia's as the years went by, and she was often a guest in our home. This relationship continued even after Sam's retirement from private practice in 1976. She made it known at that time that he was to remain her private physician. He did continue to take care of her, using our home as an office.

We were also guests of Georgia's, both at Rancho de los Burros on Ghost Ranch and her home in Abiquiu, N.M. One of the first dinners to which we were invited was at her home in Abiquiu. Just the three of us were there. Georgia said as we were being seated at the dining room table, "Now, the dogs are used to being by me when I eat, so if you don't mind, I'll let them in. They'll stay under the table, and they won't bother you. Just don't move your feet while you are eating."

Georgia had two chows with reputations for being mean. Phoebe Pack referred to these chows as "man-eating dogs" that needed to be taken very seriously. She said, "While Georgia was not one to fall in love with the animals, she wanted people to stay away from her place, and these dogs helped considerably." We sat very still during dinner that night!

Georgia kept things very simple at her homes in Abiquiu and Rancho de los Burros. All the rooms were adobe color and the few furnishings were done in black and white. There was nothing in the rooms but basic necessities. I did not really feel I was in a woman's quarters when I saw these rooms, certainly not a woman's bathroom, which is usually full of pretty bottles, with many items sitting around.

I seldom saw Georgia in anything but a pair of slacks and a coat like a man's coat. She wore black most of the time. Under the coat, she wore a white shirt and a string tie. This was her usual costume and she was always well groomed. I saw her with her black cape and a black toreador's hat with a small flat brim in the winter. I never saw her wear any other type of hat. She changed from black to white coat and slacks occasionally in the summer months, and very infrequently appeared in a loose-fitting white dress.

A young woman by the name of Maria Chabot was often with Georgia when we came to dinner in the early years. Maria was a tall, husky woman who did everything from home repairs to grocery shopping. She seemed to be a jack-of-all-trades. We enjoyed Maria. She was always straightforward in conversation and pleasant to be around.

Sam and I knew other people from Abiquiu who worked for Georgia. Dorothea Martinez was devoted to her. She cooked and cleaned and did general housework for nearly twenty years. Her husband, Frank, helped with maintenance work. Sam and I attended their 50th wedding anniversary celebration in Abiquiu on August 19, 1978 when they were remarried and had a feast dance. It was quite a festive occasion. Their remarriage took place in the Abiquiu Catholic Church, with Dorothea wearing her original long, yellow wedding gown, her hair still quite dark and her figure very slim and trim. Frank looked elegant standing alongside her in his dark wedding suit.

We were escorted to the local school gymnasium following the wedding ceremony. There a feast of native foods including beans, chili, posole, tamales, tortillas and other good things were served along with drinks of all kinds. A band began to play while we were still eating, and in the Spanish tradition, the men each in turn asked the bride to dance, and the women the groom. As was also the custom, each guest pinned money to the dress or coat of the bride and groom. Sam pinned money to Dorothea's dress and danced with her as I did with Frank. Their clothing was covered with money before the evening was over.

We felt privileged to have been invited to share this occasion with Dorothea and Frank. We were graciously received and had a nice time with all the guests.

We also knew Pita Lopez who became associated with Georgia in the 1970s and was one of her most devoted and capable employees. She functioned as her driver, secretary, bookkeeper and general helper. Pita would often have tea with me when she drove Georgia down to see Sam at the house in Española. We found her a most likeable person.

A lovely young woman in her early thirties named Margaret Wood stayed with Georgia in the late 1970s. We liked Margaret very much. She was not the forceful personality that Maria Chabot had been. She was rather quiet and almost shy. She planned and cooked all of Georgia's meals, and we were privileged to share a number of them with Georgia and Margaret. The times we were together were usually private occasions, the meals themselves simple vegetarian cuisine. The chow dogs were there, as before, under the table.

At other times, there would be just the three of us, Georgia, Sam and me. We would have a simple meal of herb soup and bread. Georgia sometimes had a fish or chicken dish served with a salad, the preparation of which she directed with close attention. We occasionally had wine. Georgia enjoyed a wine that she had selected, and I thought the wines were very good.

What Georgia saw to paint was quite different from what I might see. She looked out to the east from her bedroom window, over the distant cliffs that she loved. She called them her "curtains." Once while talking with me, she spoke of New York at night. She said that the time she loved best was when she could look out the windows of her apartment and see the buildings with their lights. She especially loved the snow in the winter and spoke of the snow flakes "standing in the air."

Georgia came into Sam's office with airline tickets to India one day in 1959. She wanted Sam to go to India with her. She did not include me in the invitation. I have often said in jest to people, "Georgia adored Sam and tolerated me, though always with respect." I really believe she did adore

Sam. She valued him highly as a physician and thoroughly enjoyed his presence and his company.

Not being of a jealous nature, I encouraged Sam to go with her. I thought it would be a wonderful experience for him, perhaps in more ways than one, but Sam demurred. He told Georgia that he could not get away because of his busy schedule. He really would have been a help to her. She fell off of a donkey while she was in India, and did need medical attention.

Sam and I planned a sit-down dinner for Georgia and eighteen other people at our home after we had known her for some time. Among the guests present were Hamilton and Jean Garland from Swan Lake. The dinner seemed to go fine, but Georgia came up to me immediately following, and said, "Please walk me out. I must leave." I was surprised and called Sam to help escort her to her car. When we were outside, she said, "The dinner was delicious. I enjoyed myself very much, but I can no longer take any more of Jean Garland. What you are not aware of is that Marie Garland, Hamilton Garland's mother, is a very close friend of mine. Marie and Jean do not get along. They are at swords' points with each other most of the time. I will tell you about this situation some other time."

Georgia later told us that because she was a good friend of Marie Garland's, Jean would be insufferable to her whenever she had an opportunity.

Georgia invited Sam and me to a small dinner party at the Abiquiu house in the early 1960s. Elliot Porter, the photographer, and his wife were there along with several other guests. It was a pleasant gathering with good conversation. During the course of the evening, Georgia led Sam and me to her studio. She turned toward us as we entered, and pointed to an immense painting that covered almost the entire south wall, saying, "I call that a painting. What do you think?" I do not remember exactly what we replied, something to the effect of "how interesting." I was actually overwhelmed by the immensity of the painting and the striking formations of what appeared to be clouds floating on a great vastness. Georgia proceeded to explain that the picture was indeed of clouds as she saw them from an airplane. She said she was calling the painting "Sky Above Clouds." It was really overpowering.

We began to wander leisurely about the studio after looking at this painting. Georgia did not seem to be in a hurry, nor did she seem concerned about her other guests. She pointed out some interesting early paintings of hers done in the years between 1910-1920. Several of them seemed almost primitive in character.

We came upon a painting of a purple iris hanging on the wall near a door. The painting was 24" x 30" in size, with striking colors. We admired it and said so to Georgia. I thought it was lovely. "What are you doing with that painting, Georgia?" Sam asked.

She replied with a wave of her hand, "I am going to burn it."

"Why?" we exclaimed. She only shrugged her shoulders. Sam finally said, "It would look great in our new living room at home."

I thought that would be the end of the matter. Much to my surprise, she said, "Why not?"

Georgia brought the painting down a few days later, and said we were welcome to hang it in the house. We had recently remodeled our home and built a large new living room. The room came alive with the painting. It hung in this room for the next sixteen years, and was enjoyed by everyone who came to the house. Georgia appeared at the house one day all those years later with a young, new driver and announced to me, "I have come for my painting."

There was not much I could say except, "Georgia, we will certainly miss your painting." The room seemed empty without it.

We had never thought seriously about trying to acquire the painting. We knew Georgia would refuse an offer because she had already committed herself to burning it. We also knew we could not afford to buy it at her current prices.

Georgia left a large black and white charcoal drawing of a Banana Flower in place of the painting. She said as she presented it, "The black and white pictures are my favorites." The drawing will be a reminder of our friendship with Georgia. It is unsigned as all of her works. The sad end to this story is that we have never seen the purple iris anywhere since that time. We do not know how Georgia disposed of it, or if she really did. Somehow in Georgia's eye, it was not perfect, not up to her standard and not meant to be admired as an object of beauty. We shall always miss the purple iris.

We were with Georgia one evening in early 1966 when she had a gathering at her home in Abiquiu. There was a good deal of talk about her up-coming retrospective show to be held at the Amon Carter Museum in Fort Worth, Texas in March. The show was to cover fifty years of her painting. Everyone was saying how nice it would be to attend. Sam and I had rather dismissed it from our minds because of his busy schedule.

Georgia called a few days later saying, "Mrs. Ziegler? This is Georgia

O'Keeffe. I just want you to know that I will be expecting you and Dr. Ziegler in Fort Worth for the showing." She added, "I have made arrangements for your stay. Your plane tickets will be delivered to you. You are to be my guests, and I am so looking forward to your coming."

Sometime later we were talking with Phoebe Pack about Georgia, and Phoebe made a rather perceptive comment. She said, "Well, you finally find out that with people like Georgia, it's a heck of a lot easier to do what they want." Sam and I could not have agreed more.

We had a nice time at Georgia's show. It was exciting, fascinating and beautiful all at the same time. I kept choosing those paintings I felt we should purchase as a way of entertaining myself, only to find they had already been spoken for. Stieglitz had encouraged Georgia to be aloof and to keep her social presence to a minimum, but Georgia welcomed all of the attention she received at the opening in Ft. Worth. She found a place to stand where she felt comfortable greeting the guests. She wanted Sam by her side most of the evening. "I know I am in good hands," she said, and she never seemed to tire during the long affair.

Georgia and I would often talk about organic food, about which she was quite an authority. She told me that most people did not know how properly to cook vegetables. "They usually overcook them," she said. She told me how to grow alfalfa sprouts in a drawer. Her instructions were:

> Boil a Turkish towel, lay it on wax paper or something to protect the drawer. While the towel is still damp, sprinkle non-sprayed alfalfa seeds that you can buy at the health food stores, over the towel. Then cover the seeds with part of the damp towel. Close the drawer, leaving just enough open for air. The seeds will root in the towel, and you can easily pull out the sprouts. They are wonderful eating.

Sam came home one day saying he had admitted Georgia to the hospital. He thought I should take something to her. Flowers did not seem appropriate. I finally decided on a pudding my mother used to make called Floating Island. I felt Georgia would be unhappy with the hospital food, and Sam confirmed that she was a very picky eater. She lived primarily on herbs, soups, gelatins and chicken, diets which were very bland. I made the pudding and placed it in several small glass dessert cups, then took it to the hospital and asked the nurses to see that she got it. I made it for her several times, and she loved it.

Georgia later wrote a nice letter, thanking me for the pudding. She said:

> I came home to Abiquiu Monday afternoon and your pudding was the only thing I ate that day until I got dinner. I had eaten one of them (a cup of pudding) the night before. They were so delicate and delicious it was really a pleasure to have them, as you yourself must know how "just right" they are for the "not so well one." I am sure you must know how much I enjoyed them. I will one day ask for the recipe, with the hope that they can one day come from my house as well as yours.[18]

I sent Georgia the recipe for Floating Island. It is as follows:

2 cups milk
2 egg yolks
1 whole egg
1/8 tsp salt
4 T sugar
½ tsp vanilla
Scald milk in a double boiler
Heat slightly 1 egg, 2 egg yolks, sugar, salt and vanilla
Add hot milk to egg mixture
Stir constantly until egg coats the spoon
Cool, and turn into custard dish
Beat eggs whites with 2-4 T sugar for meringues
Drop meringues on top of custard as "Floating Islands"

There were times when Georgia seemed interested in telling me about personal things, such as how she did her exercises. She said she loved to go out walking, where she could gather her rocks and pieces of wood, and clear her mind before approaching her next painting. She was intent on keeping her feet in good condition, and she showed me the foot and ankle exercises she felt were beneficial for her.

She felt that eye exercises were also important. She spoke of putting pressure at the inner corner of each eye by the bridge of the nose and then moving her eyes to help maintain their health. She seemed to enjoy sharing these kinds of things with me.

Georgia appeared attentive and concerned about me as well. I received a card from her on one occasion when I had not been well, with a note saying, "I overheard that you're not well. This is just to greet you and say that I hope and trust you will be alright soon." [19]

We invited Georgia for dinner one Christmas. We learned that she was going to be alone and we thought she might enjoy our company. She accepted, and seemed most appreciative of our hospitality. I distinctly remember how she looked when she arrived in the late afternoon. She stood at the entryway in her black Flamenco hat with a black scarf covering her head under her hat. She wore a dark blue serge suit, white shirt, and her favorite silver pin at the neckline. I call her suit a blue serge because it reminded me of one my father wore. It was midnight or dark navy blue and made of a strong fine twill fabric. She handed me a gift when I welcomed her to our home. It was Stieglitz's book of photographs he had taken of her. Our evening together was most enjoyable. We shared a delicious Christmas fare with Georgia and a few other close friends.

Claudia, one of Georgia's sisters, was also a patient of Sam's. She got to know him well enough that she also wanted him to be her physician. Georgia called to make an appointment to see Sam one time when Claudia was visiting with her. No sooner had he put down the phone from talking with Georgia than it rang again, this time with Claudia calling. She wanted to see Sam, too. They came down together from Abiquiu. Georgia refused to come into the house with Claudia when they arrived. She had to come in first and alone. Claudia was forced to wait in the car while Sam attended to Georgia. I finally invited Claudia in for tea to help the situation, and Sam spent some time with her after seeing Georgia. Claudia and Georgia had apparently been arguing all the way down from Abiquiu.

Phoebe Pack told us that Georgia did not know what she would do with her sister when she first came to New Mexico. Phoebe urged Georgia to have Claudia start a vegetable garden. Claudia really took to this suggestion, and began raising prize vegetables. We had some very delicious red raspberries from her garden.

There were many sides to Georgia. She lived primarily within her world as an artist and could be very single-minded and calculating about her relationships with people and much aware of her own advantage, but she also had a sincere, philanthropic side. She was quite concerned about the local people with whom she came into contact in Abiquiu, many of whom worked for her in one capacity or another. Sam received a letter from her on one occasion about a young girl:

> Dear Dr. Ziegler:
> This little girl—is only on her third week with me but I think she needs some attention from you—
> She is a very nice little girl and is very eager to go to college which is an event in Abiquiu—
> I send her to you not just because I think she is ailing but because I think she is worth the effort—
> Thank you and all best wishes
> Sincerely[20]

We were at Georgia's home for dinner one time, and she put something into Sam's pocket just as we were leaving. She looked at him and said, "Here, this is for you. You do as you think best with it." There was a check for $5,000 in his coat pocket. She had made the check out to Sam, and he gave it to the Española Hospital. This gesture was quite genuine on Georgia's part. I am sure she felt certain we would see that the hospital benefited from her gift.

We were acquainted with the Santa Fe artist, Barry Atwater, and his wife, Helen. Barry said one day, knowing of our friendship with Georgia, "Sam, I would like to meet this famous lady, but I do not think I ever will unless you set the stage for me." Sam told Barry he thought he could arrange a meeting for him.

We spoke to Georgia about Barry and his great desire to meet her one day later when we were with her. Sam explained that he was an accomplished artist with one of his works hanging in the United Nations Building in New York City. She said she would be willing to meet him and she set a time for 2:00 p.m. the following Sunday afternoon.

We drove Barry to Rancho de los Burros for this occasion. We were greeted by a very aloof Georgia, who was short on conversation and warmth. Barry was immediately uncomfortable. He indicated after a short time, that he was ready to leave. We bid Georgia good-bye, both Sam and I feeling embarrassed and not knowing what to make of Georgia's coolness.

Sam had occasion to see Georgia in his office several weeks later. As she departed she remarked, "Sam, don't ever bring any of those calendar artists around again." We never did bring another local artist to see Georgia, and we never told Barry what Georgia said about him either.

We saw changes in Georgia as she aged. She softened a great deal. She knew she was growing old, and wanted to be in the company of friends. This was one of the reasons she appreciated Sam and me. She knew us well and could rely on us. We were part of her world, so to speak. She seemed to be able to relax around us.

Georgia began to take an intense pride in her skin after Juan Hamilton came into her life. She was out in the sun so much she was predisposed to little skin blemishes on her face and arms. Sam spent a great deal of time over the last years of her life gently caring for these spots.

Phoebe Pack said Georgia told her that she had never cared anything about her looks before she met Juan. Juan made her into a different woman. He began to choose her clothing, and she started to put on lipstick, attend to her hair, and be very concerned with appearance.

We would see her many times clutching Juan's arm as she walked outside when he was with her at her home during the later years. We rarely saw them together in public, but Juan occasionally drove her down to see Sam.

We never felt curious about Georgia's relationship with Juan. The rumor of marriage arose, and Sam was questioned at some length by lawyers who were involved in the settlement of her estate, about whether he knew if they were married or not. I had never thought about a physical relationship between her and Juan. In her younger years, Georgia had quite a beautiful body and her face was striking and had been photographed many times. The nude pictures Stieglitz made of Georgia are a tribute to her beauty as a young woman. But she was no longer a young woman in the days that we knew her, and certainly not during the time Juan was with her.

Georgia began to have nightmares toward the latter part of her life. She would call Sam in the middle of the night, at one or two o'clock in the morning, and say that she had to see him right away. There wasn't a time that Sam did not go when she called. These incidents usually happened some time after midnight, and most often when she was at Rancho de los Burros, not at the Abiquiu house.

Her dreams were often filled with the presence of a long dark tunnel through which she had to try and pass, and with a gate which seemed to block her path and which she could not open by herself. She also had the feeling that she was whirling in space in a maze of clouds and was frightened. Often, too, Sam said that she had forgotten the circumstances of the dreams by the time he arrived to be with her.

Georgia's sister, Anita O'Keeffe Young, lived in Palm Beach, Florida. She invited Georgia to visit in March of 1984, two years before Georgia's death. Georgia was having problems with congestive heart failure at this time, and she developed fluid at the base of both lungs. Dr. Cutler, a competent internist in Española, helped with this problem. Juan was to take her to Palm Beach and they planned to stay a month. They returned within two weeks because of Georgia's health. Georgia said that her visit with her sister had not been as pleasant as she had anticipated, and the stress she had been under appeared to have contributed to her condition. She had a mild heart attack while visiting there. She was put on medication when she returned to New Mexico, and shortly after, Juan arranged for them all to move into an enormous residence in Santa Fe, with twenty-four hour nursing care for Georgia.

Georgia's health began to take a sharp turn for the worse following her return from Palm Beach. Sam insisted that she be placed under the care of a competent cardiologist in Santa Fe because he could not see her regularly. A young physician by the name of Dr. Brad Stamm was chosen to assume this responsibility.

Dr. Stamm saw her daily for some time, then dropped off to seeing her every couple of weeks. Sam was seeing her about every week from December of 1985 through early March of 1986. She had been able to walk about with help prior to this time, and then used a wheelchair. She eventually settled into a semi-coma. She was totally confined to bed during the last six months of her life. She lost a great deal of weight and looked quite frail.

Seldom was Juan there when Sam made his visits. It appeared that

Juan's wife took care of what food Georgia needed, but was otherwise completely detached from her care.

I was advised not to go to see Georgia. Sam wanted me to remember her as we had known her in years past.

Georgia left an order for Sam in the early 1980s, making it legally binding that when she died, nothing was to be done with her body until Sam pronounced her dead. This order caused some turmoil because Sam and I occasionally traveled out of the area. On many of these occasions, we were too far away to be reached easily, or to be able to get back to Santa Fe in a reasonable time.

Fortunately, Sam was in Santa Fe when Georgia died in March 6, 1986 at the age of ninety-eight. He was able to fulfill her wishes and pronounce her dead.

We were sure that Georgia appreciated what we did for her and welcomed the friendship we extended. We will always be grateful for her allowing us to hang her painting of the purple iris in our home for those many years. Her painting filled our living room with great warmth and color.

Sam remembered sitting quietly beside Georgia in those early days of 1986. She lay on her bed in her black cap and white gown amidst the black and white of her bed covers, her face quite peaceful, almost as if sculptured in pale white marble. Georgia had been a person of such great inner strength, conveyed to others through the beauty and power of her paintings and by her personal example. She faced a reality now which she no longer controlled.

Georgia's visual perceptions about what she saw and experienced, which she presented as she spoke and then represented in her paintings, helped to transform the world for us and to increase our joy in it. We felt privileged to have been associated with this very special person and cannot help but feel that within herself, she remained always very much vital and alive.

Isabel's sister, Paula Williams, and her husband, Arthur, alongside Georgia O'Keeffe's painting of "Purple Iris." Taken June 16, 1969 in the living room at the Ziegler home. A gift from O'Keeffe, it hung in their home for 16 years. Then one day she asked for it back. The Zieglers sadly parted with it, accepting a black and white charcoal of a banana flower in its place.

18

A Special Friend from Santa Clara Pueblo

I received a call from Dr. Molly Radford Martin one day in the fall of 1952. Molly asked if I would be interested in having Caroline Dozier, a woman from Santa Clara Pueblo, work for me at the house. Caroline had been with Molly and her husband, Bill Martin, for many years, living with them in Santa Fe and working at their home during the week, then returning to Santa Clara Pueblo on the weekends. Molly told me Caroline's mother had become ill, and Caroline needed to be closer to home where she could take better care of her. I immediately expressed an interest, and Molly said I should go to the pueblo and talk with Caroline.

Molly gave me directions to Caroline's home which was situated on the outskirts of the pueblo at its northern edge. I drove out the next day with our daughter, Julie, then almost two years old. We pulled off the highway leading to Los Alamos about a mile south of Española, and followed a sandy dirt road that ran in a straight path due southeast toward the pueblo. The driveway to Caroline's home turned off this road a half mile along, and moved up a short incline into a small open area before a mud-plastered adobe house. An old, barbed-wire fence in some disrepair wound its way around the yard, enclosing the house in a semblance of privacy. Several elm trees stood about the space, and provided a dappling of cooling shade from the New Mexico sun. An Indian oven (*horno*) sat to one side some ten feet from the front doorway. Off to the east rose the Sangre de Cristo mountains, hazy blue in the distance.

I remember being uncertain about how I would be received as I parked my car and got out with Julie in my arms. I knocked at the front door and waited for someone to answer. The door soon opened a crack and a face peered around its edge. I introduced myself, explaining that I had received a call from Dr. Radford about Caroline, and that I had come to talk with her.

The woman who had answered the door immediately open it wide, her face smiling broadly. She looked from me to Julie and back. Julie was now beginning to wiggle in my arms. She introduced herself as Caroline Dozier and asked us to come in. She smiled readily, her eyes large and black and filled with interest and intelligence. Her hair was black, parted down the middle and worn shoulder length, the sides curled out in a gentle turn. She wore a simple smock dress of calico and loafers. Caroline looked Indian, but I noticed she bore some European features.

Caroline led me into the living room of her small home. Everything appeared neatly placed. The thick adobe walls of the rooms and ceilings of dark pine vigas carried a pleasant welcome I had come to appreciate about New Mexican homes. The room was cool and quiet in the afternoon heat. Two women were seated in the room when we entered. Caroline introduced her mother and her sister, Ramona, to us. We all seemed quickly at ease with each other. This initial meeting marked the beginning of a very close friendship between Caroline and me that lasted over fourteen years. Caroline readily accepted my offer of employment and soon became a trusted and valued member of our family.

I believe what prompted Caroline to accept my offer was my coming to see her with a child in my arms. Caroline was forty-three years old when she came to work for us. She had never married and had no children of her own. She told me some years later that she had fallen in love with an Anglo man when she was younger, perhaps in her late twenties or early thirties. The man had been divorced, and being a devout Catholic, Caroline had asked her priest if she could marry this man. The priest would not grant her permission. Caroline had to break off the relationship, and she never again became involved with a man. I think part of her went out to Julie when she saw her. She became Julie's second mother in the years that followed.

Caroline's father was a Frenchman whose family had immigrated to the United States and settled in Kansas. He had studied to be a teacher as a young man, and was sent by the U. S. Government to Santa Clara Pueblo to teach. He fell in love while there with a Santa Clara girl, whom he married. They had seven children—five sons and two daughters.

One son, Mike, lived at Santa Clara. He occasionally helped us at the house in Fairview. He was an excellent carpenter and a very nice man.

He never married and always remained close to the Pueblo. His four brothers chose careers in Anglo society and married Anglo women. They were all successful in their chosen endeavors. One brother, Edward Dozier, was the first American Indian to graduate from the University of California with a PhD in Anthropology. He became a professor at the University of Arizona in Tucson. His daughter, Wanda, later returned to live in Santa Clara Pueblo.

Ramona, Caroline's sister, also never married. Ramona, Carolyn and Mike comprised the Dozier household at the Pueblo following their mother's death. I understand that it was because of their mixed heritage that their family home was placed on the outskirts of the Pueblo. Only full-blooded Santa Clarans were allowed to live in the interior of the Pueblo.

Caroline spoke to me about the importance her father had placed on education for his sons. Their schooling had come first. Less emphasis was put on Caroline's and Ramona's education. Instead of going to school, Caroline had worked, first at San Gabriel Ranch in Alcalde, New Mexico, then at another guest ranch in the area, from which she gained valuable training in cooking, preparing dinner parties for a large number of people, waiting on tables and taking care of guests. She also received excellent training in food preparation and catering while she worked for Dr. Molly Radford in Santa Fe.

Caroline was an extremely polite and refined person. I am sure she gained her manners from her upbringing at the Pueblo. She brought this refinement along with a quick intelligence and warm personality to her work with us, making her both an adept and fine companion. Perhaps the combination of the Indian and French gave her the stoic qualities of her mother and some of the flamboyance of her father. She was proud of everything she did, and made a special effort to be a perfectionist. We could sit together and plan a dinner party in every detail. If we were having a sit-down dinner, she would cook along with me, taking it upon herself to make special rolls and beautiful butter patties with a butter flower on top. She served elegantly and was always proud of what she did.

If we were going on a trip, she would be right there helping me prepare, making sure that everything was ready and properly packed. She wanted to be part of our family, and we tried hard to make her feel welcome. We took her with us on some of our trips so that she could baby sit the children and allow Sam and me to have some time to ourselves. Many of those trips were to Arthur and Phoebe Pack's Ghost Ranch Lodge in Tucson where the children enjoyed swimming, and where their favorite breakfast food quickly became cherry pie, a specialty of the house. Julie began attending Valley School for Girls in Tucson in the mid-1960s, and Caroline accompanied me when I took Julie to school and when I visited her there. Caroline's brother, Edward, lived in Tucson, and she could spend time with him while I saw Julie.

Baseball was one of Caroline's real interests. She loved the sport. We would sit in the TV room during baseball season and particularly during the World Series, and watch the games together. Sam made a special effort to get home for lunch to be with us. Such times were special because Caroline loved the games so much.

The Dozier family always invited us out to the pueblo at sundown during the days leading up to Christmas and on Christmas Eve, to watch the lighting of the *luminarios* (little wood fires) throughout the pueblo. We would climb up on the roof of their house to see this spectacle. It was customary for fires to be lit each of the nine nights before Christmas, beginning with one fire on the first evening at sundown, then two, then three, until on the last evening, nine fires were lit at each home. All the fires made a breathtaking sight. This tradition was "lighting the way" for the Christ child. If one were some distance away from the pueblo on these nights, a large dark cloud of pitch smoke from the burning piñon wood could be seen hovering over the area.

We traditionally ate posole and tortillas on Christmas Eve which Caroline had prepared. Caroline's posole was the best we ever tasted. She brought posole from home after the corn kernels had been bleached with lye, and cooked the posole with chuck roast for several hours.

Caroline told me how she baked bread in the *horno* in her front yard. She made a leavened bread adding salt and lard to flour along with the yeast, and then plenty of water to mix. She built a wood fire in the oven before the bread dough was completely made, and allowed the fire to burn until the coals were white. The oven was then hot enough for baking. She swept out the coals and ashes, cleaned the oven floor with a damp cloth, and placed the loaves of dough on pans (either pie pans or lard can tops) and set these in the oven using a long handled wooden paddle. The loaves were left to rise for a few minutes after being placed, then the door to the *horno* and the hole in the top were covered with damp cloths, the one over the door held in place with a board. A truly wonderful bread emerged in about twenty to thirty minutes. Caroline said the people of the pueblo used a fifty pound sack of flour for weddings and feasts to make enough bread for all the guests. She said that amount of bread would last a family about three weeks.

Caroline brought us the most delicious watercress. It came from a fresh spring on their "summer home place." Each Indian family was granted a "summer" place (which she called their "escape" place) along the river not too far from the pueblo. Here they could do a bit of farming for the family. These plots were kept in the family, and could not be sold or transferred to anyone outside of the pueblo. Only another Indian family in the pueblo could possess them.

One day while working at the house, Caroline complained of severe chest pain. Sam was fortunately home at the time. He examined her and listened to her heart with his stethoscope. He was concerned by what he heard. He later told me that he had almost fainted when he put his stethoscope to her chest. He immediately made arrangements for a specialist in Denver to examine her. We drove her there for the evaluation. The doctor said that she had been born with what is called a patent ductus arteriosus, and that at her age, then about fifty years, surgery was not indicated. She should be treated only with medication.

Caroline lived for several years following her visit to the Denver specialist. She finally died of heart failure in 1966. Sam and I were out of town when she was admitted to the Española Hospital after suffering a heart attack. Dr. Merle Yordy took care of her until we returned. I went to see her and was able to spend some time with her. We did everything we could to see that she was comfortable.

We attended her funeral at the Santa Clara Catholic Church and at the Indian burial grounds, where an Indian priest offered a beautiful prayer.

I was often reminded of my own mother when I was with Caroline. We thought so much alike about so many things. Perhaps it was the French in us which brought us together. I traced my French ancestry from my mother, and she from her father. My heart was broken when Caroline died. It was a difficult time for all of us in the family.

Caroline was with us for fourteen years. We loved her very much.

19

INVOLVEMENTS THROUGH THE GARDEN CLUB

I had reached a time in my life by 1953 when I needed more creative stimulus in my life. My first approach to a change of activity was to inquire if I might become a member of the local garden club, Amantes de Flores. The club welcomed me with open arms, and I was very pleased. The club's annual flower show was approaching when I joined, and I was encouraged to enter something in the Horticulture Section, if I did not care to do a flower arrangement.

Sam had begun growing Peace Roses in our garden. I cut a nice long stemmed rose with a beautiful bud which was just about to open, placed it in a vase with water, and took it to the church where the show was being held. Entries had to be registered and in place by 10:00 a.m. the morning of the show. Garden club judges were to appear for the judging around 11:00 a.m. I placed my entry on a display table for horticulture entries as directed, and left the building full of anticipation about the results of this new adventure.

The church had no air conditioning, but its interior seemed airy and comfortable. It was a beautiful summer day, warm but not too hot. I had little concern about my flower holding up for the judging. The judges made their rounds, and we were then able to go and see who had won ribbons, and to read the judges' comments about individual entries. I rushed anxiously to my entry to see if at least some comment had been made. I found my rose bud with its head drooping and its petals badly wilted. What a shock! I had cut the rose fresh that morning. I could not believe my eyes!

I wasted no time in talking to the judges about what I should do to learn more about showing flowers. They told me that the quickest way to gain an overview would be to attend one of the flower show schools that the local garden clubs presented. I immediately enrolled in two classes at the Los Alamos Garden Club, one about horticulture and the other about flower arranging. These classes were excellent. I was so impressed that I asked members of the Española Garden Club if I might report to them on one portion of the Horticulture course. I had paid special attention to the discussion about "hardening of flowers" for entries in the Horticulture Section, and I thought that there was information everyone should know. Members agreed, and afterwards, my talk became part of preparation instructions before every flower show.

It was not long before I became president of our garden club. I served several terms over the years. I was there to learn and to have fun, and I made every effort to participate. We had meetings with information and advice about how best to arrange and display flowers, and evening workshops with guest speakers discussing dried and fresh flower arrangements, how to make Christmas wreaths, special tips on flower cultivation, and discussion of requirements for taking First Place in a State Garden Club flower show. We put together a scrapbook with all of this information for members' use. I still have a copy of the scrapbook, and it is a good resource. Our club moved ahead, and before long began to be taken seriously at the state level.

To raise a little extra money for the club, we created special arrangements of wreaths and figurines to be sold during one Christmas season. We did very well with this venture. Members created beautiful nativity scenes along with papier-mâché angels edged with gold paint. These were very special items and all were of interest for our sale. These were fun times as club members worked together. The garden club was one group in which I could participate and feel good within myself.

I came to know a number of interesting women through the garden club. Belle Becker joined the garden club not long after I did, and I was soon aware of her artistry and skill in working with flowers. We became friends and worked closely together on many of the club's projects. I came to appreciate that Belle not only has a good artistic eye, but is a capable businesswoman. She had worked for Joe Becker in his clothing store in Española before her marriage. Then Isabelle Archuleta, she quickly became knowledgeable about the clothing business and began to buy for the women's department. Her artistic bent served her well here. Her business association with Joe developed into a lifelong partnership. They were married and have a beautiful family with four daughters and one son, all of whom Sam delivered.

Joe Becker is from Denver, Colorado. He came to Española as an eligible bachelor around 1949 to establish his business and introduced a fine line of clothing and shoes for men and women. His first business was a small clothing store near the "Y" in Riverside. He later moved to a new and larger location in the Yates Shopping Center in Riverside, with the name BECKER'S proudly displayed over his store front. Joe also came to Española with a reputation for being an avid fly fisherman and a real expert at tying flies. Sam saw some of these one time, and said they were excellent.

Joe had an early interest in Indian art and artifacts, and developed this interest into a sideline in his business. Belle joined him in this interest, and dealing in Indian pottery, jewelry and other artifacts developed into a full-time business, with frequent trips to buy and trade with the Indians. Belle and Joe knew of our appreciation for Indian craftsmanship, and they began to call our attention to fine pieces as they found them. We spent a number of enjoyable evenings at their home looking over their new acquisitions for the store.

I met Adeline "Sue" Barbo (now Adeline Harvey) at an Amantes de Flores meeting in Española in the mid-1950s. Sue was an alert and enjoyable person, always full of good humor, who was interested in being involved and pursuing a worthy cause with vigor and determination.

Sue and I were active in the garden club at the state and local levels. We served on the state committee for judging Program and Year Books that were submitted for awards. This work was a rewarding experience, because we were able to gather a good deal of information about judging and arranging that was of benefit to our local club. Sue and I made many friends at the state level, and when the yearly state meeting was scheduled to be held in Santa Fe one year, she and I were asked to prepare the floral arrangement for the Speaker's Table for the final evening. This was a special evening filled with great excitement because the awards were to be announced.

The Speaker's Table was set on a platform at one end of the banquet room, and we were asked to prepare a low flower arrangement which required a special container, which neither of us had. We decided to contact our local florist for advice. The florist casually mentioned while we were at the shop, "Now, you realize that for something this long and low, you must approach your flower arrangement differently from your regular arrangements. You must first place all of your low flowers round the edge, and then gradually layer in the other flowers." We found his comment to be good counsel.

We had planned to use garden flowers, and fortunately, club members were able to supply us with gladioli. They are long-stemmed and sturdy, and we inserted these into the arrangement almost in a lying down position, with the blooms still visible. They gave side width and extended color out toward the audience. We filled in the center of the arrangement with smaller flowers, keeping in mind that the arrangement would be placed in front of the person who was to speak. It was to provide color, but not distract from the center of attention. We chose pinks and lavenders and whites as our colors.

We turned out a real "masterpiece" which met all of the length and height requirements. When we looked at it, however, we decided it was more suited for a funeral casket than for a banquet table. Sue and I had done our duty, but we laughed all the way to the banquet and many times since. Our arrangement did serve its purpose. We received many thanks for it and no ill comments, so we breathed a sigh of relief.

Sue and I became supportive of each other's interests, and we worked closely together on a number of projects that branched out from the garden club. Our biggest project involved an attempt to acquire permission from the Santa Clara Indians to landscape and beautify a piece of land along the west bank of the Rio Grande just as one crossed the bridge into Española. We envisioned a shady park with benches and a small path along a stream with bridges across for walking. I had even envisioned a bridle path, for people were still riding horses in and around Española. The soil conservationists agreed to handle the work, but alas, we were not able to convince the Indians of the merits of the scheme. Sue talked with the Pueblo Governor and we attended several meetings of the Tribal Council, with their permission, to discuss the project. The meetings were conducted in Tewa, Spanish, and English, the discussion repeated in all the languages while one individual sat to the right of the Governor and talked softly in his ear. We were politely told, after sitting for many hours at these meetings, that the Council would not grant us permission to develop a park by the Rio Grande near the Española bridge.

Sue, Ruth Trapp and I were interested in sitting in on legislative sessions at the Capitol in Santa Fe. Ruth was aware of the bills being legislated, and we would make plans to attend a session when she informed us that issues in which we had interest were scheduled for discussion. If Sue were driving her blue VW bug, she would take that car down the highway at top speed. I always worried about parking, and would say as we approached the capitol and saw the myriad of cars along the streets, "Sue, where do you think you'll ever find a place to park?"

She always answered, "Don't worry. This little bug will squeeze in almost anywhere!"

It did! I held my breath as she worked that VW bug into half of a parking space. I marveled at Sue's ability to handle this maneuvering.

Ruth met us at the capitol many times because of her tight schedule with the *Rio Grande SUN*, and following the session, the three of us would head for the Bull Ring Restaurant for lunch. The Bull Ring was located on College Street (now Old Pecos Trail) near the Capitol Building or "Round House." It was one of the favorite meeting places near the Capitol. We waited for the Legislators and their friends and followers to come in, as we discussed what we had heard in the session. We felt that we could solve all of the problems the Legislature faced, of course, had we only been approached for our opinions.

Dorothy Erickson owned the Western Holiday Motel during this time. She and her husband, Gordon, had purchased it in 1960. It was painted an eye-catching bright, warm turquoise and marked an ideal place to stop for a night's lodging as one entered the Valley from Santa Fe. My first introduction to the motel and to Dorothy was while attending a meeting of the garden club. Dorothy was a prospective new member, and had invited us all to her motel for lunch.

I was seated at a table by the pool, and a woman approached me with a big, friendly smile, and said, "I'm Dorothy Erickson. How nice to meet you." I had been waiting for the moment to meet and greet Dorothy, but she beat me to the "punch." Her greeting was well received.

Dorothy was a bundle of energy, always ready to take charge and hold your attention. She dressed with an eye toward appeal with a stunning hat, a captivating necklace and many fingers adorned with diamond rings. Dorothy was a loquacious person and a very sharp businesswoman with a calculated awareness of all that surrounded her. She set the stage for conviviality when she entered a room and greeted everyone with her cheery, "Hello, everybody! I'm here!" followed by a hearty laugh.

Dorothy was a welcome member of our Garden Club, and was active in it and other civic organizations in the Valley including the Chamber of Commerce. The various organizations to which she belonged held many of their meetings during the warm weather outside by the motel's pool, with swimming following the meetings. A number of us, including Dorothy, decided in all seriousness, of course, that her motel should become our retirement headquarters because complete relaxation and enjoyment really seemed possible there. Sam was to be attending physician and Ruth Willard McKinley the nurse on duty, with the rest of us taking turns cooking and managing the motel office during the day. We did not reach a decision about how we would handle things at night, but we had fun imagining.

The best laid plans do not always materialize. Dorothy's husband, Gordon, is now gone. Some years after his death, Dorothy married Hugh Tucker. Hugh was a most hospitable Southern gentleman, friendly and level-headed, but with an eye toward business politics. He had his "say" upon occasion while in the Valley, for he was a man of firm conviction who was not shy about taking a stand on issues in which he believed. He had a definite opinion about most.

Dorothy loved to entertain. She was known especially for her green chili casseroles which were the "hottest" in town. She always said, " I don't know any strangers." This was true. Her home was always filled with people, old friends and then new ones. She had time for all of them. Hugh has since passed away and Dorothy now lives in Sun City West, Arizona, just near Phoenix.

20

ONLY THE BEST

I had been looking for clothes to take on the trip to Seattle for the National AMA Meeting in May. Godey was one of my favorite places to shop in Santa Fe. Thelma Huff, the owner, was an excellent buyer and always had interesting things. Sam enjoyed going to Godey because he could relax and have a style show as I tried on dresses, then say, "I like it. Buy it." or "I don't like it. Forget it." Thelma arranged her shop with comfortable chairs for the men to sit while the women tried on clothes.

Thelma had a beautiful brown, heavy woven silk, two-piece suit with a tailored skirt and an Eisenhower jacket. I tried it on and it seemed just perfect for the trip. I thought I better talk to Sam before making a final decision. The suit was not inexpensive!

I told Sam about the suit when he came home. Instead of pausing to discuss the issue, he went right to the phone, asking in an excited voice, "What time does the store close?" I thought about five o'clock and said so. Sam called Godey. "Thelma, this is Dr. Sam Ziegler," he stated enthusiastically when she answered. "Don't close the shop. Isabel and I are coming right down to see the suit she tried on earlier."

I noticed Sam's excited and enthusiastic behavior, but really did not think much about it at the time. I was excited myself about being able to go back to Godey.

We drove to Santa Fe and Thelma was waiting at the door. I tried on the suit once more for Sam. The minute I walked out of the dressing room, he exclaimed, "I like it. Buy it!" He seemed quite pleased. Thelma picked up on his mood right away.

"Well," she said. "You know, Isabel is also going to need a coat to go with that new suit. The weather in Seattle is different from our weather here in Santa Fe. It's a bit cooler. Isabel should have a light-weight coat. If she doesn't have one, I have a lovely one to show you." She brought out a beautiful, off-white cashmere coat and helped me put it on.

Sam said as soon as he saw it, "I like it. Buy it!"

Thelma was right on top of matters once again, and brought out several other items for me to try on, saying, "Well, these might also come in very handy."

Sam was quite animated by now, and when he saw them, he said without a second's hesitation, "Buy them!" Everything I tried on to show him, he said, "Buy it!"

When he said to buy it, I would walk over to him and point to the price tag and ask, "Are you sure?"

"No problem," he would answer with a reassuring nod. "Buy it!"

We returned home with my many packages in the car. As we entered the house with all of our things, Sam suddenly turned to look at me, and said, "What have I done? How did we end up with so many boxes?" At that point, I was not sure whether to laugh or cry, nor was Sam.

I found out then what had led up to our buying spree. Sam had not been feeling well earlier that day. He had come down with a bad cold, with all the usual symptoms of fever and chills and general malaise. With a full day's work ahead of him, he knew he had to do something to help himself feel better. That year one of the leading pharmaceutical firms had come out with what they considered a "wonder drug" for treating colds. One of the firm's detail men had given Sam some samples to try. He did just that, and within a short time was feeling just great. During the day he began to feel achy again, so he took another pill. By the time he got home from the office and found me wanting to go back to Godey, he was in a fine mood. He has since said that the evening was an interesting lesson about the influence of a potent medication on behavior! He certainly did not use this "cold remedy" again, nor did he prescribe it for any of his patients.

We did laugh about what happened at the time, and we laughed many times afterwards when we thought about that day. Every article I purchased was lovely and just perfect for the occasion. I have used them all many times.

Sam received many payments in kind in the early days of his practice. These payments were usually in the form of chickens and eggs, or other farm produce like the big Tom turkey we got before Thanksgiving in 1949. Patients often asked if these would serve as partial payment of their bills. On one occasion he received something very different in kind. I will never forget the knock on the front door one cold winter evening. I opened the door to find a handsome young Indian man standing there with his wife. They came in, and Sam noticed the man was holding two small dolls. After talking for a few moments, the man asked if "the doctor" would accept the dolls in payment for the delivery of their child. He told Sam that Mrs. Cata from San Juan Pueblo had made the dolls. Mrs. Cata was well-known for her dolls of the various Pueblo Indian dancers, authentic in every detail. The young man had a deer dancer and an eagle dancer with him. They each stood about twelve inches high and were handsomely made. Sam was happy to take them because he knew of Mrs. Cata and her work, and recognized that these dolls would someday be of real value.

Mrs. Cata made only a few dolls of each type of dancer. The one person we knew who had a complete set of all these dolls was Jean Garland of Swan Lake Ranch. We felt fortunate to have our two. I still include them among my prized possessions.

We acquired some other fine possessions through Gilbert Maxwell of Farmington, New Mexico. We became acquainted with the Maxwells in the early 1950s when Gilbert brought his wife to see Sam about a surgical problem. He later operated on her successfully, and we became good friends.

The Maxwells came to New Mexico from Chicago to allow Gilbert to get away from the pressures of his accounting business. Gilbert cultivated a keen interest in Navajo rugs in Farmington. This interest eventually developed into the Maxwell rug business. Gilbert became one of the best informed men not only about Navajo rugs, but about all kinds of Indian weaving.

We were sitting in the living room with a fire going in the fireplace one cold winter night when a knock came at the front door. Who was standing there but Gilbert Maxwell. He had been to Santa Fe on business with his rugs and was now on his way home. He said he had some special rugs to show us, and asked if he could come in for a cup of coffee. We looked at a lot of beautiful rugs in the course of the evening. I could not believe how reasonable his prices were.

We ended up buying four rugs including a large rug from the Chee

Dodge collection, a Kinteel and a Two Grey Hills. We were not in a position to pay for them at that time, but Gilbert was quite agreeable to monthly payments. We asked Gilbert to spend the night after concluding our business, and he gladly accepted.

We went out to the lovely guest ranch, Rancho del Rio near Alcalde, on occasion in the early 1950s. The ranch was a nice escape for us, a place to get away and enjoy excellent food and a pleasant atmosphere, but close enough that Sam could get back to the hospital easily, if called. Bill and Helen Delano managed it at the time. Helen did much of the cooking, and her preparations were quite wonderful.

We met the artist, Bernique Longley, during one of our visits to Rancho del Rio. Bernique was living there at the time, and beginning to make a name for herself. She had grown up in Chicago and graduated from the Chicago Art Institute in 1945, coming to northern New Mexico in 1946 after a year traveling and painting in Mexico under a Bryan Lathrop Foreign Traveling Fellowship.

Bernique was doing wonderful pencil portraits then. We asked her to do portraits of our children after getting to know her and her work. These turned out nicely for all three of the children. Sitting for a portrait was quite a new experience for them, and Bernique was most attentive. We enjoyed Bernique's work very much, and appreciated her use of vivid color, her interesting subject matter from Mexico and Guatemala, and her fine drafting of figures of men, women and children. We are fortunate to have one of her early 1953 oil paintings of a young Mexican boy. The boy stands full-face, dressed in a wide-brimmed straw hat and a collarless white cotton tunic shirt and plain white pants. He carries a toy wooden horse in his right arm. The painting is done in light pastel tones of green, chartreuse, yellow and pink which work nicely with the flesh tones of the skin and the straw color of the hat.

We became acquainted with Lee and Dean Gulnac and their daughter, Penny, in this period. Dean Gulnac was an engineer employed at the Los Alamos National Laboratory. Sam and I found we shared many common interests with them. Lee and Dean were both musically inclined. Dean had a fine, rich voice, and he eventually took over direction of our choir at church. Lee and I became close friends through our interests in music and art. We sang duets and performed at the local churches upon request. Our singing voices were on a par.

Lee and I were also much involved in creative projects, some of which involved fund raising for the church. We called our first fund raiser, "Rags and Tags." So many people gathered for the sale that we had to call the police to keep order in the waiting line. Our "window teasers" had included some rather expensive "rags."

I had read about an Easter Egg Tree to be used as a centerpiece. I told Lee about the tree, and she immediately became interested. We prepared the eggs by punching a small hole in each end, then carefully blowing out the yolk and white from the shell. There was more blowing than we anticipated, and we became light-headed and found ourselves laughing uncontrollably after preparing a dozen and a half eggs. The small holes in the eggs allowed us to draw narrow ribbons through in order to hang the eggs on the tree branches. We decided to color the eggs, and in some we broke out a section of shell and filled the inside with small flowers. We finished our project after much laughter and much huffing and puffing and decorating. It proved to be a most attractive and appreciated one.

With such a close friendship, it seemed only natural that I would call Lee about a "surprise" purchase Sam made for me in 1955. A new car! He came home one afternoon and handed me a set of keys, saying with a big smile, "A surprise is waiting for you in the driveway." I found a beautiful new Ford Crown Victoria with automatic drive. Sam had bought the car that morning from C. V. Hunter at Hunter Motor Company in Española. It was a first. I could not wait to take it for a drive.

I asked Lee to ride to Santa Fe with me for a late lunch. She was as excited as I was about riding in the new car. Our drive started out fine. The car did nicely on the way to Santa Fe until we reached Tesuque, where the old road passed by El Nido and moved on up a hill and into town. I stepped on the accelerator to gain speed to pass an old Hudson in front of me as I began to drive up the hill. The car gave a quick spurt, then slowed back down. I tried again and pulled even with the Hudson, staying with him for about a half mile while trying to get up enough speed to pass. The man driving the old Hudson was in hysterics, laughing as he watched me try to pass, his old car able to outdo this brand new shiny automobile.

I never did get up enough speed to go around, and I was not laughing as I pulled my car back behind the Hudson and chugged on into Santa Fe. I was furious. I drove to Hunter Motors when we got back to Española and handed C. V. the keys, with the words, "When I am in a car and want to pass another car, I expect to be able to do that. Please have someone drive me home. The Crown Victoria is yours."

C. V. arranged for someone to drive me home, and he had a new Mercury in the driveway within an hour. The Ford Motor Company later acknowledged that the motor for the Victoria was not big enough to provide sufficient power for passing on the highway, and recalled these cars. He made sure other cars performed properly before he handed them over to us.

The years have brought changes into the lives of these friends. We lost contact with Dean after he and Lee separated, but through the years a beautiful and enduring friendship has continued with Lee, filled with laughter, tears and song. Time and distance seem instantly to fade away when the phone rings and Lee is calling. We immediately pick up where we left off. She married a fine man by the name of Robert Gerlach, who is a prosperous California realtor. They live in California when they are not spending time in New Zealand, where the fishing appeals to Bob and the scenery is an inspiration for Lee's painting.

Sam and I took a trip to Denver with Dr. Michael Pijoan and his wife, Barbara, several years after Mike joined Sam in practice. Sam and Mike had been working very hard and needed a break. We left for Denver with a firm order from Winfield Morton, a close friend and a wealthy oil man from Texas, that we were to stay at his apartment in Denver and have fun.

We gladly accepted Winfield's offer. His apartment was beautiful and very comfortable. We drove to the Buckhorn Café for dinner after settling in. The Buckhorn was in its prime in the 1950s. Mike said we should drop by the old Windsor Hotel on Larimer Street following dinner for an after-dinner drink. He noted that the Windsor Hotel was an historical point of interest. The Windsor Hotel had been built by Horace Tabor, the silver king, whose fortune came from the Matchless Mine in Leadville, Colorado. He and his wife, Baby Doe, had lived at the Windsor in a spacious apartment. Horace died penniless because the monetary standard changed from silver to gold. Baby Doe then moved back to the mine. She was never really accepted in Denver society, being Horace's second wife and now penniless.

Horace had said to her, "Hold on to the Matchless," thinking the value of silver would return, but the gold standard held, and Baby Doe died in poverty at the mine.

The hotel seemed quiet as we entered. We found our way to the bar and took a seat in a booth while we waited for service. We saw only two men present, both quite drunk and one trying to play a guitar. The one not playing found his way to our table and asked me to dance. About the time I was going to say, "No, thank you," the hotel manager appeared. He quickly saved the moment and asked if we would like a tour of the hotel. We readily accepted his offer. The tour turned out to be fascinating.

There was a large ballroom with beautiful parquet flooring and a mural covering the length of one wall. The eyes of the figures in the mural followed us wherever we went in the room. We saw what at one time had been the Green Room, the room where ladies gathered to talk following dinner, while the men moved to the Smoking Room. The hotel manager had turned the Green Room into an apartment for his mother.

Most of the rooms in the hotel had been dismantled, all the furniture being placed in the basement for storage with the exception of several diamond dust-backed mirrors, each 3' x 7' with elaborate walnut frames. The manager offered to sell these for two hundred and fifty dollars apiece. We were not in a position to think of buying one. The manager did tell us about the mirrors and how to recognize them, which we found most interesting. He said that a Frenchman in Chicago had made all the diamond dust-backed mirrors at the request of Horace Tabor. The Frenchman died with the formula for the mirrors, and those still in existence were very rare.

The manager then took us on to the basement, a huge underground storage area piled high with stacks of furniture. Then again, we could have selected anything we might have wanted for what was a very nominal fee. He pointed out a passageway as we were leaving the basement, that led from the hotel to the Legislature Building on Capitol Hill and afforded an easy escape for the legislators who needed a break and a drink. He said with a bit of a twinkle in his eye that there was one habitual drunk who came to the bar every day, who figured prominently in decision making on Capitol Hill. The legislators would stand this drunk up against the wall when they arrived to discuss a knotty problem while having a drink, and which ever way the drunk fell would determine the solution to their dilemma. We all laughed. The tale fit nicely with many stories of the Old West.

We saw the bullet holes Calamity Jane had made in the ceiling of the bar as we made our way out of the hotel.

Our evening visit to the Windsor sparked our curiosity about Colorado history, and instilled an interest in diamond dust-backed mirrors.

Years later when returning to Española from Denver by way of Farmington, we stopped to see our good friends, Dr. and Mrs. Crosby. Evalina Crosby said while we were there, that an antique shop was going out of business in town and we must stop in before leaving. We paid a visit and found a number of mirrors stacked along a wall in one room. Sam searched through them and found the diamond dust-backed mirror that now hangs in our home. The shop owner did not realize what it was. We asked how much he wanted for it, and he said, "Oh, how about $35.00."

Sam replied in as measured a voice as he could manage when he heard the price, "I'll take it."

The owner followed with, "I'm going down to Santa Fe next week. Be glad to drop it off for you."

Sam quickly responded, "Thank you, but no. It will fit nicely into our car." Away we drove with our mirror.

We were really pleased with our find. A diamond dust-backed mirror can easily be spotted by holding a lighted match to the mirror glass. An unmistakable clear sparkling will appear as the light catches the facets of the diamond dust. We had checked all mirrors we saw in antique stores this way for years.

Because he was so excited, Sam checked this mirror twice to be sure it really was diamond dust-backed. Knowing what it was, he was not about to let the shop owner bring it to Santa Fe in a week or so. I was afraid the owner might wonder why we wanted this particular mirror and decide to keep it.

Our mirror may be the only diamond dust-backed mirror between Scottsdale and Denver. I say between Scottsdale and Denver because I am aware of a beautiful one in the Lulu Belle, a fine restaurant in Scottsdale, Arizona.

21

HORSE SENSE AND THE KENNEL KLUB

Some of the first rodeos we attended in Española were held in a big fenced-in field. Clemmy Denton and I went to watch, and sat on the fence rails or just stood alongside the fence to see the bronc riding and the ropers. It was all a very down-to-earth, "Howdy, pardner," chap-slapping affair. We managed to sit on or stand along the fence until the bull riding event. Then we moved back. The bulls were wild and mean-looking. We thought it better not to be so close.

Clemmy was a good teacher. She explained about the short rope called a "pegging string" used to tie a calf's legs after the calf had been roped and thrown to the ground. The secret to the cowboy's success was how well his horse backed up and kept the calf on a taut rope after its rider had dismounted. Pretty tough business, but exciting to watch.

The rodeo grounds were moved in 1953 to a new location along the Taos Highway at the edge of town. Regular stands with bleachers for spectators were built along with chutes for bronc and bull riding, calf roping and steer wrestling. The Rodeo Association sponsored a calf riding contest that first year as a special event for boys under fifteen years of age. Every boy who rode was guaranteed a $1 prize. The boy who managed to stay on his calf the regulation time would be entitled to some real prize money. Word about the calf riding event quickly spread in town, and it was not long before Sammy and Norman heard about it and wanted to ride. They were pretty good horsemen, and had some experience dealing with cattle and calves. We had been to Ghost Ranch to take part in the annual fall roundup. The roundup was a three-day affair for the boys, up early in the morning and riding all day on the drive, then helping with the feeding, and with the dehorning, branding and castrating of the calves. They had taken Mouse and Midnight to the ranch to ride, and had a wonderful time under the watchful eye of the foreman, Herman Hall.

Sam and I gave our consent to the boy's riding at the rodeo. They were very excited! Even Julie, as young as she was, seemed to understand that something special was going to happen. She smiled and bobbed her head up and down, her two little braids flapping alongside. I took a deep breath, not knowing what I was getting into.

We rode out to the rodeo grounds together that Sunday afternoon. The boys were off to register for the calf riding as soon as we had parked. The event was placed mid-way through the afternoon, so we had some time to watch other events, and I had some time to start worrying. I got excited and then calmed down, then started worrying again. I wanted the boys to ride, but I did not. I guess I was a bundle of nerves.

The announcement finally came for all riders to report for the calf riding event. Sammy and Norman turned to Sam and me and Julie, gave quick smiles, and were off running for the chutes. The Rodeo Association set up a special chute for this event to accommodate the smaller calves, and the boys gathered around to wait their turns to ride. Several boys came out of the chute amidst a great deal of shouting and clapping from parents and spectators, who had crowded around to watch. Those calves sure bucked, and none of the riders seemed able to stay on very long.

Sammy's name was then called. I could not believe my ears when I heard his name, but there he was getting on his calf with the help of several cowboys working the chute. And ride he did! For about three seconds! The calf took two or three quick jumps out of the chute and dumped Sammy right off. Sammy landed on his side in the dirt, jumped up smiling and waving, and ran back to the chute.

The announcer then called Norman's name. The next thing I knew, Norman's calf was jumping out of the chute with Norman firmly seated, his left hand holding the rigging, his right hand up in the air to give him balance. What a cowboy! But then he started to slip to one side on the calf, and then slip some more, still holding on tight, the calf jumping and bucking. I felt myself clutch the front of my shirt. Before I realized what was happening, the calf did a twisting jump and bucked Norman off. We all saw the calf's hind legs kick Norman as it jumped away. Norman picked himself up off the ground, both hands reaching back where he had been kicked, a grimace across his face. But he was quickly up, too, running back toward the chute with a slight limp in one leg and a forced smile on his face. I realized I was still holding my shirt. I took a deep breath and let go, joining the others cheering and clapping.

Sammy and Norman came running up soon after, each holding a brand new $1 bill, big smiles on their faces. I saw Norman favoring his left side, and asked if he were alright. "They told us to hold on tight and not let go," he said. "That's what I did. It's OK, Mom." That was all. Then he and Sammy were gone again, off to watch more rodeo, each proud as punch.

I was proud, too. I thought I had made it through the event in fine form. I heaved a great sigh of relief. Sam, of course, had been called to the hospital and was not there to calm my nerves.

Sammy and Norman began asking to have another dog not long after our Springer Spaniel, 'Laska's, death in 1952. The Garlands from Swan Lake Ranch had often talked to us about their Standard Poodles. Sam did not care for Poodles, thinking of them as "sissy dogs" because of their French grooming. We learned that Poodles were anything but "sissy" dogs after we were exposed to the Garlands' poodles. Their dogs were big and strong, and made excellent watch dogs. Ham and Jean had to greet us at the door when we visited, before the dogs would allow us to enter, and the dogs kept a watchful eye on us while we were in the house.

Ham said we had not lived until we had owned and enjoyed a Standard Poodle. We thought about his comments and their dogs. Ham then appeared at our door one day in 1954 with a darling brown female puppy. We were immediately taken with the small bundle of fur he presented to us. Ham told us that the puppy was out of a line of champions, a male grandsire named *Rumpelstiltskin* having taken many Blue Ribbons. He said that the puppy's brown fur would lighten in color as she was older. We tried to think of a good name for her. Her color would become a light cocoa when she grew older, and we immediately thought of the name "Cocoa," but we felt we needed a more glamorous name considering her pedigree. We finally settled on "Forever Amber of Rocking Z." That was a fine name, approved by all! Despite the fancy name, "Cocoa" became her nickname, the name by which we always called her.

Dr. William Westen, an orthopaedic surgeon from Santa Fe and his wife, Freddie, called not long after we acquired Cocoa, to see if we would consider taking their white male Poodle, Wooly. It seemed that one of their children was allergic to dog fur. They knew we already had a Poodle, and felt Wooly might fit into our household. Wooly was a large dog who liked to run, and the grounds at our house would offer him plenty of room.

We agreed to take Wooly. He was an elegant, white male Standard Poodle who held his head high and strutted around the house with great show. While he was friendly, we were unsure if he would bond to us and our home, but we were game to try. We thought we needed a strong male dog around the house to watch things, and Wooly was indeed a beautiful, powerful dog.

I made plans with Lee Gulnac, a close friend from Española, to go to Oklahoma to visit Lee's parents shortly after we brought Wooly into our home. Sam then decided he would take the boys and the dogs camping overnight in Santa Clara canyon while we were away. They drove up to the Canyon and found a good campsite near a stream. The boys were able to go off exploring and play with the dogs when the tent was pitched and the campsite was in order. The dogs remained close by at first, but later, as Sam and the boys were making dinner, Wooly took off roaming in the hills with Cocoa close behind. The dogs did not return as the evening progressed, and the boys and Sam began to call and call, but there was no response.

The dogs did not return during the night. The boys and Sam continued to call the next morning, but no amount of calling or whistling brought the dogs back. Sam had to be at the hospital that day, so they finally left the canyon by mid-morning, only to return to their campsite each evening for the next two days to call and hope the dogs would return.

When Lee and I returned from Oklahoma and learned the news, we were off immediately to the canyon to try and find the dogs. We went to the campsite two and three times a day for the next several days in the hopes of finding footprints or some clue that might indicate the dogs were in the vicinity. We called and whistled and yelled for what seemed like hours. I think our calling could have made us outstanding candidates for the State Fair calling contests. Lee and I really got into the spirit, trying to make our voices carry as far as we could. We really believed our singing voices and our strong lungs would help our calling, and that Cocoa would hear us and return. But all of our efforts seemed to no avail.

Finally, on the fifth day of our search, we arrived at the campsite to find the small footprints of a dog by the stream. We were sure they belonged to Cocoa. We immediately began to call and whistle, and kept on until we were near a state of exhaustion. Then all of a sudden, a small beige, bedraggled bundle came bounding toward us. We could not believe our eyes! Then we were hugging her and she was kissing us. We were so glad to see each other again.

Wooly was not with Cocoa. We did not find him for several days. It was clear that he and Cocoa had become separated, and that Cocoa, who could not match his pace, had fallen behind and then followed her trail back to the campsite. Smart little girl she was! We knew that Wooly did not have the same loyalty to us. We advertised in the local paper and on the radio to find him, offering a reward for his return. A rancher up above Abiquiu made contact through a friend in the Valley, saying he had found a big white dog on his ranch who answered the description of Wooly. We drove to his ranch to see the dog. Sure enough, it was Wooly. He had run a long distance before stopping and was in bad shape with a bedraggled coat and evident loss of weight.

Wooly begin to settle in with us after the Santa Clara canyon incident. He made the rounds of our property, seeming to stake out his domain within its boundaries. Our neighbors to the east, the Stampfers, had a small, feisty black and grey Schnauzer named Roddy, who would come charging out of his dog door whenever anyone came near the fence that divided our two properties. He barked and yapped most irritatingly. The first time Roddy barked at Wooly, Wooly just pranced up to the fence stiff-legged, fur bristling, and gave a deep, gruff "Wooff." Roddy immediately turned and retreated into the house, tail between his legs, that being the last of his Schnauzer barks.

Wooly continued to roam. Keeping him behind our wall became impossible. He was eventually hit by a car and had his right hip broken, necessitating a pinning. He survived the surgery and seemed to calm down a bit afterwards, but I worried about his leaving again and taking Cocoa with him.

Wooly had been with us for two or three years when Sam came home from the hospital one day saying that Dr. Valerie Friedman McNown had a young patient who was partially blind, whose parents were looking for a large dog to be her companion. Valerie knew I worried about Wooly, and thought if Wooly were kept indoors and close to the young girl, he might be a good companion for her. We gave Wooly to this family. We heard very good reports about him afterwards. He seemed to take to the child and settle into the home.

Cocoa became a solid member of our family. The boys took her to the Barn at night with orders that she was not to sleep on their beds. This order lasted only until I was out of sight. The boys loved having Cocoa as a pet and had great fun playing with her.

Her place in the family was certainly evident one evening when I was feeding the children at the kitchen table while waiting for Sam to come home from the hospital. Norman and Sammy were ten and eleven years old, and Julie just three. The boys started teasing Julie and annoying her unmercifully, neither one paying attention to my command that things quiet down. Cocoa sat quietly and patiently by the table, looking on, her head moving from one boy to the other, then to Julie, then back trying to follow what was going on. I attempted a healthy swat aimed toward their backsides when the boys became too boisterous, with the words, "I'll have to swat you if you don't behave." Julie picked up on the word "swat" and managed to say, "Whop them, Mommy, whop them." Cocoa, seeing her two charges in trouble, did a quick about face. She did not want to be a part of a serious reprimand. She retreated, tail down, ears drooping, to the safety of the back room. Smart dog!

Cocoa loved the family and much preferred our company to that of other dogs. She and Julie would play Hide'n Seek out-of-doors. Julie would make Cocoa stay by the wall near the carport on command, saying to her, "STAY," and then run off to hide, often way around the other side of the house. After hiding, she would make a noise or give a low call, and off Cocoa would bound to find her. She always found Julie very quickly, much to everyone's delight.

Cocoa resented our leaving her at home alone. We did leave her for several hours by herself in the back room one time when she was still a puppy. We found when we returned, that she had knocked several flower pots off a window sill by the back door and chewed the wood around the French door, trying to get out. We felt her frantic behavior was due to her having been lost in Santa Clara canyon during the rain storm. We left her outside thereafter while we were away. She remained at home, and eventually befriended a male dog. We soon had our share of puppies.

We watched Cocoa carefully through her pregnancy. I called the Vet at delivery time, to see if I should bring her in. He told me that she would undoubtedly want us close by, and that she would probably do better at home. I said with some concern, "Sam will probably be at the hospital when she delivers. What if she has complications?" He simply said, "Don't' worry. If she should have a 'footling first,' just take hold of the legs and give a little yank."

Sam was at the hospital, of course, when she went into labor. She was in the back room, where our cat had delivered so many of her litters. We made every effort to keep Cocoa comfortable. The first one finally began to arrive after a lengthy labor during which I could tell Cocoa was struggling, and all I could see were back feet and legs. A footling had come! I felt almost paralyzed for a moment. How could I possibly take hold of those legs and yank? But I did, feeling all the time that the leg and body would come out without a head! The yank worked perfectly, much to my surprise. Cocoa responded immediately to the pup, licking it and cuddling it. What followed had us all in a state of shock. Cocoa delivered eleven puppies. Her first came around 11:30 a.m. I finally went to bed exhausted at 11:00 p.m. that night. She delivered her last pup around midnight.

Cocoa was an excellent mother. Her puppies were beautiful, but we had to give them away. We found good homes for all of them except one black male pup, which we decided to keep. The black puppy showed good promise as he developed. He was a handsome dog and had a beautiful coat. He was good around us and became an excellent watchdog, but we began to notice that he was too aggressive toward strangers. He bit an electrician who came to the house to do some repair work. We could not seem to break him of this aggressiveness, and decided we could not keep him. A rancher in the area learned we were looking for a home for the dog and agreed to take him, because he thought he would work out well on the ranch. We were sorry to see him go.

I took Cocoa to Claude James' Grooming Salon on Canyon Road in Santa Fe when she was to be trimmed and groomed. Claude recognized her fine features, even as a puppy, and she insisted that we enter Cocoa in the Dog Show. One year we did, with Claude leading her up and down the show ramp with great delight. She took a Blue Ribbon!

Cocoa's personality seemed to change after she had her fur cut and trimmed and shaped. She would sit up straighter beside me in the car on the way home. I would say, "You are beautiful, Cocoa." She seemed to know exactly what I meant and would lean toward me with her nose and give me a kiss on the cheek. After all, she had just been to the Beauty Salon.

We loved this gentle, fine and intelligent companion.

Cocoa was with us for fourteen years. She sleeps peacefully now on our property on Fairview Lane.

We tried to make sure the boys had plenty to keep them occupied during the summers. We were especially anxious to see they continue their riding and their experiences out-of-doors. We learned of a fine summer camp called Glorieta Pass Ranch. Jackson Space, an ex-forest ranger, and his wife ran the camp. It was located in the mountain area between Santa Fe and Las Vegas, New Mexico. The boys went for three weeks each summer of 1953 and 1954, and returned with glowing tales of three-day long horseback rides back onto the mesas, during which they camped out, went arrowhead hunting, saw porcupines and wild mustang horses, and learned how to chop down trees with a double-headed axe just like real forest rangers. They said Jackson Space could chop down a pine tree faster than Superman. "He is Superman!" they exclaimed, their eyes wide with wonder. In the midst of all this, Jackson also used to read them poetry. Quite an experience for them.

I know they matured as young men through their experiences at camp. The Spaces both remarked on how much they liked the boys and how helpful they were at the ranch. We appreciated the Spaces as people. They were intelligent and knowledgeable, and they seemed sensitive to the needs of young boys. Mrs. Space gave special counseling to gifted children in addition to her routine duties at the camp. We felt privileged to have our boys under their guidance.

The second year they went to camp, the boys took their own horses to ride. They had new horses now. Charlene Hartell's father, Mr. Bradley, had a couple of young Palomino geldings he wanted to give Sam in exchange for a bill he owed. We agreed, knowing Norman and Sammy were ready for younger horses they could train on their own. I remember how excited the boys were to see the Palominos. A young cowboy brought them over from Mr. Bradley's ranch. He said one of the horses was a bit rough and still needed some breaking. That horse sounded like one for Sammy. The horse was a small, compact good-looking animal with a white blaze down the front of his face. Sammy named him Don Solo. Norman, who had ridden bony old Mouse for so long, was really proud of his new horse. His Palomino was long-legged and slim, and though a bit gangly, had nicely rounded features and was much more comfortable to ride than Mouse had been. Norman called him Flight.

Sammy and Norman would take off on their horses and ride up into the hills with their bedrolls and camping equipment to sleep out over night. They were ready to go one Friday afternoon, with everything neatly packed, saddle bags full of food and water for overnight, when Sam walked out into the corral to see them. Sam had gotten home a little early from the office which was unusual for him. He saw Sammy putting a pair of wire cutters into his saddle bag. He asked Sammy, what are you doing with the wire cutters? He turned to his father and said with some perplexity in his voice, "Daddy, they're starting to put up fences all over the place around here. How are we supposed to go riding anymore?"

Those were really great days for us, watching the boys grow, watching them bond with their horses and take responsibility for them, and seeing them venture out on their own, to ride and camp and explore.

Julie became a fine rider like her brothers. She started at an early age, and began with Poncho.

Poncho was her riding horse. He was a big, tall, gaited palomino standing some fifteen hands high and gentle as a lamb to ride. For us older folks, however, he could be rather rambunctious, and always was a problem catching him in the corral. All except for Julie, of course. She would stand in the corral in front of Poncho, and he would put his head down on her shoulder as she calmly slid the bit into his mouth and bridle up over his ears. Julie could do almost anything with Poncho. She talked to him like she talked to her best friend. They had a wonderful relationship. Poncho knew that when men came to bridle him, that meant work, but when Julie wanted to bridle him, he was not going to have to work very hard. He was a fine horse with a personality of his own.

Julie probably spent as much time talking with Poncho as she did riding him. She talked with Poncho like she talked with our dog, Cocoa. They both loved her and knew that somehow, they belonged to her.

Horses were a big part of growing up in the Ziegler household. Sammy Ziegler and Norman at summer camp at Space Ranch, in Santa Fe, New Mexico.

Kennnel Klub. Isabel with Muffin and Coco (the white poodle).

22

THE *COLLIER'S* ARTICLE
(JANUARY, 1956)

There had been a time, a scant half-dozen years before, on Ziegler's first arrival as a mission doctor in the Española Valley, when a local person would have avoided a hospital as a plague house. Hospitals were where you went to die. Now, more and more, the people were viewing the new hospital as a place to get better.

Since Ziegler's arrival, the Española doctors have established not only an ever-expanding clinic, but also one of the best little hospitals in New Mexico (run by the Evangelical United Brethren, the church that first brought Ziegler down from Pennsylvania) and a first-rate medical library. They have lured other fine doctors into the area, and now minister to a territory of at least 10,000 square miles, with 35,000 inhabitants, mostly in adobe mountain villages.[21]

Thus wrote Albert Rosenfeld in his article entitled "Modern Medicine—where 'the clock walks'." This edition of *Collier's* magazine reached the newsstands on Wednesday, January 18th, 1956. Sam and I had gone into Santa Fe that day to the artist, Barry Atwater's, memorial service. Abe Silvers, a good friend from Santa Fe, came running up to us waving his hands as we were leaving the service. He said with obvious concern in his voice, "Don't go back to Española. *Collier's* magazine has hit the newsstands."

We knew an article about health care in northern New Mexico was to be published in *Collier's*. A number of the doctors in Española had been involved in interviews and discussions for this article sometime earlier, and were looking forward to seeing it in print. We were perplexed about why Abe was so worried.

We tried to reassure Abe and then drove back to Española, stopping in the Riverside Drug Store to obtain a copy of the magazine. We found that the drugstore had sold out of all its copies. Several Hispanics in the store turned a cold shoulder to us as we entered, refusing even to acknowledge our presence. Some were people we knew and considered friends. The phone was ringing when we arrived home. Callers were angry about the article, and many who did not identify themselves threatened us with reprisals.

A friend brought a copy of *Collier's* magazine for us to read. We knew something had gone wrong as soon as we saw the title of the article: "Modern Medicine—where 'the clock walks'."

Albert Rosenfeld, a free-lance writer, had approached the physicians in the Valley including Sam and Drs. Friedman, Pijoan, and Yordy, some months prior, asking if he might write an article about medical practices in the area. He informed us that the article was to be published in *Collier's* magazine. The magazine wished to have a feature about local medical practices, the impact of the new hospital and the work of the physicians in this rural area. All the local doctors including Sam were generally pleased because all of them were proud of the work they had been doing to provide better medical services for the people of northern New Mexico.

I felt the article would be a worthwhile and interesting study because it could educate the public at large about what was being done. The doctors thought that such an article should provide a fair and balanced account of medicine as it was practiced in the area, and they stipulated that they would agree to participate only if allowed to edit the article prior to its publication. They were aware of potential problems and the need to be sensitive about local feelings. Concern about these issues prompted their request to ensure the article was accurate and fair. Albert Rosenfeld readily agreed to this condition.

Rosenfeld then came to the Valley with the photographer, Cal Bernstein, to do the background work following initial talks. They stayed several weeks, interviewing a number of local people including celebrities like Georgia O'Keeffe and Oliver LaFarge, both of whose pictures were included in the final article along with a comment about them. Photographs were taken of the doctors at work with their patients, and of local people using various folk remedies common to the area.

Albert Rosenfeld did provide an initial draft of his article for review. The doctors were allowed to suggest changes they felt necessary regarding language and information that was either inaccurate or offensive. The draft was returned with comments and suggestions for necessary revisions. The final, published version, however, completely disregarded the "editing." The sections that had been changed or marked "DO NOT PRINT" were those prominently included in the final article.

The article as published correctly portrayed many of the realities with which the doctors dealt in providing medical care to the people of northern New Mexico. It stated, for example, that before the doctors had arrived, hospitals had been places where people went to die, not to be healed, but that now, more and more people were beginning to recognize the benefits of modern health care. Sam was certainly aware of this perception, especially among the older generation of Hispanics. He was also aware of the poor roads, isolation and lack of transportation that often prevented people from getting to a hospital in time to be treated.

The article spoke of the use of free clinics in the rural areas, referring to them as "vanishing clinics." These were clinics to provide temporary services in the remote areas in order to show local people what services were available and help educate them about the benefits of good medical care. The clinics were designed to encourage people to come to the hospital when they were ill. They worked well and they "vanished" as people began coming to the hospital on their own, and the need for them declined.

The article mentioned the educational work being done with local healers (medicas) and midwives (parteras) to help them understand the importance of modern health care standards and practices, and it mentioned throughout the significance of local values and cultural considerations in the provision of care. It concluded:

> The Española doctors perform their healing functions in a manner that might profitably be copied, in its overall attitude and approach, in other medically backward areas. True, it requires a special breed of men to carry out such projects. Men who love people, and who love their work. Men who are dedicated, and willing to make sacrifices.[22]

The article also favorably noted that:

> The Española Medical Center, although only one of several thriving medical centers in New Mexico, is a unique—at times,

almost bizarre—institution. Drs. Ziegler, Pijoan, Friedman and their newest colleague, Dr. Merle Yordy, with the consultative assistance of a number of Santa Fe specialists who spend part of each week in Española, are doing what they are doing for three good reasons: they love the challenge of practicing medicine in an area where it is so badly needed. They love the country and the climate. And they love the people—a quality indispensable for introducing new ideas to an area which, through isolation, has done things differently for centuries.

The people here keep their homes and children scrupulously clean and neat. They maintain a great personal pride and dignity. Their manners are gracious and charming. They are serene, yet full of fun.

And, as direct descendants of the Spanish Conquistadores, they are the inheritors of one of the oldest cultural traditions in the Western Hemisphere.

"And we respect that culture," adds Pijoan. "If there are practices which we feel are medically harmful, we try to root them out—gently, gradually. But we leave everything else alone."[23]

These portions of the article appeared to be straightforward investigative reporting, but the positive, informative comments were set alongside statements about local practices and beliefs which were uncomplimentary and insensitive to the local Hispanic population, and which overshadowed the balanced reporting elsewhere. The article made reference, for example, to superstitions about the night air which led to the improper ventilation of houses. It mentioned placing blue tobacco stamps from cigarette packages on the forehead as a cure for headache, tying a copper wire around the wrist as a cure for rheumatism, and recognition of 'mal ojo'—the evil eye—as the cause of disease.

The examples chosen and the wording used were thoughtless and unfortunate. They inflamed local Hispanics by portraying them incorrectly as ignorant, superstitious and backward. The article chose to emphasize the "unique" and "backward" as if these were the norm for the area. This was not the case, and as a group, the physicians had spoken out against this aspect of the article before it went to press.

The practices mentioned were present locally. Isolation and lack of outside services contributed to the use of local remedies and to the practices of the *medicas* and the *parteras*. Sam saw people in his office with blue tobacco stamps on their foreheads. Celestino Gallegos, the custodian and handyman at McCurdy School who was photographed for the article with the stamps on his forehead, was a patient of his. I do not know if Celestino ever put a stamp on his forehead as a cure, but he willingly agreed to model because of the common local practice. I know that Celestino received threats of reprisal because of his participation.

The degree of local reaction made for several very stressful weeks for all of us. There were moments when Sam thought he should resign from his practice. Calls came from local people, and from the relatives and friends of these people who lived all over the country. One call came from Peru. Many were more open to the real purpose of the article once they heard Sam's explanation.

I remember the calls very well. They were threatening and degrading, and they frightened us. My Española beauty operator was a lovely Hispanic girl. She told me the latest gossip when I went to her shop to have my hair done. She was concerned because she heard people say the doctors should be tarred and feathered and hung from telephone poles. She was frightened. "Mrs. Ziegler, you and Dr. Ziegler must get out of town," she urged.

Sam and I were living on coffee and little else. Sam lost twenty pounds and I lost ten. I slept with a pillow propped under my head at night. Every time a car drove by, I listened to see if it stopped. We sent the boys to spend several days with Angus and Reecie Evans, while Caroline Dozier, our house keeper, took Julie to stay with her at Santa Clara Pueblo.

Two weeks passed and the furor continued. Sam finally called State Patrolman T.J. Chavez, who came by the house to talk with us. We had been invited to attend a wedding in Santa Fe the next day and T.J. said, "You attend the wedding and make arrangements to spend the night in Santa Fe. "We'll patrol your place all night."

Sam was grateful when Dr. Tobias Espinosa, the elderly Hispanic general practitioner in Española, said to him, "Sam, this is the best thing that could have happened. These people need to be awakened to the fact that there is better medicine than they have been getting."

We received comments from other people as well saying they wanted us to know they were not upset by the article and did not blame Sam for anything.

The FBI called Sam and said they would be willing to step in and check on threatening calls and acts of reprisal. Rocks were thrown through our living room windows, and callers threatened to burn our house. We asked the FBI not to intervene, at least for the present. General Corlett went to one of the Catholic priests and asked for his assistance. The Father was very amenable and his actions seemed to help a great deal in calming local tempers.

Sam kept his regular schedule and never missed office hours. He always had an office full of people. Some of them had no serious complaints, but had come to say to Sam by their presence, " Doctor, we are with you. We have no grudge against you."

Sam received one string of phone calls from a man whose voice he recognized. The man ran a small business in Española. His calls were always very hostile. "I will get you!" he threatened in a voice filled with anger. The man's call was unsettling. We could not understand the reason for his hostility, for Sam had gone out of his way to help a relative of this man's who was suffering from severe headaches. The relative had been seeing one of the local osteopaths, but had been unable to obtain relief. Sam examined him, and discovered that he had a probable brain tumor, a potentially very serious condition.

There were no neurosurgeons in New Mexico in those days, but Sam had been fortunate to become acquainted with a neurosurgeon in Denver named Dr. Charles R. Freed. He called Dr. Freed and asked if he would examine the man. Dr. Freed agreed, and late one night, Sam drove the man, free of charge, to Denver in our car and stayed with him while Dr. Freed examined him and performed an emergency decompression of the brain. Sam then turned around and drove back to Española so he could get ready for his regular surgery schedule and office hours. The patient remained in Denver for a period of time, and was picked up and brought back home. The ultimate outcome of the case was a sad one, but at least Sam had acted as he felt was right.

Concern about these calls preyed on our minds. Sam felt he needed to do something to settle the matter. One evening as he was coming home from the hospital, he saw a dim light through the windows of the man's store, and decided to stop and see him. He walked into the store and found the man sitting at a small table with four other men. The room was lit with a single bare light bulb dangling from the ceiling. The men all turned to look at Sam whose first impulse was to turn around and walk back out the door. But retreating would be a real sign of defeat, possibly even an indication of guilt, and Sam was not about to allow this. He told me that he walked up to the man looking as brave and determined as he could. He grabbed him by the shirt, stood him up and said, "You have forgotten what I did for your family." He then pushed him back in his chair, and turned and walked out.

The phone rang at home the next day, and the same voice said, "Doctor, I'd like for you to stop in my store and buy something. Just don't do it for a couple of weeks. Okay?" Sam had no more calls. He never took care of the man or his family again.

We received words of support from many friends and acquaintances. Sam sent a copy of the *Collier's* article to Dr. Earl L. Malone of Roswell, New Mexico, then President of the New Mexico State Medical Society, and asked for his review and opinion. Earl wrote back thanking him for sending the material and saying, "I find no unreasonable things in the article." He also stated that he felt complaints and remarks that came would "be motivated more by jealousy or something akin to it than by other more responsible motives."[24]

Miguel Gutierrez, then Governor of Santa Clara Pueblo, wrote a very positive note, saying he felt the Collier's article "did a fine job of paying due tribute to you and your staff," and that the people of Santa Clara were thankful to have the services of the medical center.[25]

Judge Milton Scarborough provided a great deal of personal support in a very visible way. He wrote a strongly worded letter against the *Collier's* article and its author, Albert Rosenfeld, which was published in *The Española Valley News*. Milton said that one of the results of this "malicious article" was that our doctors were being wrongly blamed for the writing and publication of the article. Milton said that we deplored the unkind and unfair statements in the article. He placed blame on the shoulders of Albert Rosenfeld, whom Milton felt intended to write a sensational piece to attract reader attention. Milton concluded his letter with these words:

> I have handed this statement to the Editor of the *The Española Valley News* with the hope that it will be printed for two reasons. First: So that people of the Valley may know that those of us who are

newcomers to this area do not share the feelings expressed by the author of the *Collier's* article, and Two: So that the public generally may know that neither Dr. Ziegler nor his associates approve the article or believe the matters therein contained.[26]

Milton's statement soon reached Albert Rosenfeld, who proceeded to sue both Judge Scarborough and Sam. Milton and Sam met with Rosenfeld and his lawyer one evening in a law office in Santa Fe, where they had a very heated discussion. Sam never forgot Milton's support that night. His actions were those of a fine lawyer and a true friend. Milton would not back down from his statement in the newspaper. Confronted with Milt's firm stance, Albert Rosenfeld and his lawyer agreed not to pursue the matter and dropped the whole suit.

Albert Rosenfeld did write an apology for his article which *The Española Valley News* published. He said:

When all is said and done, the fact remains that many people did feel offended and insulted, and there is no getting around it: I wrote the article, and I must shoulder the blame. I therefore offer, without excuse or qualifications, my full and sincere apologies to anyone anywhere who felt hurt or insulted by anything contained in my article. I only ask you to believe that neither I, the doctors, nor the editors of the Collier's, had the remotest intentions of making fun of anybody.[27]

I kept a diary during this period. I look back at my entries now with both interest and concern. I include several here which describe our feelings as the crisis unfolded:

Thursday, January 19
Collier's mag. Article on Drs. in Española and people of the community on news stand. Seems to be causing some ill-feeling—

Friday, January 20
More trouble today about *Collier's* article. Anonymous calls coming in—blaming doctors for contents of article.

Saturday, January 21
Life seems to be a nightmare. More calls—threats made on doctors' lives. Surely 10 years of service in a community can mean more than this!

Sunday, January 22
Milton and Hollis [Scarborough] here to discuss undue publicity. The help of friends is more than appreciated.

Thursday, January 26
[A local man] called to ask us not to buy gas from him. He fears his own group will think he is favoring our side now.
Hollis had anonymous call this morning because of Milton's article.

Monday, January 30
Life seems to be nothing but a nightmare—calls and more threats—now trouble with Rosenfeld because of article written about doctors by Milton.

Tuesday, January 31
No peace and no rest—how can one not worry—some [friends] have been so wonderful. Sam losing weight fast.

Sunday, February 5
Tears and words—what to do next. Sam will not make further statement against Milt. I think he is right.

Tuesday, February 7
Final statement to Rosenfeld. His rebuttal due.

Wednesday, February 8
Esp. Valley News out with slander about Sam and Milt. Anonymous call warning of further local meetings and threats. State Police investigating— relieved to know some help available. Milt and Hollis here for evening talking with Officer T. J. Chavez.

Tuesday, February 14
Pressure letting up—but Santa Fe Co. Med. Society making something of article in *Collier's* now—possibility of advertising.

The furor largely quieted down within a month to six weeks after *Collier's* magazine had been on the newsstands. Only a few individuals tried to keep tempers stirred up for a longer time.

A friend of ours from Otterbein College, Monroe Courtright, visited us during this time. He was a reporter for the *Public Opinion*, a weekly publication in Westerville, Ohio, and was on his way back from a national newspaper meeting in Arizona. Monroe later wrote an account for his paper of his reactions to the *Collier's* article and his assessment of the local situation. Monroe correctly noted that Sam's greatest concern was that local people "will think we are making light of their native superstitions and will be resentful of our efforts in the future" and that this resentment will set back the progress being made in bringing modern health care to the area. Monroe interviewed several people in Española. He found, as one businessman remarked, that there were a few scattered objections, but generally, people realized the benefits of the hospital's work.[28]

During the crisis, Sam wrote to his father in Dayton, Ohio and asked him what he should do. He told him of his concerns and of his personal anguish, saying that there were a number of times that he felt perhaps he should leave Española, that he was no longer welcome here. His father's counsel always provided great solace and his letter brought a prompt reply full of common sense and good advice. His father wrote, in part:

> You indicated in your letter that you and Isabel learned a valuable lesson. You said, "We have been through a time when our faith in God has helped us more than we can say." That is worth something, Samuel. The only way to learn how great and how good God is, is to be conscious of His presence at such a time. May I suggest that maybe there was some lesson God wanted to teach you and this seemed an opportunity . . . since it happened by the ambitious plans of men He took the occasion to show you how real and close He could be at a time like this. Remember that gold is refined by fire, and great characters are made by trials, hard situations, testing which at times seem beyond human will or strength to endure.
>
> As I see it, I would not leave now. Since it is not a moral or ethical issue there is no reason why you should leave. The publish-

ing of this article as I see may have been a mistake in judgment. But where is the man who never makes them? Another reason why I think you should not leave is because I do not believe you will respect yourself for it in later years. If you run away it is a question whether you will ever gain what you say you seem to have lost temporarily in your self-confidence. If you regain it in the midst of this turmoil it will stick so fast that it will take a storm many times worse to shake it loose again. I am writing this 1500 miles from Española. Perhaps if I were there and knew what you know I would advise you differently. It may be God is trying to see how much iron is in His man. By this time you see that I interpret my life, every man's life, in terms of God.

. . .

Time has a way of healing things. . .

. . .

I have written at much length and perhaps have not given you any particular help in your trouble. But be sure of this my son. I wanted to help you.

With love and our prayers for God's guidance in these days of turmoil.[29]

Time does heal wounds. Sam's office continued to be just as full of patients and his surgery schedule just as busy as it had been before, and the babies kept coming and coming.

Many times Sam would comment that he thanked God for the privilege of serving the people of the Española Valley and for having been in some small way, a part of His greater plan.

This series of events was undoubtedly the most difficult and stressful of our time in Española. I had great admiration for my husband, Sam, who withstood the anger and hurtful comment from those whom he treated and made well. We were close to walking away from the problem. I was very proud of him for standing up for what he thought was right and just.

There were no negative comments from other doctors in the Medical Society during all of the furor. However, a prominent Santa Fe internist then began to push for Sam's removal as vice-president of the State Medical Society just as matters seemed to settle down. He lobbied among members of the Santa Fe County and the State Medical Society saying he felt Sam had been using the *Collier's* article to advertise his practice.

The physician had established his practice in Santa Fe in the 1940s. He was well thought of locally and seemed to be a competent individual. He did a lot of talking, but he did not convert many doctors. Most thought the *Collier's* article an interesting study in folk medicine. Sam was advanced to the position of president-elect with no opposition at the annual meeting in May of 1956.

After all of the uproar generated by the *Collier's* article, Sam became president of the State Medical Society in 1957. I know that for him, his presidency was the culmination of many years of hard work on behalf of the Society and the medical profession in New Mexico.

He traveled a good deal as president, usually with Ralph Marshall, Executive Secretary of the Medical Society, who set up a schedule of visits to all the County Medical Societies, trying to make their visits coincide with their monthly meetings. I accompanied them on many occasions since I was secretary/treasurer of the State Medical Auxiliary. I met with the women involved with the various auxiliaries while Ralph and Sam met with the doctors.

I finally suggested that Sam have Jennings Doak, pharmacist from Pueblo Drug in Riverside, who was a pilot, fly him around to the different meetings because of the many demands on his time. This suggestion turned out to be a great idea!

Sam's presidency took him away from his practice a good deal. He still tried to keep up with surgery and a heavy obstetrical load. He was with Ralph Marshall when Tessa Cimino, a patient and a close friend, was near her due date. Sam had promised her that when she went into labor, he would get back to deliver her baby NO MATTER WHAT! The call that she had gone into labor came around midnight. Sam and Ralph were some distance from Española, so "flying low" as I called it, meant some fast traveling by car to get back to the hospital in time. Sam made it and Tessa Cimino and her husband, Carl, named their newborn son, Samuel, in honor of Dr. Sam.

Sam and I were both ready for a change of pace following his busy and tiring year as president. We planned a week resting in Colorado Springs at the Broadmoor Hotel. We had learned by chance in early 1958 that Helen Atwater was Social Director at the Broadmoor. She had dropped out of sight for a time following Barry's death, and we were glad to know of her whereabouts. We contacted her and told her we hoped she would have some time to spend with us.

You would have thought the King and Queen of England had arrived when we walked in to the lobby of the Broadmoor the first of May. Four bellhops surrounded us at the registration desk, picked up all of our luggage and would not let us do anything but follow them. We walked down a long hallway and took an elevator to the 2nd floor, then proceeded along a short hall to stop before an imposing carved door which opened into a large, beautifully decorated suite. A marble-topped table sat in the center of the sitting room, filled with a huge bouquet of beautiful flowers. We could not believe our eyes, and as we were trying to recover from our excitement, we turned to see Helen Atwater standing in the doorway. She was obviously pleased with our enthusiastic response.

Our week's stay at the Broadmoor was restful and exciting. We had a tee time on the golf course at 9:00 a.m. the second morning we were there, but snow the night before made play that day out of the question. Imagine! Snow in Colorado Springs in early May !

We were able to golf the next morning, the snow having magically melted over night. We were told at the pro-shop that we were part of a four-some. The other couple were about our age, and as we were being introduced, we apologized to them, saying we were not the best golfers. They quickly responded, "Please don't worry. We are also 'amateurs'."

The woman volunteered to tee off first. She proceeded to hit a ball that traveled a country mile, sailing straight as an arrow down the middle of the fairway. It was soon obvious that her shot had not been a "lucky" one. Her obvious good play continued for the full round of golf. We found out later that she was the California Women's Amateur Golf Champion. The man was also a fine player, but not as good as she. We did not do too badly, much to our surprise. I did not hit the ball very far when teeing off, but I hit it right down the fairway with very good placement.

We were fortunate to be able to spend some time with Helen, who had done well in arranging her life after Barry's death. She seemed happy and content with her job at the Broadmoor. We lost track of her after that visit. We later heard indirectly that she had remarried and moved back East.

The visit to the Broadmoor was a nice change of pace and Sam was soon ready to get back to the hospital and his patients.

23

OUR FRIENDLY GHOST

There were many things that had to be done to our home to make it more livable after we moved in. The room off of the kitchen to the west was originally a garage. Paul McFarland had closed it off and made it into a laundry and furnace room. We turned it into our TV room when we acquired our first TV in 1950. We had a carpenter make custom-fit knotty pine cabinets for the room so that it would be more functional and presentable. The carpenter who did the work was with us off and on for about five years. We called him our "drunken carpenter" because he would start jobs, then mysteriously disappear for several days, then return when he was ready to work again. He told us that he had been in the Navy during World War II, and had worked on ships in Honduras. It was there, he said, because of the weather and the conditions under which he lived, that he had become an alcoholic.

He really was a master craftsman. He finished the back room, and then built the stables for our horses and the carport for our two cars. We placed the carport in the area where Dora Giron and I had planted our first garden.

Our carpenter was knowledgeable about other things as well. He knew exactly how to treat the beautiful hand-carved antique boards from Antigua that Mrs. Sylvanus Morley gave Sam. We were about to scrub them with diluted soap and water when he said, "No, by no means. Don't ever do that. You are supposed to brush them with a little white kerosene. I believe that I am correct in saying that." We did brush them with white kerosene, and incorporated several of these boards into the handmade wooden front door when our house was remodeled. Martel Livermore made the door. It is a work of art.

Sam and I felt we were able to think seriously about enlarging and re-modeling our home in 1960. We selected Allen McNown, Dr. Valerie Friedman McNown's husband, as our architect. Allen did excellent work, but he liked odd shapes and angles and was quite contemporary in his thinking. I felt the addition to our house should continue the feeling of the old adobe and the pueblo architecture of the original parts of the house. We bandied back and forth for some time before we came to a meeting of the minds. Allen called after he had returned from a trip to Mexico, and said, "I believe we can pull our thinking together now." Plans were then completed and put out to bid. Much to our delight, our favorite contractor, Albert Livermore, came in lowest.

The main addition to the house was to be a large new living room extending off to the east and measuring 36' x 40'. Other parts of the house were also to have changes except for the original master bedroom in the southwest corner. This room was to remain intact so that visitors and guests could see an original part of the house. It has a lovely corner fireplace and adobe plaster on its walls. Hand prints in the original plaster are still quite visible.

Before beginning construction, we had our contractor remodel the Barn out back first, turning it into a livable apartment for Sam and me and Julie. We removed the second floor balcony and bunks along with the staircase, and dropped the bunks to the west end of the main floor. We had a kitchenette installed facing the south, with a full set of windows for light, and behind the kitchenette, portable closets and a dressing area next to the bathroom and shower.

Lucille Winks, a fine local decorator, guided us in our choice of colors for the Barn. She helped select matching fabric for wallpapering and drapes.

We had huge, firm pillows made which could be propped against the wall on the bunk beds for extra, comfortable seating. The colors and fabric design for the sleeping/sitting area of the large room were all coordinated in a rich, medium blue. The woodwork was painted white as were the kitchen cup-boards. The kitchen windows were hung with curtains of soft pastel colors, creating a cheerful and pleasant work space for preparing meals.

It took a year to enlarge and remodel the house after we moved into the Barn. I would walk toward the house each morning after Sam left for the hospital, saying "Good morning" to all the workers. Some were Indians, some Hispanics and some Anglos. They were not too sure how to respond to me at first, but after several days, they began to greet me in turn. I would go on into the house, talk with the contractor or architect, whoever was there, observe, discuss if necessary, and marvel at what was taking place. Mr. Livermore would often call me in and say, "Are you sure this is what you want? If not, now is the time to say so and change it, before it is too late." The plans were so well done that there were very few changes to be made.

The telephone man who was installing the many telephone jacks in the house, came into the empty living room when it was completed, and sat on the floor, saying, "Mrs. Ziegler, this is the most beautiful house I have ever been in. I hope you and Dr. Ziegler have much happiness here." His good wishes came true. We lived in the house for many years after, always with great love and happiness.

Ben Talachi, our gardener, arrived one morning carrying a small wooden door set in a wooden frame with a sill at the bottom. The door swung on spindle-like projections fitted into holes in the frame. The door and frame were of pine that had grayed and dried with age. A leather thong hung from a hole in one side and worked the latch. It, too, was brittle with age. Ben came up to me with the door, and said, "Mrs. Ziegler, Mrs. Talachi and I would like you and Dr. Ziegler to have this door for your new home. This door came from Yunque Yunque."

I was amazed and thrilled by the gift, but I said, "Oh, Ben. This door is very old and valuable. Are you sure you want to give it to us?"

There must have been something about the tone of my voice that made Ben feel I doubted the door's authenticity. He seemed upset at my reply, and quickly responded, "Mrs. Ziegler, when the Spanish left Yunque, the San Juan Indians went over and took everything they could carry. This door has been in my family for three hundred years. The sill on the frame attached to the door was worn by hard-soled boots, not by moccasins. We want you to have this for your home."

I called our architect after receiving the door, and told him about it, saying we had to have a special place for it in the new addition. We decided to put it by the fireplace and to add a small enclosure on the out-side to house firewood. The door would give access to this small addition. The door, frame and sill together measure only 28" by 61", the door itself just 25 ½" x 58", a good size for this setting. We looked at the door after it was set into the wall, and wondered that such an historical piece was now part of our home. This gift from Ben and his wife was very special indeed.

Everything seemed different and new to me when Sam and I were able to move back into the house, even the sounds. I tried to settle in that first night, but was strangely restless. I finally dozed into a half-sleep, only to be awakened suddenly by the sound of heavy boots clumping around the bedroom floor. The steps came to rest at the foot of my side of the bed. I sat up with a start. Before me stood a Spanish Conquistador in full armor. I said in fright, "You don't belong here!" Almost as quickly, the conquistador disappeared.

We then began to find the Baluchi prayer rug which we kept on the floor near the old Spanish door, moved out of place, as if someone had walked on it and shifted its alignment. We were always particular about the placement of the rugs in the house, wanting them straight and in position. The movement of the rug was curious. We asked our housekeeper, Caroline, to be certain it was in place before she left at night, and we checked each morning following. We continued to find the rug out of place. Its movement occurred regularly, night after night, for a long period of time. We would place the rug to within half inch of the wall in front of the fire place, and each morning we would find it moved six to eight inches away.

We decided the ghost of the conquistador was responsible. He could only have come through the Spanish door from Yunque Yunque. We felt he was a friendly ghost who may have brought friends to sit by our fireplace and chat. He returned many times while we were living there, and he has returned on occasion now that our daughter, Julie, and her husband, Ken Langille, live in the house.

My mental picture of the conquistador is still very vivid. The deed abstract of our land goes back to the Conquistador Don Diego de Vargas, one of the leaders of the Spanish settlement of New Mexico, so we named our ghost "DeVargas" after him.

Sam took a liking to Ben Talachi, our Indian gardener from San Juan Pueblo. He was a big, tall, fine-looking, San Juan Indian, standing over six feet in height and weighing over two hundred pounds. His skin was dark bronze, reflecting the many years he had worked under the hot New Mexico sun. He had a graceful walk, and a gracious and personable manner.

I will never forget the hot summer day in the early 1960s, after the remodeling of the house had been completed. Sam came home an afternoon from the office to spend a little time in the yard with Ben. They worked a while and began to sweat. It got hotter and drier with every minute. The sky was a beautiful blue, clear as a bell, not a cloud to be seen anywhere, and the sun just kept beating down.

Ben and Sam got to talking about how hot and dry it was, and Sam said jokingly, "Ben, don't you think we ought to do a rain dance?"

Ben thought for a second, then replied, "Yeah, Doc, good idea you got there."

"Okay, Ben. You lead the way, and I will follow. I'll do the rain dance with you."

So Ben started dancing around the yard, chanting as he moved, "Oom, boom, boom, boom," with Sam close behind. They danced until they were both sweating pretty good. They stopped after some time and sat on the portal, both breathing heavily from their exertions. Suddenly, about two minutes after sitting down, whoosh! it started to rain like the dickens! Pouring down rain! Ben's eyes started getting bigger and bigger as he looked at the rain, and said to Sam, "Man! I've really done it." He slapped his hand against his knee. They both laughed and sat in wonder, listening to the rain. There was not a cloud in the sky when they started dancing. The sky was still cloudless as they looked out from under the shelter of the portal. A lone rain cloud had apparently been hovering in the portion of the sky, not apparent from the portal.

Ben worked for us a number of years. He pruned all of the trees in the orchard, took care of the vegetable and flower gardens, and cared for the lawns. He had a wonderful touch with gardens. We visited Ben and his wife, Margaret (Maggie), an Hispanic woman, on several occasions at their home in Ranchitos. Our visits gave us an opportunity to admire Ben's beautiful gardens. We took the boys with us whenever we could because Ben had developed a strong attachment to them and was always interested in seeing how they had grown and hearing about what they were doing.

We knew very little about Ben's background. He was a very private man, and we enjoyed him just for the person that he was. Through the years we lost touch with Ben. We later learned that his wife, Maggie, died in 1994. The year after, Ben was selected to be Popé in the Española Fiesta Parade, quite an honor for him. Popé was the medicine man from San Juan Pueblo who led the Pueblo Indian Revolt against the Spanish in 1680 that drove the Spanish from northern New Mexico.

24

EAGLE SCOUTS,
A BROKEN WRIST AND A SPECIAL DINNER

Sam had been active in scouting when he was a boy, and wanted his sons to have the same kind of experience. He became Scoutmaster for Santa Cruz Troop 134 when they were of an age for Boy Scouts. The McCurdy EUB church sponsored the Scout troop.

The Boy Scouts held competitions among the different scout troops state-wide in swimming and first aid. These competitions were among the most exciting times for all of the boys in the troop. They worked hard that first year for the First Aid Contest. Members of the team included Sammy and Norman, Hugh Prather, Angus Evans and Lisle Rogers. They had to develop basic competencies in the care of open wounds, splinting broken limbs and artificial respiration.

The boys felt pretty sure of themselves by the time the competition rolled around. Coming from our little scout troop in Santa Cruz, however, they may have been a little daunted by competition from the large scout troops in Santa Fe and Albuquerque. But they did not let it show. And by golly, they walked away with FIRST PLACE in the state competition! I think the special training and attention they received from their Scoutmaster, the doctor, may have played a part. But we were all so pleased. We gave a great shout of joy! The boys showed a lot of pride that day. They put Troop 134 from Santa Cruz on the state map.

The boys managed to continue their scouting in the midst of their other activities. They were pushing to become Eagle Scouts and had a number of merit badges to earn. They did their work and received their promotions in a special ceremony at the end of the summer. We have a picture of the boys standing proudly in their scout uniforms, their merit badge sashes draped across their shoulders with their new Eagle Scout badges pinned on them. Sam had only reached the rank of Life Scout when he was a boy scout, one rank below Eagle Scout. Sam was doubly proud when his sons became Eagle Scouts. They had worked hard and deserved their promotions.

Sammy got a job at Hayter's Cottonwood Ranch in Alcalde the summer of 1956 and wanted a motorcycle so he would have transportation to and from work. He was fourteen years old and mature enough to handle a cycle. A number of his friends already had Cushman Eagle scooters. They had all spent some time hill climbing in the foothills along the Llano. We finally consented and got Sammy a small motorcycle at Sears & Roebuck in Santa Fe, a bright red one which cost about three hundred dollars.

Sammy was quite excited about his cycle and avidly took to riding it back and forth to work. His job at the Cottonwood Ranch involved a lot of hard work. He had to load 90-100 lb. bales of hay on trailers in the fields and pick fruit up on high ladders in the orchards. His one consolation was that he could drive the ranch tractor. Things went fine for a couple of weeks. Then one afternoon, Mrs. Hayter appeared at the emergency room with Sammy sitting in the back of the ranch pickup truck, his motorcycle lying alongside him. He was holding his left arm in a sling and appeared to be in a good deal of pain. According to Mrs. Hayter, he had been up in an apricot tree on a fourteen foot ladder, and the top step on the ladder broke, causing Sammy to fall out of the tree and break his arm. He walked a quarter of a mile from the orchard to the ranch house to get help, still wearing a big apron full of apricots which he could not take off by himself.

We were thankful nothing more serious happened, and were sympathetic with Sammy about his misfortune. But Sam and I always chuckled about the fact that it cost us three hundred dollars for Sammy to work two weeks, then fall out of an apricot tree and break his arm. I do not think he would have made enough money all summer to pay for the motorcycle. It was not an entirely pleasant experience for any of us, but it is rather amusing to remember.

I really wanted a foal from my mare, Penny, because she was such a gentle, well-bred horse. We finally bred her to Herman Hall's quarter horse stallion. What an exciting day it was when the foal arrived June 8th, 1956! We had all been waiting with great anticipation through the long months for Penny to deliver. Norman went out to the corral to investigate early one morning and came running into the kitchen, eyes bright with excitement. "She delivered! She delivered!" he exclaimed. "The baby's here!" We all ran out to see. There at one corner of the corral, standing wobbly-legged beside her mother, was a darling foal. She had a sorrel coat just like her mother's, and a small round white spot over her forehead. We began to think of names. The white spot on her forehead reminded us of a coin and we thought a name like Penny's would be very nice. We finally settled on "Sixpence."

We watched Sixpence grow up in the corral. Sammy took her in hand and broke her to the hackamore. I do not think he ever put a bit in her mouth. She did not seem to need one. Sammy handled her well, and when she was old enough, he saddled and rode her. He said, "She did not buck with me when I first rode her, but she reared and fell over backwards with me on her. Really scared me. I guess I got lucky that day. I came out without a scratch." Sixpence calmed down after that. She was a good horse.

Our home on Fairview Lane, with its large yard and corral, was in constant need of attention. The boys fed and watered the horses, kept the corral clean, and took care of the lawn in the summer, mowing the near half acre of grass. They took pride in their work, and the yard looked nice. Sam and I were aware of their efforts, and began to pay them when they reached their teens.

The boys called to me from the yard one day as I returned home from the grocery store. I set my packages down at the back door and walked over to them. They had been trimming grass along the wall near the tool house. They stopped their work and came up to me as I approached. Both seemed excited about something, as if they had a secret to tell. Sammy asked expectantly, "Would you and Dad be free Saturday evening?"

"Well, yes, I think so. Why?"

They responded with big smiles on their faces, "We would like to take you out to dinner." How wonderful and thoughtful of them. They apparently had been saving their new found wealth from their yard work and wanted to show their appreciation.

We talked things over when Sam came home. We decided we should go to El Nido in Tesuque. The boys made the reservations while I arranged with Patty Murphy to babysit Julie.

That Saturday, we dressed up for this special occasion. Charlie Besre, owner of El Nido, greeted us when we arrived and seated us in one of the booths by the dance floor. El Nido was a favorite place for us to dine, and the boys seemed excited about the evening.

The waitress gave us menus and asked what we would like to drink. We placed our order and began to look at the menu for dinner suggestions. Sam immediately said, "This is a special occasion, and I think we should begin with some hors d' oeuvres." Charlie was noted for his snails, so we decided to have the escargot. We then turned to discussion about dinner, and Sam felt that filet mignon would be perfect for the occasion. The boys, being in their early teens with very healthy appetites, could not resist steak, and joined their father in ordering filet mignon. I had the lamb.

The evening moved along nicely. Conversation was excellent, filled with dreams and plans about school and home and travel. We saw a number of our friends as we dined, and we were proud to introduce our sons and say that we were being "treated."

All went well until it was time to decide about dessert and coffee. Sam again spoke up, "We should have dessert and coffee. By all means! The Cherries Jubilee sounds good to me." He ordered this for himself, while I selected a sherbet. The boys said they did not believe they cared for anything. They then asked if we would excuse them for a few minutes.

I had been watching Sam all evening, and could hardly keep from smiling each time he ordered the most expensive item on the menu. We knew that the boys were having concerns about how they were going to pay for the meal, and had probably gone to count their money. I knew Sam had been extravagant in his ordering for a reason, but I was nervous at this point and had begun to feel sorry for the boys.

When the boys returned to the table, Sam said, "Okay, we want you to know we have had a perfectly wonderful evening with you here. We are proud to have two such thoughtful and considerate young men as our sons. Now we want to put your worries at ease. We realize you have been a little concerned about how you were going to pay for the meal. Your mother and I felt you should be exposed to some of the realities of the world, and what might happen to you some evening when you are out on a date. It is important for you to be prepared if you are put on the spot financially." He grinned broadly, then continued, "Have no fear. We'll see that you have enough money."

The boys managed to pay the bill without our help, including a tip for the waitress. After laying all their money on the table, they walked Sam and me out to the car with their chests puffed way out, making sure to open the door for me.

A lot happened with our horses the summer of 1956. Norman's horse, Flight, turned out to be a good horse that he could work with and train, but Sammy's horse, Solo, proved to have a mean streak. Sammy felt he was a handful from the beginning. He worked with the horse, trying to train and gentle it, but the problems persisted. Sammy went out horseback riding one day with me. I was on Penny and Sammy on Solo. As we rode along in front of the Stampfer's house on the corner, their little Schnauzer dog jumped up on the wall barking loudly, and scared Solo. The horse bolted and began bucking across the road, throwing Sammy on the other side in front of the cement irrigation ditch. Sammy hit his head against the saddle horn as he was thrown, splitting open his left ear, and was pretty shaken by the whole incident. Solo took off riderless for the stables and could not be caught until he stopped in front of the corral gate.

We did not know what to do about this horse. Sammy was fourteen and we felt Solo might be a little too much horse for him. Ross Medina, who worked for us as a gardener and helped care for the horses, asked if he could try to "gentle" the horse a little before Sammy got back on him. We told him to go ahead. He found himself bucked around the corral. When he came into the house afterwards to report, he said he had one heck of a ride, and that Solo was sure "snorting fire."

I had another occasion to develop my dislike for Solo. Fred Stampfer, our neighbor to the east, asked if we would keep our eye on his house while he and his wife were away on a short vacation in Mexico. We said, "Yes, of course," and wished them a safe and pleasant journey. I kept watch during the day as I could, and Sam or I made the rounds in the evening before bed, to be sure everything was alright. Sam was called to the hospital late one evening, leaving me alone at home with Julie. Julie and I made a quick trip to the fence to peer over and assure ourselves that everything was secure, then returned to the house and went to bed.

I lay quietly for some time, unable to sleep, and then began to hear noises that sounded like someone trying to pry open a window at the Stampfer house. My heart began to beat faster and I got up to go to a window and listen more closely. The noise came again, sounding like wood being bent or twisted by a crowbar. I grew concerned and thought I should go and investigate.

It was a chilly fall night, so I put on my shoes and slipped my coat over my nightgown to protect myself from the cold. Not one to be afraid, I went outside and walked toward the Stampfer's place. Half-way to the house, I heard the noise again, louder this time, and realized it was coming from the direction of our stables, not the Stampfer's house. The stables appeared quiet as I stood looking toward them from the backyard except for a periodic loud gnawing sound that issued from one stall.

I moved closer and discovered that the sound was coming from Solo's stall. The horse was chewing on the wood of the hay bin at the front of the stall, making enough racket to keep at least me awake. "That horse!" I thought angrily to myself. The other horses all seemed to be eating quietly, with Penny in the stall on Solo's left, and Flight, Poncho and Shadow on the right. Not thinking, I slipped through the rails on the corral fence and walked quietly into the corral, stopping before Solo's stall. I felt that I had to do something to make him stop making that terrible noise, so I took off one of my shoes and banged it all of a sudden against the outside of the stall, shouting at the same time, "Stop that racket!"

Was I in for a surprise! The horses bolted out of their stalls and charged into the corral. Penny was fortunately next to me on my left, and must have sensed my presence because she brushed past me and turned the other horses away toward the other end of the corral as I huddled up against the stall.

I made a quick exit from the corral, realizing I may have been a bit foolish. That Solo had made me so angry, and I now had another reason to dislike him. Imagine! Waking up the neighborhood chewing on his stall! And I had thought a burglar was trying to break into the Stampfer's house! We decided Solo was bad medicine. We sold him and bought Sammy a nice looking, well-trained white mare from a ranch in Pojoaque. Sammy rode her a few times and felt so good about her and the way she responded to his commands that he decided to call her Melody. She was a pleasant change from the rough riding he had experienced with Solo.

Eagle Scouts, (left to right) Norman Ziegler, Angus Evans, then, (gentleman who presented Eagle awards) and Sammy Ziegler.

25

NOT TO BE FORGOTTEN

Clementine (Clemmy or Clem) and Gordon (Buck) Denton were among the first local people we met after our arrival in Española in 1946. Arthur Pack introduced us to Buck when we were looking for a place to live. Buck was a realtor, insurance agent and land developer all in one. We took to him immediately. He had a quick wit and was a good mixer, and he seemed shrewd in his business affairs and knowledgeable about the area. We noticed that Buck walked with a slight limp, and later learned he had broken one of his legs some years before when he attended a local event. The bleachers on which he had been sitting collapsed, injuring his leg.

Clem was a distinguished looking woman with strong features and what appeared to be prematurely graying hair which she wore short about her face. She dressed well, and though reserved, enjoyed a good joke and would not hesitate to join in the laughter. She was a most generous-hearted person. She entertained beautifully and was proud of her antique furniture and fine china. Occasions at her home were always special.

Clem was well-liked in the community and active in our church and local affairs. She was an accomplished pianist and organist, and accompanied me for solos when I sang. She often played the organ at our church. She was especially interested in the Santa Fe Opera. We attended a benefit party for the Opera one year and both wore spring "bonnets," which were quite the talk of the occasion. Our pictures appeared in *The New Mexican* the following day. The paper noted that the bonnets that had "captured the eye and the imagination of staffer Don Meeks were worn by two party-goers, Mrs. G. H. Denton and Mrs. S. R. Ziegler of Española. The two were pictured at the much-talked-about, highly successful benefit party given by the Santa Fe Opera Guild at the Bishop's Lodge."[30]

Buck and Clem were patients of Sam's, and Sam delivered their sons, Chuck and Dalton. We were often at each other's homes for family gatherings. The boys played together, and as they grew, rode horses together. Clem and I hauled the kids' horses by truck to the local horse shows for several years. It was all good fun! The arrival of visiting relatives of either of our family's usually meant supper and an evening of fun together.

Clem often came by the house for coffee, and always brought a large purse full of surprises. It did not take Julie long, at age two, to learn what Clem's arrival meant, and she would eagerly reach for the magic purse. Clem enjoyed Julie, and loved the attention her purse brought.

Clem stopped attending church and seemed to retire into herself after their younger son, Dalton's death. Dalton had attended Dartmouth College. He came home one Christmas Holiday with friends from school, and went to Aspen, Colorado to ski for several days. He had a cold at the time, and on arrival in Aspen, called home to say he was too sick to do much skiing. Clem advised him to stay in bed and rest. He remained behind in the hotel room while his friends went off to ski. They found him lying in bed, unresponsive, when they returned to the room. They put out an immediate emergency call, but the paramedics who arrived were unable to revive him.

Sam said that according to the medical reports, Dalton died from high altitude pulmonary edema. This condition is usually seen in individuals coming from a lower altitude and exerting themselves at a higher altitude without having a period of time to acclimate themselves. Dalton apparently had a mild upper respiratory infection which would have made him doubly vulnerable. Sam explained that high altitude pulmonary edema causes an accumulation of fluid in the lungs, impairing gas exchange and making it impossible for a person to obtain sufficient oxygen to live.

Clemmie never really recovered from Dalton's death. She did find some strength from reading my father, Frank Howe's, book, *Meditations of a Laymen*, but she remained much to herself.

I was with Clem at the emergency room of the Española Hospital the night before she died. I had gone to see another friend who had fallen and broken her hip. Clemmie was brought in while I was there, having suffered a stroke. I asked the physician in charge if I might stay with her for a time, and he readily agreed.

Clemmie could not talk, but I held her hand and talked about all the wonderful times our families had shared together. The frantic look I had seen on her face when she first came into the hospital, seemed to soften as I talked. She died the morning of October 28, 1994.

We met Elmo and Bunny Tipton not long after we settled into our home on Fairview Lane. They lived near John and Mary Marsh in Cuartales. Elmo, who like to be called "Tip," was the new owner of the Rio Arriba Telephone Company. He balanced a soft spoken and congenial manner with a hard-nosed, astute business sense. His wife, Lillian, went by the name of "Bunny." She was an active member of the Amantes de Flores Garden Club in Española. I was drawn to her energy and good humor. She had wonderful ideas about gardening and flowers, and grew saffron, which is difficult to cultivate. I was delighted when she presented me with a jar of it. We formed a strong friendship. We also liked Tip. He and Sam seemed to find much in common.

The Tipton's home was a beautiful adobe with a sweeping view of the Sangre de Cristo mountains to the east and the Jemez range to the west. The house was surrounded on three sides by acres of alfalfa and orchards, and a corral for horses. They had a swimming pool which was just beyond the lovely portal, and we enjoyed swimming there on many occasions. We would also call Bunny and Tip to come over and join our family for an impromptu dinner when pots of food were bubbling on the stove. It always seemed time well-spent.

One winter weekend we made a special trip to the Tipton's cabin near Truchas, the mountain village close by. Bunny and Tip were well organized for the trip, and loaded their truck with a snow-mobile, and containers of food for breakfast and steaks to cook on the open fireplace for dinner. We drove as far as we could in the truck once we reached the Truchas area, then Tip took Bunny on ahead to the cabin in the snowmobile so that she could start getting things ready for us, while he came back to pick up Sam and me. It was cold outside and the snow was waist high, but we were warm and comfortable inside the cabin, sitting by the fire talking and dreaming. We were at an altitude of eight thousand feet, so you know we slept very soundly that night.

The cabin was well built, and warm and cozy in the winter. It was equally pleasant in the spring when the wild flowers were in bloom. The Tiptons kept their horses in a large pasture by the cabin during the spring and summer months, and the horses would come galloping up to greet us as we approached. We always looked forward to these trips.

We lost Bunny in 1991. Tip then moved to California with Bunny's brother, Joe Byrne, and his wife, Nancy. They took wonderful care of him. Tip sent us a copy of his "All Saints Day Letter" some years ago, which went out to all of his friends. He said in closing, "I think of you often and miss seeing you. I send my best wishes to all of you. May the good Lord bless you and keep you. May you have a great holiday season which will soon be on us." [31]

Enclosed with the letter was a note from Joe Byrne about a new lecture hall at the College of Santa Fe to be named "Tipton Hall" in memory of Bunny. Joe included the text of the plaque which was to be hung in the hall. It reads:

"This gift of Tipton Hall is done in memory of my wife, Lillian Tipton (1903–1991). She was born Lillian Byrne on the Monday before Easter and was known to everyone as 'Bunny.' The College of Santa Fe is on land once owned by her father on which her brother, Verne, ran an airport and flying school. On that land, Bruns Hospital was built. Bunny and I never had children of our own, but we believed in education and youth. With the help of the Lord, whenever Bunny and I did something, we tried to do the best we could. I wish that you who use Tipton Hall will do the same."

It was wonderful to receive Tip's fine letter and know that he was well, and to read of his memorial to Bunny, a fine tribute to a vibrant woman who was our dear friend.

Tip is gone now also. We talked with him on his 100th birthday. His mind was still clear and sharp. We remembered as we talked, the special times we had spent with him and Bunny.

In the late 1950s, Senator Horace DeVargas and his wife, Nathalia, bought the house next door to us from Earl and Nan Fullman and moved in not long after. We were neighbors for many years and became close friends, sharing many experiences together.

We were at each other's homes on many occasions. Nathalia would often call when Sam came home from the hospital and say, "Let's get together!" We gravitated toward wherever food and beverage were most readily available, either in their kitchen or ours. Conversations were always current and interesting. Horace would talk about his background with a great deal of pride, but he was very proud to call himself an American, not just an Hispanic. He had an intelligent and free-thinking spirit which he brought to all of his personal and political involvements.

Horace was a most refined looking man, always well-dressed, gracious of manner and sensitive in demeanor. He was well respected for his ability to represent his constituents. He loved to entertain in his home, and he was a good dancer.

I learned that Horace was a descendant of one of the first Spanish conquistadors in the new world, General Diego de Vargas Zapata Luján Ponce de León. He was born in 1908 and had one brother, Diego, named after this famous ancestor. Horace was raised in Ojo Caliente to the north of Española, and began his career as a grade school teacher. He advanced to become a superintendent of schools, but eventually left to go into the insurance business which he continued while he served as New Mexico State Senator from 1947–1972.

Horace divorced his first wife, and tragically lost a son in an automobile accident in 1949. His second wife, Nathalia, was devoted and faithful to his every cause. She was a tall, stately woman of Ukrainian descent, very generous-hearted and pleasant to be around. Nathalia seemed to blend with the Hispanics as easily as she did with the Anglos, and was accepted by all.

Our lives seemed to develop a spirit of friendly competition as neighbors. It was not long after we had remodeled the Barn and our home in 1960–1961 that Horace and Nathalia began to remodel their outbuildings and construct a large new living room with a sizeable fireplace. Remarkably, there seemed to be a great deal of similarity between what we did and what they did. We laughed many times about this friendly competition and enjoyed each other's efforts. One could say that this rivalry even spilled over into entertaining.

We cherished Horace and Nathalia as neighbors, and felt that our relationship was the way it should be with neighbors, with a lot of give and take and mutual support and admiration.

Alan Vedder and his wife, Ann, were among our very close friends in Santa Fe. We think of them and our association over the years with great warmth.

Alan came to New Mexico in the mid-1940s from Delaware following his graduation from Yale University. He was Curator and then Conservator of the Museum of New Mexico for many years until his retirement in 1979. He was internationally recognized as a conservator and a specialist in Spanish Colonial arts and artifacts, and was author of the work, *Furniture of Spanish New Mexico.*[32] He was much involved with the identification and restoration of furniture and religious artifacts of the New Mexican Santeros. A tall, good-looking man of lean frame, with light brown to graying hair, a rugged face and heavy eyebrows, he spoke softly with constantly smiling eyes, his voice always filled with excitement about the world around him. We came to appreciate this quality in him.

Alan married Ann Healy in 1962. We knew Ann from the early 1950s, when we became acquainted with her father, Dick Healy. Dick was the owner of Santa Fe Book and Stationery Store, located for many years on San Francisco Street just off the plaza in downtown Santa Fe. He was one of the first Santa Fe businessmen we encountered, and his welcome greeting in his store was memorable. We were often customers of his. We knew Dick and his second wife, Mildred, from our association in town, and from our occasional vacationing together at Arthur and Phoebe Pack's Ghost Ranch Lodge in Tucson, Arizona. Dick was killed in a tragic accident in the late 1960s, but Mildred remained a close friend.

Ann Healy was a bright and sensitive woman with a formal, dignified demeanor. She attended a prep school in New York State, and then went to Stanford University in California where she graduated "with distinction" in Business. She served on the Board of Directors of St. Vincent Hospital and the Santa Fe Opera for many years.

Ann met Alan one evening at a party he gave at his home. Mildred said that a friend told Alan there was a lovely lady, a "real Santa Fean," whom he thought Alan should meet. Alan said noncommittally, "Fine." They met and immediately after began dating. They were married within a short time. Mildred thought they were an ideal couple, interested in each other, never trying to outdo or compete, and always supportive. We felt this way about them, too.

A favorite avocation of Ann's was gourmet cooking. Alan would call when Ann had time and energy to spend in the kitchen, and say, "Come on over. Ann has just made a special 'something' you must try." Sam and I would then be off to their place for an evening of fun. They were both interesting, outgoing people who entertained wonderfully, and who added greatly to any gathering of which they were a part.

They were both much involved with the Santa Fe Opera, being knowledgeable about opera and supportive of the Opera and its activities. We would meet at the Opera Club and have a wonderful evening of music. Ann always arrived in a beautiful, long evening dress with a hibiscus flower in her hair. Alan grew these flowers in his garden, and hibiscus became her trademark. She looked lovely beside Alan, who was always dressed properly with black bow tie and tux.

The Vedders were very much a part of the social set in Santa Fe, but Alan had the dubious distinction of being a perpetual "late arrival." He said jokingly in his own defense, "You must never arrive on time at a party. You might find your hostess still fixing her hair." He then smiled broadly and chuckled.

Alan and Ann were to come to our home for dinner one evening. It was a sit-down affair, rather formal. I said on the invitation that dinner would be served at 7:00 p.m. All the other guests arrived promptly, but Alan and Ann did not arrive, and then still did not arrive. The rest of us took seats and started dinner, when the phone rang. It was Alan, his voice sheepishly apologetic, saying, "My God ! I believe in being late, but not this late. I am lost, and Ann cannot find your address. Please forgive us." We reminded them of the way, for we were living in Española then—and gave warm congratulations mingled with some laughter when they finally arrived.

Sam and I moved to Santa Fe in 1984, and Alan and Ann called to welcome us. They said that their lives had been brightened spending time with us, and that they were looking forward to more occasions together. Sam and I were touched by their thoughtfulness.

Ann fought a battle with breast cancer for fifteen years. She followed treatment protocols with great exactness, determined to carry on as though nothing were wrong. She remained quite active physically, and much involved with local business and cultural affairs. We would often call and offer to take them to dinner or to spend an evening together during the last year of her life, when real difficulties began to set in. They would accept our offer sometimes. At others, Ann said she much preferred to be at home, and she invited us there.

Out last time together was when we returned from Scottsdale, Arizona in 1988. They called to invite us to dinner at their home, insisting that we come. One other couple, also very close friends, was present with us. Ann was beautifully attired in a lovely chiffon dress, but appeared quite thin. She had prepared most of the dinner herself, and we spent a pleasant, rather quiet evening. We were thankful for that time. Ann died in January of 1989.

Alan had begun having occasional spells where he blacked out before Ann died. These spells continued after her death and took quite a toll on him. We had dinner together on one occasion, and I remember taking his arm as we walked after dinner and sensing how frail he had become. He lingered not even a year after Ann's death, passing away in December of 1989. Mildred feels that he lost his will to live when Ann died.

Eugenie Shonnard became a close friend from Santa Fe in the mid-1950s. She was a painter and a sculptress of exceptional talent who had studied under Rodín in Paris. We had been privileged to see some of her work at a showing at St. John's College in Santa Fe before we came to know her. Eugenie knew Mike Pijoan's father, and when Mike joined Sam in practice, she sought him out for medical care. Mike referred her to Sam not long after as a possible surgical case. Our relationship developed from there.

Eugenie was a jolly, laughing spirit who seemed constantly bubbling over with enthusiasm. She had a pleasant round face framed with snow white hair gathered into a bun on the top of her head. She always wore a smile.

Eugenie was no longer painting, but she was deeply involved with clay sculpture which dealt primarily with altar design and large bas-reliefs for placement behind pulpits and for use in gardens. Sam often dropped by her studio when we were in Santa Fe just to say hello and talk about her latest ventures. Sam, a surgeon and artist, became interested in doing some work of this nature as time went along and was intrigued with the tools she used and fascinated by what she could do with her hands.

Eugenie became excited when she found out Sam was interested in trying his hand at sculpting, and began to make plans for him to come and work with her. She bought and presented Sam with a beautiful set of sculpting tools. She promised that she would give Sam the secret of how she mixed her clay. Eugenie had a sculpting medium she mixed herself, a secret formula she had learned from her husband years before.

Eugenie continued her bi-yearly check-ups with Sam, but I know she was very disappointed they were never able to start a project together. Somehow, the office and hospital always interfered with plans. She died a number of years ago. Her tools lie in an honored place in our den at home. They are a tangible reminder of a wonderful woman, and of a marvelous experience that might have been, had fate not ruled otherwise.

I still have two pieces of Eugenie's sculpture that she gave us. One is a magnificent St. Francis of Assisi holding a turquoise bird, and the other a beautiful Madonna.

After reading *The Wind Leaves No Shadow*,[33] one cannot help but wish to meet the author, Ruth Laughlin. Her novel is filled with excitement and historical facts about an early period of New Mexico and carries one on a non-stop adventure.

Sam attended a County Medical Meeting and dinner one evening in Santa Fe. While there he became acquainted with a very interesting doctor by the name of Alexander, who said he was originally from England. He had come to the United States and, of course, to Santa Fe. There he met and married Ruth Laughlin.

A short time after the Medical meeting, the telephone rang and it was Ruth Laughlin Alexander calling to invite Sam and me for dinner. We accepted, of course, and found the evening with Dr. and Mrs. Alexander delightful.

They were living in a beautiful home located on the outskirts of Santa Fe. Their home was set on a high hill and faced to the north. The living room window was exceptionally large, looking out over a landscape that carried ones eyes almost to the Colorado border. It was a breathtaking view.

While in conversation and enjoying the endless scene before us, Ruth said, "I grew up in Santa Fe, living in a down-town area surrounded by houses and buildings. It was a confined area, where one was not really aware of weather, except to know that it was either raining or the sun was shining. It was not until moving to the present location that I really began to enjoy and appreciate the beauty and excitement of a rain storm and the lightning that accompanied it." Listening to her describe a storm as she watched it from her window, with its bolts of lightning and gathering clouds, and hearing her talk about their movement across the sky, was almost like watching her become involved in writing another chapter for a book. I loved to hear her speak.

My dreams of meeting Ruth, the author, had come true. She was everything I imagined and more, and it was always a pleasure to be in her presence.

Her 1948 First Edition of *The Wind Leaves No Shadow*, which is in our possession, includes her autograph and note, "With gratitude that the Zieglers are now New Mexicans—Ruth Laughlin."

J. I. Staley was a wonderful man. His father, J. I. Staley, Sr., had founded Staley Oil. J. I. later became president of the company and ran it with help of his two brothers. J. I. divided his time between Santa Fe and Wichita Falls, Texas when we knew him. He was a prominent benefactor of the Santa Fe Opera, St. John's College and the School of American Research in Santa Fe.

J. I. gave lovely parties and provided many good times for us. He had a special way of keeping people laughing at his priceless jokes. He entertained beautifully and lavishly. One could be with the Duke and Duchess of Bedford at his parties as easily as a next door neighbor.

He was constantly doing "crazy" things that contributed to the fun, like driving around in his car with a bumper sticker that read EAT MORE GOAT. We exchanged Christmas gifts, and J. I.'s bumper sticker stimulated one of our more memorable gifts to him. We sent him a poem entitled "A Goat's Prayer" that I had cut out of a magazine and saved especially for him. The magazine had printed the poem on an 8"x 11" sized page along with the picture of a goat. Sam and I had the page matted, and then mounted under glass with a frame of rough wood bark. J. I. later told us that our gift had stolen the show that year.

J. I. spent most every summer at a chateau in France. We always had a standing invitation to visit, but Sam could not easily find time to break away from his practice. We finally decided it was time to join J. I. in France, when he sent an invitation to his seventieth birthday celebration at the Ritz in Paris in 1982, and we made plans to attend. It was an exquisite affair. Guests from all over the world came for the occasion.

Tom Milne was J. I.'s companion. He was a tall, slender nice looking man with dark, curly hair and dark eyes. He was always ready with a warm greeting and a friendly laugh. Tom was a long time employee of the Staley Properties, and while in Santa Fe, had a remarkable career. He came to the area in 1953 and over the years served as a Justice of the Peace for Pojoaque

Valley, was on the Pojoaque School Board, and helped to found the Pojoaque Volunteer Fire Department and the Visiting Nurse Service. Tom was a lover of the arts. He was on the International Folk Art Foundation and the Board of the Santa Fe Opera Guild. He had a special interest in collections, especially of costumes and textiles.

Tom suffered from arthritis which progressively crippled his hands and body. He never openly complained about his discomfort, but when the pain became unbearable, he would call Sam, usually in the middle of the night, asking for help. Sam arranged for him to be seen in the emergency room at the Española Hospital, where the nurses gave him medication for the pain.

Sam never said anything to Tom or J. I. about the emergency care he gave, but there would be a knock at our door and Tom would appear, holding a basket full of gifts. We found six very nicely wrapped crystal goblets one time, placed among the other things. A heart-warming gesture!

We knew Tom was often in great discomfort, but he seemed to manage well, and he never complained, even after he was confined to a wheelchair.

Norman Rosen was the owner and manager of a liquor store in Los Alamos when we first met him and his wife, Ivy, in 1954. He was of slight build, with curly black hair and luminous, laughing brown eyes. He dressed immaculately and was always appropriate for the occasion. He had a keen mind and a contagious laugh, and he loved to tell Jewish jokes, poking fun mostly at himself.

Ivy was a slender woman almost as tall as Norman. Her face was finely chiseled, her hair very blond and cut so short that it hugged the sides of her face. She had an eye for style. Norman "moaned" about her extravagances, especially to his male friends, but he really enjoyed indulging her. She was the daughter of a Methodist minister from the Midwest. She left home following college, and being strong-willed, made her way to Denver where she took a job in a jewelry store. It was there that she met Norman, who was then a jewelry salesman. Norman's family was upset when they learned that he had married a Christian girl. They eventually gave their consent, but Ivy never felt that they accepted her into the family.

Sam and my introduction to the Rosens came through Barry and Helen Atwater. We had stopped in Tucson, Arizona to visit them at the time Barry was having a one-man art show there. Barry mentioned that he and Helen were on their way to Alamos, Mexico after the show, and invited us to come along. The Atwaters were to meet their friends, the Rosens, in Mexico and they knew we would enjoy getting to know them. Sam made arrangements with the hospital, and the next thing we knew, we were on our way.

Norman masterminded the journey in Mexico because he spoke more Spanish than any of the rest of us. He had been told about a special place to stay in Alamos with a "fabulous" chef. We finally found the place late in the afternoon. Who should be leaning against the doorway as we entered the lobby but the famous chef about whom Norman had heard. Norman stopped to talk with him, saying, "*Buenos dias*. What's for dinner?"

The chef replied, "I really haven't made up my mind yet. But I will expect to see you there." He walked off with a smile.

We met in the placita of the hotel for cocktails and hor d'oeuvres. Soft Mariachi music played in the background. We had dinner in the dining room. There were twenty-four guests, all seated at one long table set with great elegance. Courses began with Oysters Rockefeller. What a chef! The whole evening was splendid. Wine with every course and music in the background, one example of the many happenings we later experienced with the Rosens.

Norman and Ivy owned a large, rambling old adobe in Nambé for a number of years which they called The Rocking Horse Ranch. Ivy was artistically talented and had a fine ability to draft. She handled all of the architectural design for the remodeling of their home. She was recognized and appreciated for her knowledge of the arts and of local artists and their work, and she was appointed to the New Mexico Arts Commission. The walls of their home were filled with the works of many local artists. Their home was wonderful to see and explore. Ivy herself sculpted and designed goose and ostrich eggs like those of Fabergé.

Norman was born in Denver in 1914 and educated in Colorado. He received his degree in Business Administration from the University of Colorado in 1936. Following his service in the military in World War II, he and Ivy were married. They came to New Mexico in 1951, and Norman soon became a successful businessman. The enchantment of New Mexico with the peace and quiet of its mountain streams also attracted Norman, who loved to fish and was an expert at this sport. He pursued business ventures in Santa Fe and Los Alamos for a number of years, and then moved with Ivy to Acapulco, Mexico where Norman tried his hand at business south of the border.

Norman and Ivy touched our lives in a very special way. We are better people for having known them and we loved our times together.

Among the special friends we met through Norman and Ivy Rosen were the Ruthlings. We came to know Helene Ruthling, or "Ma" as she was called by her friends, at a Christmas party Norman and Ivy gave at their Rocking Horse Ranch in Nambé in 1953. "Ma" was a large woman with a hearty laugh who exuded warmth and a friendly spirit. She was from Stuttgart, Germany and came to Santa Fe in 1928 as governess to the grand-children of Taos personality, Mabel Dodge Luhan.

We always received a warm hug when we entered the delightful gift shop in Santa Fe called "Doodlet's" that Ma ran with her daughter, Theo. It had a never-ending supply of objects of interest. The Ruthlings made many of these items. The store took its name from Ma's daughter, Theo, whose nickname was "Doodlet." Theo was a tall, handsome woman with beautiful heavy black hair which she often wore in a braided ponytail. She was a warm and inviting person, making friendship with her most special.

Ma and Theo gave Sam and me a miniature Christmas tree they had made one year for the holidays. The tree was a real "labor of love." It was set on a music box stand and stood fifteen inches high. It was adorned with many tiny "keepsakes" from our past which we had given them to use for the decorations—earrings, fancy pins, track medals from Sam's high school and college years, foreign coins from our travels abroad, tiny colorful bows, small party favors saved from high school and college and more. We were thrilled to receive this unique gift, and cherish it. It brings back many happy memories when we display it each year in a special place in the house at Christmas time.

One special time we spent with Theo was in March of 1959, when we accompanied her and Norman and Ivy Rosen on a buying trip to Mexico. Decorative tiles for the shop were on her list of purchases. Our trip began in Mexico City. We hired a limousine and a driver who turned out to be a jewel of a man. The driver pulled onto a side street on the outskirts of Mexico City as we left early in the morning, and stopped by the door of a house. He left the car for a short period, only to return with hot cheese quesadillas for each of us. They were just off the stove and delicious. We have yet to eat their equal anywhere in the states.

Our plans were to travel "The Sun Circle." Theo had contacts along the way and knew exactly where the driver should stop so she could look at prospective items. We all got out of the car to explore when we reached a place where she wanted to look. Theo knew exactly what she liked and what would sell. She found the tiles she wanted, and also bought several quite elegant bathroom lavatory bowls, which were much in demand in the Santa Fe area. She had all of these items shipped back to the States for the shop. She had decided this was the best approach to buying in Mexico.

Theo had been ready for a break from the long hours spent at the shop in Santa Fe, and having us with her allowed her to relax and enjoy the buying. We were fortunate to stay in a wonderful hacienda at Morelia, owned and operated by the American, Ray Coté. Our hacienda was the Villa Montaña, considered one of the more comfortable inns in Mexico. It stands on a hill overlooking the town of Morelia. Ray Coté welcomed all his guests with exquisite taste and imagination, and believed in indulging his guests with wonderful gourmet food and very comfortable surroundings. The rooms at the hacienda were filled with beautiful antiques, all of which were for sale. We welcomed the attention and service. Our suite was luxurious. We hoped that the antique furniture would not be sold out from under us! We ended up purchasing some of the antiques.

Theo traveled all over the world to find items of interest for her shop. She spoke Spanish and German, and was able to get around well in Europe and Mexico. She first introduced into Santa Fe, I believe, the tiny white lights used on Christmas trees. These originally came from Europe.

Theo married Peter Raven, a Professor of Art, in 1968 and they moved from Santa Fe to Seattle where Peter taught for ten years at the University of Washington. Theo wrote once settled in Seattle that they had met a couple from San Francisco who reminded them of us. They were in the same "heart-department," as Theo put it. She followed this statement by asking us to make a special effort to pay the Ravens a visit in their new home. Her words were heart-warming to be sure. We were unfortunately, never able to visit. They returned to Santa Fe in 1978 so that Theo could be more of a help to Ma at the shop. She and Peter were together for nine more years, during which we enjoyed many times together talking art and travel and just ordinary Santa Fe gossip. Peter became seriously ill in 1987 and died suddenly, a premature loss for Theo and for all of us who knew him and cherished his friendship.

Theo reminded me recently that one of her fondest memories was when Sam and I knew she was planning her wedding and offered to have a party for her. We asked her to make out the guest list for the occasion. She said, "I would like Georgia O'Keeffe, Ma, my brother, Ford, and, of course, Peter."

We questioned, "Theo, you have so many friends. Surely you want us to invite more people." She answered, "Just my family and Georgia, so we can talk about art. Ford will be so pleased to be able to talk with Georgia."

Well, Ford never did arrive in time for dinner. Someone had borrowed his car and he had no last minute transportation. Theo said afterwards with some pique, "All Georgia wanted to talk about was her herb gardens!" We all laughed.

Theo's brother, Ford Ruthling, was gaining recognition as an artist when we first met. His 1964 "Sunflowers" hangs in our home. Ford's surge into prominence came in 1977 when the Postal Service selected his paintings of Indian pottery for commemorative stamps in honor of Southwest Pueblo Indian culture.

Ford is a handsome man with a sensitive personality. He is never too busy to greet us with a friendly smile and a hug.

Ma is gone now, but Theo and Ford remain special among my friends.

26

WITH A SENSE OF PRIDE

The 1960s were a busy time for me full of community involvements in Santa Fe and Española.

A group of Santa Fe men met in 1961 to discuss the need for an alternative form of secondary education in the community. They quickly moved to form an independent, non-sectarian, co-educational college preparatory school, and by December of that year, had signed articles of incorporation and completed by-laws for the Santa Fe Preparatory School.

Leland Thompson, whom I knew, was a member of the original Board of Trustees. Leland called me soon after the articles had been signed and asked if I would be interested in serving on the Board. The Board knew of my work with the Española Woman's Club and Library, the State Medical Society Auxiliary, and of my participation in church activities, and it felt that I would be able to represent the parents and students in the northern part of the state.

I was pleased to receive the Board's request, and said that I would be honored to serve. I knew the school was founded with the intention of providing students with a thorough secondary education, with equal emphasis upon the importance of the individual as a person, and of service to others in the community. Worthy standards such as these made recruiting a pleasure. Thus began a rewarding and stimulating six years for me between 1961-1966. I audited classes at the school, observed students, met with teachers and the headmaster, and was much involved with student recruitment. I talked personally with parents and students in the pueblos around Española, and in towns as far north as Chama. Many were interested. The one big problem was distance and transportation, for there were no boarding facilities provided. Those who could master these problems did so, and felt their efforts rewarded.

I was in good company on the Board. I knew many of the members and was quickly impressed with their dedication. I found my association with people stimulating and enriching. I also served on the Finance Committee of the Board with Leland Thompson, Carl Goodwin, Oliver Seth and others, all of whom moved ahead quickly toward meeting their goals and dealing with problems that arose. I felt that I profited by this experience, and gained more than I contributed. A woman's point of view was also appreciated, however.

The Board decided in 1964 to have a Parent-Faculty Reception for approximately three hundred and fifty guests. I was appointed chairperson for the event. We had a successful reception, and the enthusiastic support of Board members' wives who assisted me made this occasion quite special.

The new four-lane highway passing through Riverside and out of town toward Alcalde was completed in 1962.[34] The highway construction brought major changes to the character of Española. It was readily evident that its bare macadam and cement were great eyesores, and that the traffic islands between opposing lanes were without aesthetic quality or appeal. I missed the beautiful cottonwood trees that had lined the two-lane road through Riverside before the new highway was built. I suggested to the Amantes de Flores Garden Club that we design some type of landscaping for the islands. They thought the idea was a good one and gave me full support to proceed ahead on my own. I made an appointment with Cipriano Vigil, Mayor of Española, to speak with him about this possibility. I presented my ideas and asked for the Mayor's and the City Council's approval so that I might approach the State Highway Department about landscaping. The Mayor and the City Council gave their approval, and the Mayor asked me to plan and supervise the landscaping.

I was excited about the possibilities, but also a little daunted by what I had undertaken. I immediately contacted Jacques Cartier, a good friend from Pojoaque, and asked for his help. He was intrigued with the idea and gladly offered his assistance. I then approached the Highway Department about a traffic island project. I requested their specifications regarding landscaping and their permission to move ahead. The Highway Department seemed interested, but each time I talked with one person, I was politely referred on to someone else for additional inquiries.

This shuffling from one person to another went on for a year, and then another year. I had all I could take from the Department at the end of two years. I learned the name of the man who was in charge of final decision making regarding our project, and called him to review the treatment I had received over the past months, saying, "I am calling to ask for a definite reply from you. I expect an answer by the end of the week. If I have not received one, I will call every newspaper in the state of New Mexico and tell them about the treatment I have received while working on this beautification project for the city of Española."

I had a reply within a day! The answer was, of course, "Yes, go ahead with your plans."

I immediately called Jacques, excited that we were finally able to proceed. Jacques' fine talents now came into play. After retiring from the performing arts, he had taken himself to Japan to study landscape gardening in Kyoto with the master landscape gardener, Ogawi Jehei. Following his return, he had received the Frank Lloyd Wright Award in Landscape Design for a garden he designed in Santa Fe. He devoted himself to the landscaping project for Española with the same interest and enthusiasm he gave to any of his own projects. It was a delight to work with him. The Highway Department placed a number of restrictions on the landscaping, but Jacques said that we could accomplish a great deal with the use of rocks and native plants and shrubs.

There were sixty traffic islands along the highway with which we had to work. Jacques and I moved ahead with the landscaping with the help of the City Council, the Mayor and city workmen. Jacques was not one to stand back after the design had been made. He loved the actual arranging and planting. He indeed supervised the workmen, but he was also planting and digging right alongside them. The workmen were Joe Suazo, Bennie Montoya and Benjamin Rivera, all of whom were most helpful. Bob Trapp also took a great interest in the beautification project. He gave us outstanding news and photo coverage in the *Rio Grande SUN*. I was with the reporter and the photographer making sure that local people were recognized and photographed along with Jacques and the Mayor. *The Santa Fe New Mexican* provided coverage as well, and wrote:

> That sensitive artist with fresh dirt on his hands has begun the intricate beautification of traffic islands along U.S. Highway 84 here.

And he is donating his time and creative talents.

Jacques Cartier of Pojoaque, known throughout the Southwest for his prowess in landscape design, began work last week after the State Highway Department and the Española City Council approved the work.

Behind the whole thing is Amantes de Flores, the Española Valley garden club, and its committee on the work, Mrs. Samuel Ziegler …

Despite the rules under which he must work, Cartier launched the planning and actual landscaping with his typical enthusiasm. By the week's end the esplanades had lost their unimportance and were beginning to take on a natural beauty like one citizen put it, 'As if they had always been that way.'

. . .

'Mayor Cipriano Vigil and the council,' Mrs. Ziegler said, 'deserve most of the credit for getting this project approved.'[35]

Our beautification project received national recognition from the First Lady, Lady Bird Johnson. The First Lady especially mentioned our use of native plants and shrubs, which pleased her very much.

The Española Chamber of Commerce named me "Woman of the Year" in 1964. This honor came as quite a surprise. I learned of it at the last minute as the announcement was made at the Chamber's yearly banquet. I had been aware that Jacques would probably be recognized for his work, which he well deserved. I had not considered myself for such an honor. It all happened in an amusing way.

Sam and I had planned a trip to California at the time of the Chamber's banquet. I was weary from the long months I had dedicated to the landscaping, and suggested to Sam that we skip the Chamber of Commerce gathering and go on to California. Sam had learned that I was to receive the award, however, and that it was to be a "surprise." To allay any suspicions I might have, and at the same time to make sure I attended the banquet, Sam said that we probably should go to the banquet out of respect to Jacques. I agreed. Art and Joyce Houle then called to invite us for cocktails prior to the banquet, and Sam said, "Oh, good! Let's go to the Houles and then to the banquet. We'll take off for California right after!"

To my surprise and pleasure, Jacques was at the Houles when we arrived. I said to Sam, "He will surely be recognized at the banquet." I still had not considered that I might also be honored.

Jacques did receive a special award for his landscaping work. Art Houle presented the award, saying with a smile that Jacques "doesn't live in the Valley, but he lives in our trade area." I was quite amazed and pleased when they announced my name as the outstanding woman of the year. I received a beautiful plaque which reads:

OUTSTANDING AWARD
1964
WOMAN OF THE YEAR
ISABEL ZIEGLER
ESPAÑOLA VALLEY CHAMBER OF COMMERCE

The plaque hangs in a special place in our home. The *Rio Grande SUN* wrote of this award:

> Mrs. Ziegler, long active in community work, was cited by the Chamber as the Valley's outstanding woman of the year. Stressed was her work in getting the traffic islands landscaped in the traditional south western style, as Chairman of the Amantes de Flores Garden Club committee handling the task.
>
> In addition, she has worked with the Youth Concerts of the Valley, an organization which works to bring fine musicians to the Valley schools for performances at a moderate price so the students can learn to appreciate fine music.[36]

Working with Jacques on the traffic island project had been an enriching experience. I was pleased to do something which I felt brought beauty to our city, and I took much satisfaction in seeing the project completed. A deeper friendship arose with Jacques and his wife, Zena, through the work. Zena's untimely death several years later created a loneliness in Jacques' life, and he called at times saying, "I am lonely, but do not wish to be with many people. When Sam comes home, let's have dinner if you two are free." We made every effort to be with Jacques, especially at these times.

I was asked to speak at Jacques Cartier's memorial service at the

First Presbyterian Church in Santa Fe years later in 1991. I did so with pleasure, remembering especially our working together on the landscaping project for the city of Española. Jacques seemed delighted at the end of the project when one of the hired helpers shook his hand and called him *"primo."* I remembered this at the service, and said of Jacques:

> He took pride in that simple project... Here was a man who had won many national landscape awards, who had spent time with great gardeners of Japan. His only reward (for the Española project) was thanks from me, his friend, and the warm handshake of a native laborer.[37]

27

AN OLD FORD, ALBINO SQUASH AND A BOMB SHELTER

The boys' "teens" were up and down times, troublesome one minute, serious the next, quiet and then exciting, but there was always a little romance tucked in. Sam Jr. and Norman definitely wanted time to ride their horses with their good friends, Royce and Coy Washburn, and Chuck Denton, but girls had begun to attract their attention, too. Thoughts of dating and going to a movie or to dinner began to occupy their thinking. What they needed was transportation, a "cool" car,

The boys bought an old '41 Ford the summer of 1959. It was specifically a '41 Ford four-door sedan with a flathead V-8 engine, according to Sam Jr. It was just black and sort of beat up to me, and it rocked back and forth on its chassis as if something were amiss with its suspension. The boys paid a hundred dollars for it, and kept it out back in the corral where they were teaching themselves to drive the standard shift. They spent their time speeding up and down the length of the corral, slamming on the brakes as they turned and then peeling out doing "brodies" on the return trip. The dust sure flew and they would be laughing with their arms hanging out the windows and slapping the sides of the doors.

They spent many hours washing and polishing their car. The previous owner had removed all of the chrome. A smooth, sleek appearance seemed to be the "in" thing at that time. Sammy also removed the handle on the trunk so the back of the car would be absolutely smooth. I do not remember how they got it open after that. I believe they rigged up some kind of wire pull system on the inside by the back seat. Pretty neat!

The boys felt the interior was not nice enough for them to take out girls, so they had it reupholstered. Black and white tuck and roll. They spent more money on the new upholstery than the car itself had cost. I guess they did use the car a couple of times for dates.

Those are really great days to remember.

Our first attempt at gardening had been trampled upon by a roaming horse, but we soon started other gardens. We placed these in an open area in the corral, next to the Barn. Dorothy Burnam from Ghost Ranch came to work with us in 1950. She knew a lot about gardening and brought manure for fertilizer. I am sure that we had one of the richest garden plots in Rio Arriba.

Ross Medina and Ben Talachi worked with us in the yard in the late 1950s and early 1960s, and they were very helpful with the preparation and tending of the gardens. We grew tomatoes, golden bantam corn, zucchini, acorn squash, beets and green beans. We also had a cutting garden of beautiful flowers with gladioli, baby's breath, iris, and lilies.

There are a number of things about these gardens that are fun to remember besides how good all that fresh, home-grown produce tasted. We began to notice an acorn squash one summer that was not turning its normal green. It remained white as it developed into a full-grown squash. Sam was sure it was an albino, and to confirm his diagnosis, he took it down to Howard Morgan, the weatherman at Channel 7 in Albuquerque, who was quite a horticulturist. He agreed that the squash was truly an albino, and he showed it on Channel 7 news on several occasions. It was his custom to do this when unusual plants were brought to his attention. I still have one of the seeds from this squash.

The zucchini squash we grew were another story altogether. I went out one evening to gather corn for supper and glanced down at a little zucchini, thinking I should begin to gather the squash because they would soon be big enough to eat. I had occasion to go back out to the garden the next morning, and here in place of the little squash I had seen the night before, was a tremendous zucchini a number of times bigger than the night before. The comical thought flashed through my mind that, "My gosh, at this rate, these squash are going to take over the world!" It seemed to me an astounding rate of growth. We picked and cooked these squash before they had any chance to grow any larger. They were so good to eat!

Joe Posey, the gardener for Mary Wheelwright at Los Luceros near Alcalde, gave Sam some beefsteak tomato plants one summer. Joe had been setting tomato plants in his garden at Los Luceros and had a few left over. Sam put these plants out behind the little room off of the kitchen on the northeast side of the house, where they would get plenty of sunshine. They grew beautifully and must have had just the right combination of sun, moisture and soil because they produced really big tomatoes. They grew so well, in fact, that the tomato slices we cut were generally bigger than the slices of sandwich bread on which we placed them. Truly amazing! They also had a rich, tasty flavor.

A family by the name of Fullman lived next door to us for a number of years in the late 1950s. Earl Fullman was a scientist at the Laboratory in Los Alamos, and his wife, Nan, a nurse. Nan made the most wonderful bread. She would call when Sam got home from the hospital, and say, "Come on over and have some hot bread and butter." Her fresh bread was a real treat.

The Fullmans had seven children. All of them were very well-behaved. They would sit together in a group on and around the sofa when they came into our house, and remain almost motionless. They did not seem unhappy, just reserved and pleased to be part of the activity. Julie, who was seven years old when they moved next door, had a lot of playmates with these neighbor children. It was a wonderful time for her. She turned the little tool shed out in the yard into a play house. It actually became a "hospital" for her dolls. Sam gave her old syringes and other medical equipment he brought home from the hospital or office to use in her play. "My dolls were so full of holes from all the shots we gave," Julie exclaimed recently with a chuckle. With the Fullmans next door, she had great fun.

Earl Fullman heard all the news at the Laboratory about the situation with Cuba. He would come home when things began to grow tense, and talk about the possibility of a nuclear bomb being dropped. "We have got to begin thinking about protecting ourselves. We should consider building a bomb shelter. They have given us orders to do so at the Lab."

Sam's reply to these comments was, "Heavens, I don't have time to build a bomb shelter or even supervise the building of one." But he suggested to Earl, "If you will see that it gets built, I'll pay the costs."

Earl hired some men to do the digging. Nan Fullman and I then began planning what sort of foods, water and other necessities we should put into the shelter. We decided to bottle water. We actually "canned" the water, sterilizing it and sealing it under pressure like you would fruits and vegetables. I kept two of the bottles for the next twenty years. Sam took a jar to the hospital laboratory and had the water tested. It was absolutely pure.

We really did a good job. I still have one jar of this water.

I got to thinking about all of the people who would be in the shelter while all this activity was going on. They included the Fullmans and their seven children along with Julie, Sam and me. Then Caroline Dozier, our housekeeper, said, "Be sure and make room for me, too." I realized how many of us there would be as I counted noses, and thought, "You know, there has to be some way that we can crawl out of the shelter and back over to our house if we need to escape. We can't just be stuck in the shelter together."

Julie then started asking perplexing questions. "How are you going to get me from school? There will be cars all over the roads. Somebody will run out of gas and someone will have a wreck." I tried to calm her fears. "Don't worry, Julie. I will take Poncho, our Palomino, and the wire cutters, and I'll go through all the fields down to McCurdy and get you." She seemed to feel better about the situation with this explanation. She was really concerned that we might not be able to get her from school. We were also concerned. As it turned out, the scare dwindled and the hole in the ground remained a great big hole.

Sammy began attending Verde Valley School in Sedona, Arizona in the fall of 1956. He enjoyed his experience there. He had a bit of trouble adjusting, butting heads with one of his teachers, who happened to be the music teacher. We tried to explain to Sammy that he did not have to like all of his teachers, he just needed to be open to what they had to teach him and try to learn something from them. He changed his attitude and came to like and respect his music teacher. Sammy eventually became the leader of the school band.

The school took trips each year to Mexico and to the Navajo and Hopi Indian Reservations, in addition to tours of the Grand Canyon. Sammy loved these trips and came home each summer with tales of the sights he had seen. He always brought something interesting back with him. One year he came home with a huge, fourteen foot long leather bull-whip, which he showed us how to twirl over our heads and to crack. He told the story of a friend, Gene Shippen, racing him out of the gorge of the Grand Canyon after they had hiked down to the bottom, a five to six mile trek. Sammy took a great deal pride in his physical abilities and his endurance. I was pleased to see him developing into a fine young man.

Sammy also took an interest in dramatics and theater at Verde Valley. He discovered that he had a fine talent for acting, and was given the lead in a number of plays. We were able to get down to see him for several of these productions, and were pleased with his performance. Sammy was president of his senior class at Verde Valley, an accomplishment Sam and I also admired. I was glad to see him continuing a Ziegler tradition.

Sammy graduated in June of 1960, and we gave him a jeep for his graduation present. He came home that summer and got a job at the Ghost Ranch Natural Museum, helping to build the beaver exhibit which became one the best beaver displays, live and historic, in the world. I know that he had a good time working at the museum. He palled around with his friends, the Washburns and Dentons, in his spare time, with little Julie tagging along after her big brother.

Norman took longer to adjust to being away from home than Sammy. He attended George School, a prep school near Philadelphia, Pennsylvania, which was a long way from New Mexico. While letters and phone calls helped, they were often not enough. Sammy was out West and only a day's drive away, and we were able to visit him. We did not get back to George School to see Norman until his graduation. Sam especially would have enjoyed seeing him play football or follow one of his track meets. I know he was a pretty good halfback in football, and in track, he broad jumped and ran a good race in the low hurdles and the half mile. He also excelled academically and took part in school activities. He was an officer in his dorm his sophomore years, and a prefect in the younger boy's dorm his senior year.

Norman attended a work camp in Germany sponsored by the Friends Service Committee during the summer of 1960 between his junior and senior years. He went to Bavaria in southern Germany along with six other classmates from George School and a teacher and his wife. It was exciting! They traveled overseas on the Queen Mary from New York City, and came home on the Queen Elizabeth. Sam and Julie and I met him in New York on his return that August. Julie had just finished her fifth grade at McCurdy School, and the three of us were on our way to Florence, Italy to visit John and Mary Marsh.

Norman kept a diary that summer. An early entry read:

Am taking to the sea better than expected; so far have needed only 1 ½ dramamine pills and two aspirin. We ran into a storm and since then, it has been rough and windy. I can feel the boat listing from side to side. The wind sweeps across the deck with such force the I can hardly walk outside, and the mist covers my glasses so that I have trouble seeing. The ocean, rolling mightily against the ship, is one of the most beautiful sights I have seen, and one of the most terrifying and mystifying. It seems like an enormous body of liquid glass, so smooth, and dark like midnight blue. Waves pound against the boat, and are thrown back with much churning and white water. Great swells like rolling giants emerge and then disappear . . .

We have a letter Norman wrote during his senior year at George School, one of the few we saved. He was in the process of deciding about colleges for the next year. He had been to Haverford College near Philadelphia for an interview. He wrote about this interview and about school:

Guess what? I'm in my first penalty study hall tonight since coming to [George School]. The reason stems from the fact that I didn't sign out when I left to go off campus. So, they gave me Friday evening study hall. It is not too bad; a lot of my friends are here, too. Of course, I had a legitimate absence, but I just forgot to let the school know I was leaving. I was visiting Haverford College . . .

As for my visit to Haverford: It is a good college. It's standards are high, the facilities good, and it has a great faculty. The work's pretty hard. For example, for Freshman English students have to read a book a week and write a paper on this book. There are two classes a week plus a tutorial. In the tutorial, several students meet with the teacher and read their papers. They have to be prepared to defend their papers while others tear it up. . . I am not sure about Haverford. Good college, but I think I might like to be out West, maybe go to Stanford. It would be nice to be closer home.

I tried to read a play in study hall tonight, a play by Chekov called *The Three Sisters*. I've read other of his plays including *The Sea Gull, Uncle Vanya, The Cherry Orchard*, and now I must finish this one. They are all strange plays, filled with frustrated people trying to grasp something, accomplish something, find some one thing to complete their lives, be it love, success, whatever. Seems very much like us. I think you would enjoy Chekov's plays. Try *The Sea Gull*.

I have to go to sleep now. Been studying too hard ever since I got back from Christmas vacation. I'm tired ....[38]

I cannot say that we went right out and obtained a copy of Chekov's play at the library, but Norman had placed a thought in our minds. We did not envy him his decision about which college to attend. We had been through the same process with Sammy. Sam had encouraged Norman to apply to Stanford. I rather hoped he would go there if he were accepted, and indeed he was!

Julie enjoyed her trip to Europe with us during the summer of 1960 when we went to visit John and Mary Marsh. She was at a good age to travel and open to what she was seeing. Boys had not yet begun to cloud her field of vision. We discovered something about Julie we had not been aware of. We were in the Sistine Chapel and I was commenting on the beauty of the murals, when Julie spoke up, saying, "Mother, I don't think I see it like you do." I thought she was referring to my interpretation of the painting, but when Sam took off his glasses and handed them to her, she put them on and exclaimed, "Now I know what you are talking about."

Dr. Val checked Julie's eyes when we returned home. She had 20/20 vision. I keep wondering how she ever got through her first years of grade school, and why we had not discovered her condition before. She had developed a lot of coping skills, listening closely to her teachers and "remembering."

· Julie tells about the times Sammy took her out in his jeep with the Washburn boys (when we were away, of course), and drove into the sand hills rabbit hunting at night with 22s, with just the headlights of the jeep to guide them up and down the gullies and in and around the juniper bushes. Sounded like quite a wild time to me.

Julie did well in grade school at Española and got along well with all of her friends. There is only one incident that I remember. She was playing near a door with a plate glass window one day when a classmate accidentally shoved her into the door and her arm went through the glass, cutting it badly from her wrist all the way up to near her shoulder. Sam had to put in 289 stitches to sew up the laceration. Julie still has a long scar down her arm. Such memories of childhood!

28

Pleasant Surprises

When doctors arrive at the hospital, they are often confronted with people and events that disrupt their routines in unexpected and surprising ways. Sam remembered going to the hospital one morning at 6:30 a.m. to make rounds on the wards before starting surgery. Just as he parked and was getting out of his car, he heard someone coming into the parking lot at what sounded like a fast clip. He turned to see a car race past and skid to a wild stop, tires screeching, before a parking place. A character wearing tight faded blue jeans and a long-sleeved shirt with the sleeves rolled up high on the arms jumped out and sauntered nonchalantly toward the backdoor of the hospital. To Sam, the person seemed more concerned about the entry he made than about the possible safety of others.

Sam said he thought at first that this person was a young man and went to talk to him, only to discover that "he" was a tall, nice looking young woman with straight black hair swept back along the sides of her head. Sam let her know in no uncertain terms how he felt about her entry. All she replied was, "Oh, I am sorry. I will be more careful next time." She then sauntered on into the hospital, her arms swinging defiantly at her side.

Sam saw her on one of the wards several months later, and learned she was taking a Licensed Practical Nurse (LPN) training course at St. Vincent Hospital in Santa Fe while working at the Española Hospital. She graduated from her course with honors in 1960.

It was not long after her graduation that the young woman was assigned to surgery. Ruth Specht, the Nursing Supervisor, asked if it would be alright if she scrubbed-in as an assistant instrument nurse. Ruth said her name was Ramona Vigil and that she seemed to have a burning desire to be a scrub nurse.

Rose Reese was working in surgery at the time. Rose loved surgery and was a fine instrument nurse. Under her supervision and training, Ramona progressed rapidly and was one of the best, most dependable scrub nurses before long. She continued to work in surgery until near the time Sam retired from private practice in October of 1976.

Sam said that Ramona was a good example of what someone can do when they set a goal for themselves. Ramona told Sam that she had always wanted to be a nurse, and that meeting him in the parking lot had made her more determined in her efforts.

Ramona eventually married a young man by the name of Pablo Chavez who was a free-lance contractor in the Valley. She developed into a fine individual who is very giving and thoughtful of others. Sam was very pleased when he learned that she had become one of the driving forces behind a group in Española called Amigos del Valle. The group sees to the needs of disabled and elderly people. It continues to be very active, and is now incorporated with its own Board of Directors and fleet of vehicles to carry out its work. The service is supported through charitable contributions. The Valley View Church contributes to this effort.

I know Sam was always very proud of what Ramona made of herself. She served as an inspiration to him in the quiet, determined way she went about serving her community.

Stan Egli became administrator of the Española Hospital in July of 1965. He was the first trained hospital administrator in Española, and was a very capable man who became a close friend of Sam's.

He was a man of few words, but when he spoke, he made good, sound sense and was always to the point. He was of slight build, with graying hair combed neatly about his head, and he kept a sober face. Always dressed in a business suit and tie, he was never overly exuberant. His primary concerns were the care of the patients and the attitude of the hospital staff. His offices were located in the administrative wing some distance from the daily hospital activity, but he often walked the halls and wards when he had finished with his duties, just to be in touch with what was happening. He had a quiet, capable presence that was most appreciated.

Sam had been aware of problems with admission procedures at the hospital prior to Stan's arrival. Patients of his complained to him about the poor reception they received, and he had difficulties when he called to inform the hospital about an admission. We had talked about the situation, and Sam asked me if I would consider helping. After Stan came on board, Sam spoke with him and asked if he would consent to my being involved. Stan was most appreciative of the offer.

I started by calling a friend who had been working in the admitting area, and asked her to bring me copies of the forms being used to admit patients. The forms I saw seemed inadequate, but I quickly realized I needed more guidance in order to proceed. I spoke with Stan and he made arrangements for me to spend time in the Admitting Department of Presbyterian Hospital in Albuquerque. I returned to Española with a good sense of what changes needed to be made in forms and procedures to bring the department up to standard.

I realized that the small room being used to admit patients was inadequate and inappropriate. I explained to Mr. Egli that the department needed to be redesigned with open booths allowing accommodation of several people at a time. The redesign was quickly accomplished.

Hospital employees who handled the admission of patients worked out of the Business Office. The primary duties involved handling patient insurance. They filled in at the information desk as well. They had minimal training for admissions work. I started teaching them basic medical terminology, and for this purpose, asked Sam to make a list of the most commonly used terms. I gave the staff several new terms each day and had them write each of the terms ten times along with their definitions, and turn their work in to me. The staff learned quickly, and to my dismay, I soon found that they were being hired by doctors and enticed into other areas. All at once they had skills that were in demand. They were knowledgeable in medical terminology. I talked with Stan and said to him that we were losing ground, that we needed to hire someone who would be in charge of this area full-time. Stan agreed, and after interviews with several interested people, we finally hired Mary Miller Smith, a very capable and dedicated individual. Laura Lucero was one outstanding admitting clerk. Her homework was always the best, accurate, neat and on time. She was eager to learn and to help. She worked closely with Mary Miller and remained with the hospital for many years.

I began my work in the Admitting Department in 1966, the year after Stan took over as administrator. I was at the hospital every morning, Monday through Friday, checking on the staff, looking over homework and making certain that the admission of patients proceeded according to protocol. I often filled in as a clerk when the department was busy. After Mary Miller was hired in 1969, I felt that my responsibilities were really no longer needed, but I kept checking on the department and its work, and was involved over a period of some five years in all. I finally said to Mr. Egli that I thought the situation was under control, and he gave me his sincere thanks for my time and efforts. The staff in the department held a luncheon in my honor and presented me with a lovely statue of St. Francis of Assisi.

Deer hunting in the mountains of northern New Mexico can be an exciting experience. It can also be dangerous. I learned about one particular incident late one afternoon in the fall of 1972. There was a knock on the door at our home. When I answered, I found a nice looking young man in his early thirties standing there. He held a heavy, wrapped package in his hands. He looked expectantly at me and said with a smile, "Mrs. Ziegler, I know you don't know who I am. One year ago, Dr. Ziegler saved my life. I was shot when I went hunting. I just came back from hunting this year, and I have some venison steaks for you and the Doctor."

I was surprised and pleased by what this man said. I gladly accepted the venison steaks and thanked him for his thoughtful gift. I said I would tell Dr. Ziegler about his visit when he got home from the hospital. Sam very seldom, if ever, discussed his patients with me, so I knew nothing about this man or what had happened.

Sam later explained to me what had happened. The phone had rung one evening at the house just as we sat down to the table for dinner. Sam remembered that he had just come home from a long day when he had had a heavy surgery schedule. An emergency room nurse was calling to say that a young man in serious condition with a bullet wound to the chest had just been brought in. Sam had taken a deep breath, gulped down a few bites of dinner and hurried back to the hospital.

He realized as soon as he did his examination that the man was in very serious condition. He had the nurses start fluids as quickly as they could to increase blood volume and prevent the man from going into shock. He then tried to piece together a history from the friends who had brought him to the hospital. The State Police were present, but all they knew was that a "shooting victim" had been brought to the hospital. The friends said that some young thugs who were apparently out to make trouble, had shot the man while he was hunting near Tierra Amarilla. There had been no feud involved nor had the man done anything to precipitate their action.

The man's friends fortunately had not wasted any time in bringing him the fifty miles into the hospital. It was obvious that the man was in critical condition and would not survive a long trip to Albuquerque, where hospitals were more accustomed to caring for injuries of this type. Sam said he had a bullet wound to the left chest with possible cardiac trauma, and needed emergency surgery at the Española hospital. Sam had him prepared, and did the surgery that saved the young man's life.

What a delight for me to meet the young man and to hear what he said. We did enjoy his venison steaks.

29

FAMILY HAPPENINGS, "FLOWER GIRLS" AND NOTABLE ARTISTS

M_y father, Frank Howe, came to visit us in 1955 following a trip to see relatives in the Midwest. He seemed to have a lot on his mind. "I am very lonely without your mother," he said. He then asked what we thought about his getting married again?

"No one can ever take Mother's place, Dad," I said. "But we realize life is difficult for you all alone, and we want you to be happy."

The woman he wanted to marry was a distant cousin named Mary Kuckucks, whom he had known as a young man in Forest, Ohio. Mary had never married and her family felt Dad would fill a void in her life as she would in his. Dad and Mary were married soon after and were together for five years. Mary died of a stroke in 1960.

Sam and I talked with Dad about his coming to New Mexico to live with us after Mary passed away. Dad gave the matter a great deal of thought and made several trips out by train before he decided it was the right thing for him to do. Dad was having problems with his business at the time. He had hired on a young man and his wife to help him, who were not entirely honest with him. The young man's wife worked with the books, which enabled them to take money on the sly, leaving Dad in some debt. It was too late to recover anything by the time we knew what was going on. I went to California in 1961 with our attorney, Milton Scarborough, and his wife, Hollis, to meet with Dad's attorney and the young man. Milt and Dad's lawyer finally decided not to bring any charges. The building Dad had purchased for his business was then sold for enough to pay off his mortgage. Dad sold his house in Fresno shortly thereafter, and moved to New Mexico.

Dad was eighty-two years old when he came to live with us in 1963. He was a big man over six feet tall and weighing over two hundred pounds. He looked well and seemed in good physical condition except for his advancing arthritis which caused him difficulty walking. He was taking at least eight to ten Anacin each day to control his pain.

He settled in with us and was anxious to be of help in any way he could. He needed to find a way to occupy his time and quickly devoted himself to the yard. He found it easiest to sit on the ground with his legs outstretched and scoot along on a piece of old carpeting as he worked. The carpeting helped to protect him as he moved along digging and cleaning and pulling up weeds. Later, when he became more wheelchair bound, he managed to roll his wheelchair out into the yard to rake leaves or pull weeds. He also went out in front of the wall along the road to work. People would stop their cars to talk with him and marvel at his accomplishments.

I had Dad sorting music for me and mending sheets that needed repair within a short time after his arrival. He soon joined the choir at church and began to sing with us. He mended much of our choir music. One day a church member gave him a hand-carved cane for walking. Dad said the cane was a tremendous help. He carried it with him and used it from that time on. Dad was a welcome addition to our church and was often asked to share his thoughts during religious discussions. People quickly came to respect his opinions.

Dad joined us whenever possible on trips to Santa Fe or Albuquerque. He marveled about the beauty of this area, and I was heartened that he remained alert and interested in the world about him. He became well-known at the bank and grocery store which we often visited.

There were occasions when Sam and I would be away traveling. We felt it best to have someone look after Dad during these times, to be sure he was alright and to help him prepare his meals. Inez Miller agreed to stay with Dad when we were away. She was a warm and sincere person whose help we greatly appreciated. She was also a good cook and was able to prepare everything Dad liked. They seemed to enjoy their times together. Inez's presence at the house and her care for Dad made our travels away much more enjoyable.

Dad did a lot of remodeling for us, especially on the Barn. We had talked about adding an additional room to the Barn for some time, and I had gotten a cost estimate from a contractor. His quote came in at ten thousand dollars. I did not feel we could spend that amount of money. Dad kept telling me that he could do the work. We finally said, "OK," and by golly, he did! There was only some remaining work that needed to be done by a finish carpenter who put in the windows and door frames so they fit snugly.

Once when Sam came home on an afternoon off, Dad was working on this addition putting on the roof. He was sitting up there pounding away. Sam went up on the roof to help him. He got a hammer and started putting in nails. But he developed a tennis elbow in about half an hour that hurt so much he could hardly lift the hammer and had to quit.

Sam's attempt to helping Dad became a family joke. Dad put the matter in perspective, however. He said, "I certainly could not be of help to you at your surgery."

My father received a well-deserved recognition from the community in 1972 when he was just one month shy of his 91st birthday. I wrote my sister, Paula, at the time, saying:

> Dad is doing pretty well. Actually, he is very well except for his arthritis and that is slowing him down a great deal when he walks. I think next week we'll start some whirlpool baths to see if they will help.[39]

Dad was recognized by the Española Chamber of Commerce with a Senior Citizen Award for his contribution to helping keep our town clean. People had seen him out in front of our place with his little cart, faithfully cleaning up the never ending collections of trash that was dropped along the road. There were times when his back bothered him enough that he chose to sit in a wheelchair while he raked up the debris.

Dad had written for as long as I can remember. I was able to read some of his poems while he lived with us. Many of them dated from our years in Westerville, Ohio. He had begun writing what he called his *Meditations of a Layman* a number of years before he came to live with us. Those who were privileged to read these *Mediations* felt that others would enjoy them and benefit from them. Dad started compiling handwritten notebooks of the *Meditations* with this interest shown in his work, and sent them to people all over the United States. I suggested that he type his compositions when he could not sleep at night, and he began using his trusty old manual

Underwood and his time-tested hunt and peck method. We considered having copies made of sheets he had typed, but he felt he should do all of the work himself, and of course, this project kept him very busy.

I include one of Dad's *Meditations* here. It is one of my favorites:

> Every morning lean thy arms awhile
> Upon the window sill of Heaven and
> Gaze upon thy Lord.
> Then with this vision in thy mind,
> Turn strong again to meet thy day.

The Tschicoma Chapter of the Los Alamos Dale Carnegie Alumni Association also awarded Dad a Certificate of Honor. This honor came for his contribution to human relations in this community through the gifts of his *Meditations of a Layman*. It was wonderful for him to receive such recognition at his age of 91.

Julie had started going to McCurdy school in 1959 when she was in the 5th Grade. She liked the school right away and felt comfortable with the students and the teachers there. She tried out and was chosen as one of the school's cheerleaders when she was in the 7th Grade. She continued her cheerleading for the next two years, and had a lot of fun cheering for the school teams and being involved in student activities.

Julie took part in the rodeo parades between 1962-1964 and had a lot of fun with these, too. She washed and groomed and brushed Poncho until his palomino coat shown in preparation for the parades. She was smartly dressed in her riding outfits, and she and Poncho were often near the front of the parade.

Julie met Olga Velasco when she started the eighth grade at McCurdy in the fall of 1962. They became close friends. Sam and I did not get to know Olga until the following spring. Julie came home as Easter vacation started, saying, "Mother, there is the nicest girl at school. I would like to invite her to stay with us for Easter vacation. She has to stay at the dormitory all alone if we don't. Can't she come and stay with us?" Sam and I discussed the matter, and then called Superintendent McCracken. It was not long before Olga joined us at home.

Olga's stay with us went very well. She and Julie had fun together, and Sam and I enjoyed having her. She was a vibrant young woman with flashing dark eyes and an emotional temperament. She did not want to leave when it was time for her to return to school, nor did we want her to go. Sam and I decided it would be good for Julie to have a "sister" around. Olga moved in with us after lengthy discussions with the school, Olga's aunt in Santa Fe, and our attorney. She lived with us for the next two and a half years.

Olga is Cuban. She came to the United States with her father, Carlos Eduardo Velasco, in 1961. Her mother, Maria Josefa Sotelo, was not allowed to leave at the time, but was able to come some years later. Olga's father was a political refugee who had been involved in a conspiracy to subvert the Castro government. He sought asylum in the Uruguayan Embassy in Havana in 1961, when three other Cubans with whom he had been involved were taken prisoner by the authorities and executed. He remained in hiding for a number of months. Olga wrote of this time:

[My father] had been missing for some time, and while [he was] at the Embassy, I received news of him. He was still alive, and he asked me to contact my grandfather to arrange for my departure with him. This involved the Ambassador for I could only enter the Embassy in his car. I had permission to leave for I was still a minor. We flew to the Yucatan Peninsula for one night on Cubana de Aviacion, and from there to Miami, where my father stayed to work. He was a chemist. I went on to Santa Fe, New Mexico to live with my aunt and her husband. I went to school in Santa Fe, then transferred to McCurdy [in 1963].[40]

Olga was well liked at McCurdy. She made many friends, but she became closest to Julie. Thinking about that time, Olga said:

While at McCurdy School, I made many friends. But there was a girl I particularly liked who also took a strong liking to me. Her name is Julie Ziegler. Our friendship grew into a family situation as we became best of friends. She changed my life, for even though I had taken English in school in Cuba, she always corrected all the mistakes I made when I spoke. Her friends became my friends and her family my family. We grew up believing we were sisters. We played together, studied together, got into trouble together, dated together and traveled together. Real sisters never had the home we had.[41]

I worried about the girls' growing up and starting to date. Their choice of boys happened to be the twin brothers, Larry and Terry Norris, from down the road on Fairview Lane, which helped to put my mind at ease. They could not have chosen nicer boys. Larry and Terry were both well-mannered and trustworthy. They were so identical that when they came to the house, we ended up just saying, "Come on in, Lar-Ter." They would laugh and come on in.

The girls did a lot of studying after school at the kitchen table while I was preparing dinner. Talking and laughing were all part of "study time" with the radio on, of course. If a certain song would come on the radio, the girls would be on their feet dancing around the kitchen. I found myself getting into the rhythm, stirring the gravy in time with the music as I listened and watched the dancing. We were all laughing hilariously before we knew it. Such fun times to remember! What a crew we had! "Never a dull moment," I used to say.

Olga learned to ride horses while she lived with us. She recalled:

First thing in the morning, Julie and I would get up, jump into our cut-offs and run barefoot out to the corral, where we caught Poncho and climbed aboard him bareback. I had a tough time. He was so tall for me. I always had to climb up on the fence to mount. Julie had an easier time. She's taller. We would [often] ride into the center of town to the old Tastee Freeze to get an ice cream cone. I remember that Julie liked to chew on those long red licorice sticks while we rode Poncho. I was never able to acquire a taste for the stuff, but to this day my heart warms at the smell of it. It brings back so many memories of my growing up and Julie. We always rode double. Poor old Poncho. He was very patient with us, but he loved us, too.[42]

Olga and Julie had a fun-filled time while they were together at our house. Julie then transferred to Valley School for Girls in Tucson, Arizona in the fall of 1965, where another friend of hers, Nina Houle, was attending. The transfer entailed much discussion with the Houles about

Valley School, and with Olga, who was to remain at McCurdy. Olga went to live with Dolph and Gwen Pringle when Julie left for Valley School. Sam and I were sorry to see her go, but we felt while Julie was in Arizona, it was best for Olga to return to McCurdy. We knew she would have a good home with the Pringles. We also knew we would not lose touch with Olga. Olga wrote:

> God has been good to me. The Zieglers turned out to be a lovely family which I felt I could count on for all the love and advice I needed. They taught me right and wrong, and to be the very best I could ever be. I am very proud to be a part of this lovely family, and I'm very thankful that God introduced me to them.[43]

Julie became eligible to drive in November of 1965 at the age of fourteen, and could hardly wait to get behind the wheel of a car when she was home for the summer. I made her practice with my car in the corral before letting her out on the roads. I had her backing up the car and making turns and pretending to park, and the horses seemed to stay out of her way. Olga was learning to drive at the same time, and I was trying to teach her how to handle the car as well. They got a lot of practice on the Llano Road, which was more deserted then than it is today. Olga was a bit more high strung than Julie. She seemed impetuous and I found myself holding back turning her loose on the highway. I should not have been so timorous. Years later, she handled New York City traffic better than the cab drivers. She had a perfect temperament for chaotic big city driving as she chauffeured Sam and me about the city with great skill. I then realized that the Llano road in Española had really offered her no challenges at all!

Julie began pushing for a classy dream car of her own as soon as she learned to drive. We said instead, "How would you like to have our Chevy pickup truck to make the rounds?" It was an old pickup Norman bought some years before at Houle Chevrolet in Española. We purchased it from him to use around the place when he went off to college, and it seemed perfect for the girls. I had driven it quite a bit, and I liked it, but the girls were horrified. Their attitude quickly changed when they realized it was either drive the old truck or walk.

Nina Houle came by the house one day with her mother, Joyce, saying she had heard about the truck and wanted to see it. Joyce said to the girls in her quiet but perceptive way, after she had looked the truck over, "Why don't you paint flowers on it?" It was 1965, the perfect "flower" time. The girls jumped right into the project, and when the truck was finished, everyone loved it. They had more fun in that beat up old truck than they could have had in a shiny new car. The truck turned out to be the most popular conveyance in town. Everyone wanted to get to know who the "flower girls" were, and they all found a convenient gathering place at the local drive-in.

I met the artist Dean Holt one evening during a party at Norman and Ivy Rosen's Rocking Horse Ranch in Nambé in 1963. Ivy introduced Dean to me and said in a quick aside, "He may be aloof. Don't be disturbed." I actually found myself quickly involved in an interesting conversation with Dean, and as I remember, it was not about art.

I knew what to give Sam for his next birthday after meeting and talking with Dean. I wanted to have Dean Holt paint his portrait. I was familiar with Dean's work, and I admired the lovely portrait he had done of Rosalie, owner of the Pink Adobe in Santa Fe, which hangs in the large dining room at the restaurant. I called Dean to see if he would be willing to do the portrait. He said, "Yes. I believe I would enjoy painting Sam's portrait." I then told Sam. He was surprised and pleased.

We made arrangements for Dean to come to our home to discuss the size of the painting and other details. His eyes lit up when I told him I wanted Sam to be painted wearing his maroon robe from the International College of Surgeons with its hood of red and green, and he asked, "Where are you planning to hang the portrait?" I showed him the large wall in the living room where we wanted to place it. His voice rose in pleased exclamation when he saw the wall, and he moved his hands as if to encompass a large painting meant to fill the space. We made arrangements for sittings, and Sam found the experience stimulating.

Dean Holt painted Sam's portrait as he stands from two different views placed side-by-side on the canvas to present Sam himself and to display his magnificent robe. The view on the left is a facing view of Sam with his hands folded before him. The view on the right is of his back with his head turned slightly to the left, the focus being on the maroon surgeon's robe with its beautiful flowing hood. Dean used soft ochers and yellows for the background color which complements the red, green and maroon of the robe, and the skin tones of the portrait. It is a striking work 58" x 68", and hangs over the fireplace in the living room of the home on Fairview Lane, where Julie and her husband, Ken Langille, now live.

I became involved with a group in our community during the early 1960s who were responsible for organizing a series of Youth Concerts in the Valley. These concerts sponsored a number of fine young performers who were able to come and play for local people, and gain recognition for their talents. One of the performers was a Cuban-born classical guitarist named Hector Garcia. Hector gave an exceptional performance for a large group of people who gathered at our home one evening. He took a rather hasty leave after his performance, however, saying only "Gracias" with a nod of his head, and departed. I was curious about his quick departure, but was unable to find out why.

I happened to accompany Sam twenty years later to an art class being taught at Ghost Ranch near Abiquiu. We stayed overnight and for breakfast in the morning, went to the dining room at the lodge headquarters to eat. Sam and I were placed at different tables because seating space was limited. I sat with four young men and an older man in his forties. As the older man talked, I became aware of his accent and realized he was the students' guitar instructor. I knew music classes were in progress at the ranch, but I did not know what kind. I kept looking at this man and finally asked, "Are you Hector Garcia?"

He replied, "Yes."

I introduced myself to him, saying, "Years ago you gave a concert at our home in Española." He immediately stood up and took my hand and kissed it. He made apologies for not thanking Sam and me for the privilege of playing in our home, and for never having written to us. He said, "Mrs. Ziegler, I knew so little English then, I was not even able to thank you properly as I was leaving. I was so embarrassed. I rushed away. If you will forgive me, I would like you to come to my concert while you and Dr. Ziegler are here."

I expected a performance with his students, but the following evening, guests from all over the ranch gathered at the auditorium to hear Hector Garcia give a solo performance. He told the story of being at our home as he started his program, then dedicated his performance to Sam and me. He played for more than an hour and a half, beautiful, breathtaking classical guitar music. He came up to us following the program, and said, "If at any time I can perform for you, please call on me."

Belle and Joe Becker introduced Sam and me to Joseph and Theresa Lonewolf at a showing of Joseph's pottery in the early 1970s. I liked Joseph's miniature pottery and was intrigued with the delicate, finely-carved animal and bird figures in the Mimbres tradition that he worked onto the surface of these small pots. I was more intrigued with Joseph himself, however.

He is a tall man with fine features and straight black hair that he then wore shoulder length, with long bangs that reached near his eyebrows. His brown eyes seemed to carry an intense and somewhat distant expression, making me feel his thoughts were somehow far away and involved with his next intricate pottery design. I was also taken with Joseph's wife, Theresa. She seemed a thoughtful and friendly woman. She is of medium height, with brown eyes and reddish-brown hair she wore short. She appeared capable and energetic, a good match for Joseph.

We came to know Joseph and Theresa better over the following years, and we attended several of the Santa Clara Feast Days at their invitation. We were always made to feel most welcome. The Feast Day is a wonderful opportunity to eat delicious Santa Clara food and see the Indian dances.

The Lonewolfs were also guests at our home. On one occasion, I had arranged a dinner party with several friends from Santa Fe who were most eager to meet Joseph when they learned he was also to be there. I called Joseph beforehand to alert him, and said, "Joseph, please come to dinner dressed with your wonderful Indian jewelry. Friends from Santa Fe are looking forward to meeting you." Joseph replied with some hesitation and then a laugh, "Oh, Isabel, you know, the jewelry is so heavy to wear. But if you wish, I will do it for you."

Joseph made a very handsome sight when he arrived for dinner that evening. He wore a shirt of soft beige-colored material and black slacks. Over the front of his shirt hung a silver and turquoise squash blossom necklace with large turquoise stones and bear claws extending out from each stone. Complementing the necklace were a concho belt with large silver buckles and turquoise stones, and a sand-cast bracelet also of silver and turquoise. Joseph made an impressive figure to be sure. As the evening progressed with good conversation and fun, we did give him permission to remove some of the jewelry so that he would be more comfortable. I know our other guests were all taken with Joseph's jewelry, but they seemed more pleased with his friendly and pleasant manner, and Joseph appeared to feel very much at ease.

Joseph's sister, Grace Medicine Flower, and her husband, Ron Hoffman, live near the plaza at Santa Clara Pueblo. Grace followed in the family tradition and has become well-known for her Butterfly design on her pottery. It has always been fun to be with her and Ron on Feast Days. They would take Sam and me to an area close by their home where we would have a wonderful view of the dances and could see the Indians as they came out of the kiva and moved to the plaza to perform. Evening dances were an especially interesting time to be with them and feel the closeness of the pueblo, see the lights of the fires and feel the color and drama of the dancing.

We also came to know Joseph's daughter, Rosemary Apple Blossom. She is a potter and has served as Artist in Residence at the Heard Museum in Phoenix. Once when Sam and I were spending the winter in Scottsdale, Rosemary was scheduled for a pottery showing there. Her mother, Theresa, was with her at the time. Sam and I invited them both for dinner the evening of the showing. We were having such an enjoyable time at dinner that we hardly realized the hour. I suddenly looked at my watch and said to Rosemary, "Rosemary, I don't mean to rush you, but I fear you may be late for your show." She turned toward me with a smile and replied, "Don't worry, Isabel. No need to hurry. I'm working on Indian time tonight." She set her own pace and we willingly followed.

Sammy said that when he first went to Otterbein, no one would talk to him because they thought he was Mexican and did not speak English. He has dark hair and was deeply tan from being outside during the summer months, and he appeared on campus dressed in his Apache moccasins, a leather jacket and jeans, typical of what he had worn at Verde Valley School. He did not fit the Midwestern collegiate mold, and had an amusing awakening into this new world. It did not take long for him to be accepted and well-liked.

Sammy continued his work with theater at Otterbein. We were pleased when he sent notices from local papers or copies of theater programs listing billings. He held a lead in the December 1961 production of Moliere's *Tartuffe*. He wrote to us about the play and his role, which he was enjoying immensely:

I'm not idle. I'm now in an Otterbein Play which will be out on December 7-10. I play the part of Valere who is the lover. It is not a small nor big part, but a very good one. The play is *Tartuffe* by Moliere. You ought to read it. It is quite good. When you read it, read it with a taste of sarcasm and try to picture the gestures and poses of the 17th century French court. Everything is over-acted and quite funny.

The play itself takes a cut at hypocritical religious people such as Tartuffe, the lead. Tartuffe is actually a criminal who sees how religion and piety hold such a hand that it is almost a farce and he makes the best of it. The play does not mean that religion is no good, only that its real significance is overlooked and exploited for social ends.[44]

Sammy went on an educational tour to Europe with students from Otterbein College during the summer of 1963. They visited a number of countries including Italy, France, Germany, Switzerland, Austria, Yugoslavia and Greece. Sammy had some interesting adventures, particularly on his trip to Greece. His adventure there should be told in person!

Norman had begun to study German at George School, and he continued at Stanford. He attended Stanford's overseas campus in Beutelsbach, Germany following his freshman year, spending six months there with study tours to Berlin and Prague, Czechoslovakia. It was a difficult time politically in Europe. The Berlin Wall had been erected the year before, and the Russian Communists exerted an oppressive presence in the Eastern Zone. Norman saw first hand some of the effects of this presence during his visits to Berlin and Prague with the ever-present armed guards, check points and barbed wire. He sent a postcard from Prague addressed "Outside The Iron Curtain," and wrote that, "Everyone who talks says 'we know what the West is like; we are hungry.' I will tell you more later. P.S. This may never reach you, anyway." [45] I think he really felt the authorities might confiscate his postcard because of what he had written, or censure it in some way. It was hard for us to imagine the conditions under which people were living in these countries.

Norman went to Berlin to live with a German family named Beitz after he finished his studies in Beutelsbach. Rita, the daughter of the family, had been in Work Camp with him during the summer of 1960. He told us that during work camp, she had to return to Berlin for a short time when the border was closed and the Wall erected to be with her family, because there was great concern about their safety. Her father was a police officer in Berlin and much involved in what was happening. Norman lived with the family for three months while studying German at the Goethe Institut. His stay was not without difficulties due to the political tensions in the city and the problems of moving back and forth across the border between West and East Berlin. His German family had relatives in East Berlin whom they could not visit. Norman spent a good deal of his time taking care packages to these relatives and carrying messages back and forth until he was no longer able to cross the border. We do not know all of what happened, but a friend of his from Stanford, also in Berlin at the time, was stopped on the border and questioned for several hours about her activities. She apparently gave out Norman's name as someone with whom she was "associated." The border guards were very suspicious about smuggling and other "illegal" activities. It seemed unsafe to cross the border after that.

Norman finally came home in March of 1963, and spent the summer working as a busboy at Bishop's Lodge in Santa Fe, then returned to Stanford to finish his undergraduate education. He immersed himself in the study of European history on his return, intent on trying to puzzle out answers to some of the complexities he had found in Europe and Berlin.

30

CHRISTMAS AT HOME

Christmas was always a wonderful time in our home, and while we lived on Fairview Lane, the holiday season seemed to become more special with each passing year. This was one of the few times that we could all be together, especially after the children began to go away to school.

Those of us at home started to plan for Christmas in early December with discussion about the *farolitos* (little lanterns). My father was much involved in these discussions. Preparation of the brown paper lunch sacks we used for the *farolitos* was his primary responsibility. He was always eager to get to work. It was his self-appointed task to fold down the tops of the paper sacks and then stack them neatly in a corner of the back room. He would find an out-of-the-way corner and work at his own pace. "You let me do that work," he said with a bright smile and a warm chuckle. "It's about my speed." We used over one hundred and fifty sacks to line the firewall along the front of the house and the adobe wall by the road.

A week before Christmas the family would be together, Sammy and Norman having flown in from Ohio and California, where they were in college. They brought their smiles of anticipation and their warm hugs, and they, along with Julie and Olga, raised the tempo of happenings at home. I remember how the boys would make a tour of the house when they came home from school, going from room to room to look at the decorations that had been put up and making note of each new or different thing that had appeared in their absence. They remarked on the wonderful smells of Christmas, the piñon wood in the fireplace, the greens about the house, and the food cooking in the kitchen. We all liked New Mexican dishes along with roast turkey and dressing and all the trimmings.

One of the first things we did together was to set out the *farolitos*.

We carried the sacks out from their great stack in the back room and set them in piles in front of the house. The boys then brought around a wheelbarrow full of sand. My father usually sat in a chair alongside the wheelbarrow, helping to put sand in the sacks with a small shovel while Norman and Sammy and whoever else was willing, passed the sacks along to Sam. Sam stood on the ladder ready to place them along the top of the firewall of the house. The boys and Sam inserted a light bulb through the back of each sack once they were in place, and connected all the light strings so with a flick of the switch, Sam could, all at once, light up the night with the *farolitos*. We used white electric lights for the *farolitos* along the fire wall, and they worked quite well.

We lined the two hundred foot long adobe wall in front of the house along Fairview Lane with a similar display of *farolitos*. This time, the wheelbarrow was loaded with sacks that had already been filled with sand. Either Sammy or Norman pushed the wheelbarrow along while the one not pushing lifted the sacks to the top of the wall. We used candles here, and the *farolitos* gave off a soft glow at night. Lighting these *farolitos* was one of those pleasant chores we took turns doing. We did not mind the work even in the cold of the evening.

Townspeople said the house seemed a magical sight as they drove by at night. We thought so, too.

I would usually be in the kitchen preparing beans and chili and tortillas with Julie and Olga while the men worked on the lights outside. They would be a hungry bunch and would soon come crowding into the room. I kept the food simmering on the stove in readiness. Julie and Olga were runners for me. They constantly relayed reports about how the work was progressing and called me when everything was ready so we could go out and help light the candles.

"It's almost time, Mom. Do you have a tortilla ready? Norman's hungry and wants to eat," Julie would call out. Or Olga would say with a grin, "Come on, Mom," her voice going up and down enthusiastically in a mock sing-song. "The food can wait! We've got to go outside now. It really looks great. Come on! Come on!" We would laugh and grasp hands and file out into the brisk night.

Some winters were quite cold, so a good tasty food break after the lighting was most welcome. Everyone crowded into the kitchen clasping hands to cold, pink cheeks and rubbing arms and shoulders to warm up.

Being together, having many stories to share and getting to know each other again after short absences, was very special.

Our living room with its fourteen foot ceiling allowed us to have Christmas trees so tall we could not let them stand alone. We set them on a base and "hung' them with a heavy wire from one of the big beams in the ceiling.

We went with friends to the Jemez Mountains one Christmas to cut our trees. Sam spotted a tall, gorgeous tree, and being mindful of the fact that trees over fifteen feet were taboo, he circled the tree several times trying to judge its height and finally cut it, realizing that it may have been just a shade too big. An Indian ranger stopped us to look at our trees as we came back down through the Ranger Station. I thought for a moment he might confiscate the one we had cut, but as he approached the trailer, he turned to look at Sam. He immediately recognized him and then saying, "Hello, Dr. Ziegler. Remember me? You took out my appendix." He never looked at the trees after that. He just waved us through with a good-natured smile and a wish for a "Merry Christmas." Richard Cook of Española Mercantile provided us with one of our largest trees. It was an evergreen that reached the ceiling. We decided to spray the tree lightly with snow flocking, which seemed very special on such a fine, stately tree, and helped to accentuate the ornaments.

We gathered during an evening to decorate the tree once it was in place. Decorating was a real labor of love. Among our ornaments were a number of special hand-decorated, frosted glass balls John and Mary Marsh had given us. John designed and decorated these balls, and they were true works of art. They were three to ten inches in diameter, each decorated with sequins and beads. The beads were lovely onyx and bugle beads of varying shapes and sizes, and gave great elegance to each ball. We treasured these ornaments and hung them on the tree in special places where everyone could see them. We felt privileged to have them among our collection.

We used colored lights and bubble lights and blinking lights over the years, but finally settled on the small white lights which we first obtained from Doodlet's in Santa Fe, because they seemed to hi-light the decorations best. Sam orchestrated the placement of the lights and balls, wanting every-thing just so. He took great pride in his work and in how the tree looked. We placed a hand-made angel at the top of the tree, with a special white light alongside to highlight it.

I made a special place in the living room of our three English carolers. Sam and I had gone to the Rose Bowl Parade and game in Pasadena, California in 1953, and while there, stopped at an interesting shop in Laguna Beach, where we saw the carolers and decided they had to be part of our Christmas decorations. These figures stand from ten to fifteen inches tall and include a man and woman, and a young boy, each dressed with colorful nineteenth century period handmade costumes. The man and woman each hold a song book, while the boy stands alongside with a small lantern in one hand.

I placed these figures in front of a scenic backdrop depicting house walls and street lights, and scattered snow flocking about to portray a joyous and colorful wintry scene. We received the backdrop as a gift from Dick Healy of the Santa Fe Book and Stationery. Dick had used it one Christmas in a window display. Sam and I saw it and asked about it, and Dick said, "Why don't you take it home? I'll probably just throw it away when we take the decoration down." We were pleased and surprised, and said that we had a good use for it. Dick had it taken out of the window and presented to us. "Merry Christmas," he had said with a big, warm smile and a jolly "Ho, Ho, Ho." What a lovely gesture!

I asked my father to create an old fashioned street lamp for the display. He made a beautiful one using a small tin light fixture. It held a tiny bulb that cast a lovely soft glow when the lamp was lit.

I found a special place in the entryway for the papier-mâché nativity Lee Gulnac and I had created. We had worked hard on this project and enjoyed ourselves immensely. I was very pleased with what we made, and I know Lee was, too. We had made the nativity a real "production." We set up a large work table in our back room with sufficient space to allow us to maneuver with all of our pieces of material and "gooey" flour paste (glue). Here we could drape the wet material over wire or Styrofoam frames, begin to shape our figures, and allow them to dry undisturbed. Lee worked on Mary and the Christ child, while I made the Three Wise Men my project. We began to paint and decorate as soon as the material was dry. Lee shaped Mary in a sitting position so she could be placed alongside a manger. She painted Mary's robe a soft blue and edged her shawl in white so it frames her face. She left the Christ child unpainted and it is quite beautiful in the soft yellow-white natural color of the papier-mâché. The Wise Men each stand fifteen inches high, and each has a distinct personality. Their faces and beards are painted natural tones, and they are richly dressed with turbans and robes of deep green and red fabric lined with gold and jewels. They appear stately and majestic as they wait patiently to present their offerings to the Christ child.

Discarded jewelry filled the need for the elaborate costumes and the gifts for the Christ child. My handiest source for old jewelry was my neighbor and friend, Nathalia DeVargas. Lee and I were amazed to see the finished pieces, and when Sam and I arranged them in a manger scene in our entryway on top of the Mexican chest, using pieces of wood and rough bark to create a stable and a manger, we found we had a very effective display.

Norman came home one Christmas and saw the nativity, and immediately asked, "Wow, Mom, where did you get this?" I told him with a smile that Lee Gulnac and I had made it. "Really," he said, his voice rising in disbelief. "You and Lee made that? Wow! That's nice! That's really nice! You and Lee do some very special things together."

My father had seen Lee and me working together on the nativity, and remarked good-naturedly, "You two must be sisters. I don't think I have seen two women have so much fun together." Such a good time we had, and the nativity brings remembrance of it back each time I put it out for Christmas.

We found a special place in the house for the small "keepsake" tree that Theo "Doodlet" and her mother, "Ma" Ruthling, gave us one year. It is adorned with tiny treasures to remind us of things past. We also received mistletoe from Col. Bob and Jane Fate. Sam and I had met the Fates shortly after they purchased John and Mary Marshes home in Cuartales. They loved to go into the nearby mountains to gather greens at Christmas time. We always welcomed their gift of the fine mistletoe lush with white berries and hung with a handsome red ribbon. We placed other greens about the house, and had candles and greens on the large mantel over the fireplace in the living room.

An antique chandelier with Dresden china flowers, brass leaves and eleven candle holders hung over the dining room table. A beautiful, soft light graces the table and the room when the candles were lit. I decorated the chandelier with small pine sprigs and red velvet ribbons, and covered our dining table with our banquet-size damask table cloth. The cloth was a family heirloom. One time I bravely tinted it a soft, light shade of green to blend with the other Christmas décor, and it highlighted nicely the fine china and crystal we set our table with when we dined.

Last but not least, we always put wide red ribbons and a large bow with greens on the front door to the house. These decorations made it resemble a wrapped package, ready to be opened.

I tried to make certain that we had special holiday music playing when we were together in the evening or on the weekends. On Christmas day, we often played Handel's "Messiah." There were Christmas carols at other times, traditional and modern, and special recordings such as the Vienna Boys Choir and others.

Christmas Eve meant posole, green chili and hot chocolate which we enjoyed by the fireplace in the living room after a late church service. We always set out a special bowl of posole and a glass of beer for our friendly ghost, De Vargas, before we went to bed. We placed these next to the fireplace, just near the door from Yunque Yunque. Christmas morning started with Sam's reading of the Christmas story from the Bible. We sat at the table, and it was a time of great warmth and togetherness, touching hands and smiling with each other. Sam read his favorite passage from the King James Version of the Bible, Luke 2:1-20: "And it came to pass in those days, that there went out a decree from Caesar Augustus, that all the world should be taxed . . ."

I remember when the children were small, it was difficult for them to be patient while the Christmas Story was being read. They were quite eager to open their gifts. Sam prepared fresh grapefruit with red and green maraschino cherries, and this usually kept them occupied until the reading was finished. They were then allowed to open one present each, after which we finished breakfast together. Things were more relaxed and leisurely when the children were older, but the grapefruit and cherries remained on the menu.

Christmas was a wonderful time to entertain, and our Christmas of 1964 was very special for this reason. Sam Jr. was home from Naval Officer Candidate School (OCS) in Rhode Island, which he had entered in July following graduation from Otterbein College. He had finished OCS in October. His fiancée, Sandra Joseph, who had also graduated from Otterbein and was now teaching elementary school, was with him from Ohio. Norman was in his final year at Stanford, and was home on break for the holidays with his high school sweetheart, Carol Thompson. She was now a junior at Radcliffe College and had come in from New Jersey.

Our good friends, Dick and Barbara Sawyer, and their two boys, John and Ridley, nicknamed Rid, had also come from Boston for a ten-day visit. The Sawyers were all interested in New Mexico. We suggested they read some books before they came to give them a better feeling for the area, and mentioned Willa Cather's *Death Comes For The Archbishop*, Alice Marriott's *Maria, The Potter of San Ildefonso*, and Ruth Laughlin's *The Wind Leaves No Shadow* for starters. They took to these recommendations enthusiastically, and had many questions for us upon their arrival in Santa Fe. "Which are the Jemez Mountains?" and "Will we be able to see the Lamy Chapel?" and "Where is San Ildefonso Pueblo?" they asked.

We had a party for sixty people the evening after everyone had arrived to give all our guests an opportunity to meet local people. We found time for a trip to the mountains. Dick Sawyer had mentioned they would enjoy an opportunity to ski, and I drove them to the Los Alamos ski slopes because they were the closest. But Dick would not let the boys out of the car upon arrival. The Massachusetts slopes to which they were accustomed were more like hills in comparison to our mountain slopes. Dick felt it would be better if the boys filled their time doing other things. Julie introduced all of these Eastern greenhorns to our horses for a bit of riding, and we spent time exploring Santa Fe and visiting the Pueblos. We made sure we introduced Sandra, Carol and the Sawyers to the local diet, especially to New Mexican chili and posole. Dick Sawyer was so taken with posole that he wanted it for breakfast.

Young John Sawyer developed a crush on Julie during the visit. He was all of ten years old, while Julie was now fourteen. Barbara sat John in a chair to trim his hair when they returned to Boston, saying, "You should have some bangs."

John immediately held up his hands and replied, "Oh, no. Julie won't like me that way! Barbara wrote to me about the exchange with some amusement. Sam and I could not help but chuckle.

We made sure to play charades one evening before everyone left. Sam and Barbara were captains for one team, while Dick and I took charge of the others.

All of us had a lovely time, with much impassioned acting out of subjects and titles and roles, and generally good success on both sides guessing clues.

That Christmas Eve, we ate our posole late in the evening around the fireplace, and then drove to Tesuque Pueblo. We knew the Indians would be celebrating Mass at midnight, and I had heard there would be dancing.

We made our way to the church, and as we stepped inside, we heard singing above us in the choir loft, with Christmas carols in Tewa, Spanish, and English. We stood quietly at the back of the church looking out over the pews filled with Indians, women on the right and men on the left. An Indian woman rose from her seat after a few moments, to walk to the life-sized nativity at the front of the church. She picked up the doll of the Christ child and held it in her arms, then gently placed it back in its crib and returned to her seat.

Two Indian couples dressed in native costumes entered the church close to midnight, and walked to the alter. A single man along with them began to chant and slowly beat a drum as the dancers turned and moved slowly in a sacred dance. A priest made a few short statements and said a prayer after they finished and had filed slowly out of the church. People then rose and left quietly. It was a beautiful and peaceful ceremony for us to see.

31

LAS CONQUISTADORAS: A MUSICAL ADVENTURE

I took time to do personal things which I enjoyed while I was busy with civic activities. One of these was singing. I had become involved with music at our church soon after Sam and I arrived in Española, and helped to get a choir started. This involvement brought my voice before the public. I was soon asked to sing for weddings, which I loved to do. I sang for the weddings of Jeanne Voyles, daughter of Buck and Lela George Voyles, Martha Law, daughter of Bill and Peggy Law, and Vickie Hartell, daughter of Harold and Charlene Hartell. These were special occasions. I also sang at the installation of Ruby Neill as Grand Matron at the Order of the Eastern Star in Española, which was a great honor.

The Harvey twins, Janis and Janet, came from Ohio to work at the Española Hospital in August of 1962. They began attending the Evangelical United Brethren Church once they had settled in. Sam heard that they loved to sing, and he told me about them. I met them soon after, and when we had an opportunity to visit and get to know each other, they quickly became close friends and provided a new and stimulating dimension to my singing.

Janis and Janet were Registered Nurses with baccalaureate degrees from Ohio State University School of Nursing. They wanted to serve as medical missionaries following graduation, and before they knew it, they were on their way to New Mexico. They were nice looking young women with curly dark hair worn short about the neck, and lovely, warm smiles. Janis recalls:

> Sam had a little trouble telling Janet and me apart at first. When we were together. Sam would sometimes just look at us and sort of grin or chuckle. He called us both Miss Harvey then, but it was not long before he could easily identify the correct one of us.[46]

They were Midwestern "greenhorns" when they came to Española. Janet has a vivid picture of their arrival at the Lamy train station. She remembers:

> . . . feeling like I had arrived in a foreign country, sitting in Lamy with my big trunk, with all my belongings waiting for a ride to the hospital. But I quickly fell in love with the cactus, the mountains and the beautiful sunsets.[47]

Knowing of their interest in music and singing, I soon asked if they might be interested in singing with me. I invited them to our home, where we had a piano and could practice and work without interruption. They gladly accepted my invitation and we soon began rehearsing. Janet played the piano and sang 1st soprano during our practice sessions, while Janis sang 2nd soprano and I sang alto. The twins voices were, like themselves, identical, and my alto blended nicely with their sopranos. Working with a trio was a new experience for me, and I began to enjoy singing in a small group.

The twins had sung many duets together, and they brought music with them. Their favorite numbers were "How Lovely Are Thy Dwellings" and the popular song "Tumblin' Tumbleweeds." We began performing locally after we had practiced for a while. Patty McCracken Yates (now Patty Robertson) would accompany us when we performed. We were quickly in demand for church services. We spent a rich and fulfilling year and a half singing together.

Our friendship expanded beyond the field of music. Sam and I enjoyed having Janet and Janis in our home, and our children looked forward to spending time with them. I grew to like and respect them both for their fine voices and for their dedication as nurses to the mission of caring for and serving the sick. Janet says of her nursing experience:

> We lived in the dormitory by the hospital. I worked one year in the pediatric unit and one year in obstetrics. I remember how sick the babies were coming in nearly dead from Shigella dysentery or other diarrhea problems and high fevers. I was very ill in 1963 with Shigella myself. Dr. Ziegler took care of me as he did all of us nurses, and I survived.[48]

The twins were interested in the community of Española and in the people living here, and were anxious to learn about all of northern New Mexico. We made sure they attended the burning of Zozobra (Old Man Gloom) in Santa Fe and went to the Santa Fe Opera, and they became involved in rodeo parades in Española. Janis rode in the Queen's Parade, and said of her experience:

> Somehow, I became acquainted with a rancher who had a horse named "Sonny Boy." I rode in the Queen's Parade before the rodeo in 1963. As a note of humor, I remember how [this horse] loved to be the lead horse. His master was riding another horse however in the parade and it was difficult to keep "Sonny Boy" in line. After the parade, I thought I would try my roping skill (Will Roger's style, which I had learned in high school). I took out my lariat and tried to lasso a sagebrush. What a surprise! The horse took off like we were working cattle. I caught the bush and nearly got left behind. Thank the good Lord I stayed on and counted my blessings. The resolve: "I won't do that again."[49]

Janis managed pretty well for a "greenhorn." The twins also participated in a rodeo parade on another occasion, riding on the Hospital Float. They stood on the float platform twirling their ropes Will Rogers style. We took pictures of them doing their fancy roping, but Janet recalls with amusement that "I think our ropes were always twisted up each time a picture was taken."

We felt secure asking the twins to baby sit Julie when we were away from home. Sam gave them the keys to our new Thunderbird one time. They were overjoyed with the chance to drive it. Julie sought out their help giving our big Palomino, Poncho, a bath on another occasion. Poncho had other ideas, as Janis recalls:

> . . . Julie tied him to a tree. He balked when we started to wash him and the noose around his neck tightened. I thought he would choke himself. Fortunately, we got the rope off, but he never did get a bath.[50]

Janis returned to Ohio in late 1963 to marry Roger Hamrick and raise a family. Janet remained another year in Española, then entered graduate school to earn her Master's Degree in Nursing. She married Jerry Hussong in 1989. Jerry had two children, and Janet quickly took on the roles of wife and mother.

The twins will always be very much part of our family.

I realized very quickly after Janis and Janet Harvey left Española that there was a void in my life. Our trio had shown me how important singing was to me. I had both fine companionship with the twins and an avenue to pursue my music.

I soon began to think of forming a new trio. Patty Yates had been accompanying my former trio. She was a native of the Española Valley and has spent a lifetime associated with the church's work here. She studied piano under a number of outstanding teachers. One special teacher in particular was John Marsh. When I called Patty, she said she would be interested in accompanying a new trio.

Patty and I knew that my neighbor, Elberta Honstein, had a beautiful, clear soprano voice, lovely to hear, so I called her to see if she might be interested. She said, "Yes, very much so." She came right over. Although Elberta was active in many community projects such as 4-H work, she always found time to participate in our practices and performances.

Elberta, Patty and I talked about the kind of music we wanted to sing and who might be our 2nd soprano because we needed a third voice to complete the trio. Patty suggested Sandra Pomeroy. Sandra was a teacher at McCurdy, and wife of Fred Pomeroy, McCurdy High School principal. We called her and she readily accepted our invitation. Sandra was an excellent choice to round out the trio.

Our trio was an exciting combination, all three voices clear and bright and in perfect harmony. Harmony is important when a trio sings, both for the quality of the music and for the blend of personalities working together and dealing with the pressures of performing. We were fortunate in our group. We reacted well to each other and were sensitive to timing, rhythm and expression. I know Sam was biased, but he said our voices were so beautiful that he felt chills go up and down his spine when he listened to us sing. We quickly realized we needed a name for our group, and we chose "Las Conquistadoras."

We felt the name fit nicely with the history and setting of New Mexico.

Many of the numbers I sang with my first trio were favorites of my new group, and we increased our repertoire as requests for our performances grew. We rapidly developed into a polished singing group with Patty's accompaniment, and were soon in demand for special music at churches, banquets, weddings, and luncheons throughout the State.

We sang by request for weddings as well as for services at the local churches around Española, at St. John's Methodist Church and St. Francis Cathedral in Santa Fe. At St. Francis Cathedral, we were accompanied by their organist of reputation, Connie Chavez. I saw people in the audience at St. Francis Cathedral turn to look at us as we sang from the balcony, with smiles of pleasure and interest on their faces.

State Senator Horace DeVargas asked permission of the State Legislature for us to sing at the opening of the 1966 Winter Session, and we were well received. We sang on the plaza in Santa Fe at Fiesta time, and performed several numbers from Camelot for a group of women from Albuquerque, who attended a guest luncheon in Santa Fe.

Elaine Marshall accompanied us when we sang for a large gathering of church women in Albuquerque. She had accompanied us on a number of other occasions when Patty could not be with us. Kay Manley of Los Alamos also agreed to accompany us after she heard our voices and felt we qualified! She was delightful to work with.

There were times when Sandra Pomeroy was not able to sing with the trio. A close friend, Rosemary "Kue" Hunter, who had a beautiful soprano voice, would sing with us in Sandra's place. Kue was with the trio when we sang at St. Francis Cathedral in Santa Fe, and she became a permanent member after Sandra left the group in late 1967 to move to Alaska.

The trio decided to record an album before Sandra left. Sam and Roy Honstein agreed to sponsor us, and Elaine Marshall helped to arrange for the recording. She contacted Ray Avery of Albuquerque, who had recorded the Albuquerque Symphony, and asked if he would be willing to handle our recording. He agreed, but did not want to splice a tape, so we had to sing a number until he felt it was perfect. He could then use it directly in the recording.

We started our session at 8:00 o'clock on a Saturday morning and sang until late afternoon, with only one short twenty minute break at noon. Albums were soon released for sale, the release coinciding with the 20th

Anniversary of the Española Hospital. We planned to contribute all of the money made to the hospital. Carl Goodwin, a good friend and owner of the Santa Fe, KTRC Radio Station, played selections from the album on his station. We had reviews in the *Rio Grande SUN* and the *Santa Fe News*, and in our church's national publication, *The World Evangel*. I am not sure how the article appeared in the *Santa Fe News*, but I think Carl Goodwin was responsible.

The front cover of the album is a lovely color photograph of our trio with our accompanist, Patty. We are poised in front of the beautiful hand-carved wood paneled door at my adobe home. Patty, Elberta, and Sandra are seated, and I am standing behind. We all wear Southwestern dresses with turquoise and silver jewelry in keeping with the traditions of New Mexico.

The *Santa Fe News* wrote of our album:

> The recording, released to coincide with the 20th anniversary of the Española Hospital, consists of a variety of songs ranging from "The Lord's Prayer" to "Tumbling Tumbleweeds." All proceeds from the sale and distribution of the album will be donated to the hospital. The trio consists of Elberta Honstein, long-time resident of Española and wife of an Española businessman, Sandra Pomeroy, wife of the principal of McCurdy High School, and Isabel Ziegler, wife of the chief of surgical service at the Española Hospital. Accompanist is Patty Yates, daughter of Dr. Glen McCracken, long-time superintendent of McCurdy School.[51]

Requests for albums came from friends and acquaintances and others all over the United States. We were able to contribute over $5,000 to the hospital from our sales.

Our trio gave several of its more entertaining performances at the Fireman's Follies in Española between 1965–1968. The Follies were held each year from 1963–1968 at the El Rio Theater in downtown Española to raise money for the Volunteer Fire Department. Richard Cook, Fire Chief for nearly fifteen years, and C.L. Hunter of Hunter Motors, Art Houle of Houle Chevrolet, and Roy Honstein approached all of the local talent and asked them to participate in the event.

The Follies were a fun time drawing audiences of all ages, and the local performances were not to be missed. The trio was in demand, and never failed to give a memorable showing. We gave a good deal of thought to our costumes for each performance. We wanted to portray the theme of each song and its music, and dress appropriately for the occasion. We had a seamstress make a shortened version of a Flamenco skirt with a black blouse to match, and we ordered Flamenco hats from Mexico for the number "Cuando Calienta El Sol." With our hats on and a red rose tucked over one ear, we were ready to perform! Response was outstanding. We were amateurs to be sure, but we had great fun, and the audience enjoyed itself. A favorite song of everyone's was "I Left My Heart in San Francisco," which brought cheers and whistles from the audience, and we always dressed in boots and chaps and cowboy hats when we sang "Tumblin' Tumbleweeds."

We sang "Aquarius" the year of the musical *Hair*. Sam and I had seen the performance in New York, and the music had a profound affect on me. The other members of the trio also found it captivating when they heard it. We decided "Aquarius" was worth trying and that it would be a real challenge for us. The time seemed right.

Music has a way of affecting people differently. "Aquarius" is such a number. Local radio stations were giving prime time to the music, and there was an Albuquerque dance hall that featured strobe lighting for dancing along with the music. Remembering the musical I had seen and heard in New York, and wanting to convey that kind of atmosphere when we presented the music, I enticed Roy and Elberta Honstein, Kue and C. L. Hunter to join Sam and me for an evening of dancing in Albuquerque. The evening proved to be most fruitful and enjoyable. Everyone came away with great enthusiasm for producing "Aquarius" with strobe lighting. Our next step was to locate a drummer and figure out a way to handle effects at the theater on the night of the performance. Could the town of Española manage such a fete?

I learned, by chance, of a young man named Jimmy Powers who lived down the street from me. Jimmy was an Española High School student who was a member of a local band called the "Jivin'J's". He played the drums and had a setup that flashed colored lights as he drummed. He could not wait to perform with us when I contacted him. Patty would not be available for the performance, but we were fortunate to have Dr. Merle Yordy's daughter, Martha, to accompany us. The trio dressed in filmy material of light colors that blended with the flashing lights. Applause, whistles and more applause brought down the house. Our performance was one to be remembered.

Roy Honstein, Elberta's husband, was supportive and enthusiastic about our trio. He came to hear us sing whenever he could get away from his Morgan Horse Farm and Chevron Oil business. Sam had a chance to listen even with his busy schedule, because we usually practiced at our house. The blend of the trio's voices along with our outstanding accompaniment was always cause for people to stop and listen.

At the present time, 2009, a Las Conquistadoras recording display adorns the passage wall of the new addition of the Española Hospital. We are all proud and pleased.

When our trio disbanded, I became a member of the Los Alamos Light Opera which was a wonderful experience. I started in the chorus of the Light Opera, then had a minor part, and later was runner up for a lead. The shows in which I played included *On A Clear Day* and *Show Boat*. Practice for the winter shows during the three years 1968-1970 started in September at 7:30 p.m. We practiced until the director decided we could leave, which was often 11:00 p.m. or later. I remember arriving home after midnight many times.

The Don Juan Theater near San Ildefonso was in full swing with its Little Theater performances during this time. I tried out and was cast for four different character parts in Dylan Thomas's *Under Milkwood*. The director, John Mench, set up the show as a series of scenes that move swiftly from one area of the stage to another. Those of us performing had to move quickly. Our character changes involved different hats, wigs, glasses, and other props as needed. It was a fun experience, and rave reviews on the radio called for the show to continue for a second week, but the theater was under contract to another group. Our daughter, Julie, worked backstage with props during my performances with the theater, and she loved the experience, too. She learned a great deal about the nuts and bolts of stage production.

Sam was so busy in those days that my involvements did not bother him. He would often arrive home for something to eat and be off again just as I was returning. There were a lot of "hellos" and "good-byes" said in passing!

Las Conquistadoras, a vocal trio composed of (left to right) Elberta Honstein, Sandra Pomeroy and Isabel Ziegler. The trio performed at weddings and special occasions and at one opening of the State Legislative Session. Patricia Yates, accompanist, not in the picture.

32

SAM'S ELECTION
TO THE ESPAÑOLA CITY COUNCIL

Sam had long held an interest in local civic affairs, and in the activities of the mayor and city council. His decision to run for election to the Española City Council in 1966 grew out of the civic work I had been doing with the city and with Mayor Cipriano Vigil. My civic involvements over the years and the discussions about community plans and the needs of Española as a community gave Sam a greater awareness of the community as a whole, and helped him to appreciate the individuals responsible for local government. He came to know Mayor Vigil, and some of the mayor's ideas and dreams began rubbing off on him. In the latter part of 1965, Sam approached the mayor about the possibility of his running for city council.

Sam felt that the council was composed of individuals who were taking care of the day-to-day problems of a city, but were not giving enough attention to longer range city planning and to the problems associated with growth of the community as a whole. To him, there seemed to be no one with real vision or drive. He wanted to add his voice. I know he felt that he could make an important contribution.

Soon thereafter, Sam became a member of the mayor's non-partisan slate called "Citizens for a Greater Española." Cipriano Vigil was running for his fifth consecutive term as mayor. The four running for city council who joined the mayor on his ticket were Tony Lucero, Buddy Gallegos, Gilbert Vigil and Sam. Sam was duly elected to his first term as an Española City Councilman on March 1, 1966. His had been a very close race. The *Rio Grande SUN* noted:

> The closest race . . . was between Freed [sic] Seeds, incumbent councilman and Dr. Samuel R. Ziegler. Dr. Ziegler, a member

of the "People's Ticket" defeated Seeds 672-655, a 17-vote margin.[52]

The *SUN* went on to write that "Tireless campaigning apparently paid off for the [the opposing party] 'Citizen.' For weeks, members of the ticket and volunteer workers combed every nook and corner of Española making personal visits at least once to almost every householder." [53] Sam had not had time to do this kind of campaigning. He was too busy with his practice. I know he had succeeded primarily on the basis of his good name.

Cipriano Vigil was not re-elected. He appeared to be a capable leader and a man who could get things done, but he had a Council pulling in separate directions. Cipriano was replaced in office by a young man named Epimenio Vigil. Richard Lucero was elected to the Council in 1966. He quickly assumed a prominent role, and used this stage to further his plans to run for Mayor in the next election.

The old Bond House served as City Hall in the early years. The city had purchased it from the Bonds and it served a useful purpose. It had an adequate meeting room, a spacious mayor's office on the second floor, adequate restroom facilities for the public, and plenty of room for ancillary offices. It was located within minutes of the hospital and had phones readily available.

Bob Trapp, editor and publisher of the *Rio Grande SUN*, challenged the City Council in early May of 1969 to a "beard-growing contest" for the Oñate Festival, which was to be celebrated in July. The *SUN* wrote:

> The city administration has put out a lot of publicity in support of the Oñate Festival and I'm going to see how serious they are [Bob said]. We might have to establish a handicap system for those whose beard-growing talents are questionable, but the big problem is finding out if their wives will let them grow beards.[54]

The *SUN* reported with some amusement the following week on the Council's acceptance of this challenge:

> Española city councilmen, with smirks of glee, back-patting and confident laughter, Monday night accepted the challenge of the editor of the *Rio Grande SUN* to a beard-growing contest for the Oñate Festival July 11–13.

Amid the joy, however, were some glances of apprehension at the sight of Editor Robert Trapps [sic] luxurious start.

Councilman Dr. S.R. Ziegler, as highly regarded for his cutting words as his keenly edged scapel [sic], presented a resolution by the council urging that Trapp's challenge of last week be accepted.

The resolution declared the "city council has high regards for his editorial ability, but considers him incapable of raising much more than a boyish fuzz on his chin."

The slanted, and obviously prejudiced resolution, continued that the city council and mayor "were in the great part responsible for initiating the revival of the Oñate Festival and thereby should take responsible parts in helping set the mood of the Fiesta."

Following acceptance, Mayor Lucero was noted to stroke his 5 o'clock shadow and declare ominously that "This guy is always trying to tell the city what to do and now he's trying to tell us how to grow beards."

Reached at his office, Trapp said he couldn't understand what the mayor meant by the remark.[55]

Española began to look like a western town at the turn of the century as beard growing caught on. It soon seemed that every male was growing a beard. The City Council certainly rose to the challenge and City Council meetings looked like frontier "hangin'" courts. No winner was ever declared to Sam's knowledge, but the challenge made for rootin', tootin' successful 1969 Oñate Festival.

The *Rio Grande SUN* initiated a "regatta" at the Oñate Festival. The idea for this race was Bob Trapp's, I am sure. It was to start with much fanfare on the Rio Grande up near Pilar and end at the bridge crossing from Riverside into downtown Española at Oñate Street. I believe Bob Trapp and Frank Willard rowed one boat, while Scott Garner and Paul Barbo rowed another. I am not sure who else gathered up the courage and the stamina to enter the race. The Rio Grande was not running very high at this time of year, and was not too difficult for "amateur" rowers. People watched and cheered from vantage points all along the river. I believe Frank and Bob reached the Oñate Street bridge first. There was, of course, much celebration that followed from the enthusiastic crowds that had been watching and cheering along the way.

33

The New City Complex and Public Library

Sam had been re-elected to the Council from Ward 4 in 1970 as a member of Mayor Richard Lucero's ticket, "Voice of the People." Included on the Mayor's slate were Ernesto Vigil for city judge, and Eddie Rivera, Leroy Salazar, Levi Sanchez and Sam for councilmen. All were successful on March 3rd except Eddie Rivera. I know Sam was sorry Eddie lost. He felt Eddie would have made a good councilman.

The *Rio Grande SUN* wrote of this race:

> A third incumbent, Dr. S. R. Ziegler, was returned to office from Ward 4, getting 742 votes in a [4-way] race—the highest total of any council candidate.

> . . .

> Dr. Ziegler carried all the precincts handily in his campaign for a second term . . . that saw Ziegler poll more votes than his three opponents combined. He had 742 to 607 for all the others."[56]

The City began to move forward with planning for the new city complex with Richard Lucero once again in charge. The planning and building were the highlights of the early 1970s. The new city complex, named the Lucero Center, is a wonderful facility. The comfortable and spacious library with a capacity for 75,000 volumes is a befitting memorial to the early days when a small group of women worked hard to begin the first library in a small building on the Los Alamos highway. The Olympic-size swimming pool with one and three meter diving boards offers safe swimming for local youths and elders. The gym is constantly used and is frequently the scene of civic dinners, where one can find the most delicious posole, green chili, menudo, sopapillas and tamales. I have never found food anywhere as good as real northern New Mexican home cooking. There are adequate meeting rooms open to all, Democrat or Republican, Boy Scout or Girl Scout, religious or civic.

The new center has been a boon to the area, and it is appropriately named the Richard Lucero Center. Richard brought the Center into being with his continued belief that "It can be done," and his unselfish donation of time and energy beyond the usual call to duty. We all participated in many details from the acquisition of land and the initial legal aspects to the selection of architects, developers, construction companies, interior decorators, and the ultimate staffing of the building.

Richard made trips to Ft. Worth and Washington, D.C. to promote the project and to seek funding. If he had not pushed the way he did, the project may not have been realized. It was a project worth the time and effort it took to bring it to reality.

Ground was broken on February 27, 1973 and the Richard L. Lucero Center and Public Library were dedicated on March 10, 1974. Sam served as Master of Ceremonies for the occasion, and he was privileged to introduce U.S. Senator Joseph M. Montoya, who gave the Dedication Address.

The Complex was finally completed with the dedication of Valdez Park a year later on August 10, 1975. The park is a large outdoor recreational area adjacent to the Lucero Center.

The new complex was also the focal point for the new library. Reaching this point involved a rather circuitous route. I had been busy during the years from 1950 into early 1960s with many different activities, but my interest in the library continued in small but important ways. I went by the library to be sure a club member was on hand to check books in and out, and to help with questions or problems that may have arisen. We had a small committee of women who worked on book selection. The committee considered requests from local people, and then met with Sophronia Dewey from the State Library, and later Celsa Quintana, who operated the New Mexico State Library Bookmobile in Española, for advice about purchases. I talked with the Mayor Cipriano Vigil at one point about an additional room across from the two rooms we had for books, to provide better space for Woman's Club members to deal with the public and to check out books. The Mayor very nicely accommodated this request.

Outside events began to shape the scope and function of the library. Bill Carr, who advised Arthur Pack of Ghost Ranch on issues of wildlife and conservation and who started the Wild Life Museum at the ranch, had contacted me by letter in January of 1964, to say he had a private collection of some 4,000 books, bulletins and other materials with an appraised value of $30,000 he would like to donate to the Española Library. He stipulated only that the books and materials must be properly housed and cared for.

It was immediately apparent that the present library would be unable to house such a large and valuable collection, and that a new location would be needed, both because of space requirements and the need to ensure proper air conditioning, lighting, fireproofing, and security for the books. I contacted Mayor Cipriano Vigil in reference to Bill Carr's offer. The Mayor was most enthusiastic, and in turn, appointed me chairperson of a library committee to ascertain what must be done to ensure this gift.

I chose four members to assist me. Ruth Trapp served as secretary. She was an extremely well-read individual interested in seeing Española develop a library of some quality. I knew that Ruth would not serve on my committee unless she believed in its worth, and that her efforts would be sincere and dedicated to the task at hand. She and her husband, Bob, were both excited about the possibility of obtaining Bill Carr's books.

My good friend, Mrs. Leon Williams of Jacona Ranch in Pojoaque, a woman with a great appreciation for the arts and an active interest in the affairs of Española, served as vice-chairperson. David Todd, the late Lay Reader of the Episcopal Church, and Senator Horace DeVargas were the other members of the committee. Bill Carr was asked to served in an advisory capacity. Bob Trapp and Nathalia DeVargas also contributed much time and effort because of a sincere interest in the project. All of these people wanted it to succeed, and they were able to reach out and involve other interested parties throughout Rio Arriba County and northern New Mexico, which was most helpful.

We met as a committee each week to pull ideas and thinking together and then branched out to pursue leads for possible locations. Our committee went all over town trying to find the perfect place. Ruth Trapp and I found a building close by the People's Store in downtown Española that might serve. All members of the family who owned the property agreed to sell to the City except one living in California, who felt the building should remain in the family. Ruth Trapp worked tirelessly with the family, but was unable to obtain consent. We began to check elsewhere with this option closed. We even investigated the possibility of El Mirador at Alcalde, where we thought both a library and a museum might be located. Both could serve all of northern New Mexico.

We contracted our U.S. Senator Joseph Montoya with Senator DeVargas's advice and help, but the Senator did not seem overly interested in becoming involved with our project. He made us sit and wait a good three hours when we went to see him for a scheduled appointment in Santa Fe. I believe he was trying to avoid us. Horace kept saying while we waited, "You know, we just have to stay here and be patient." We were finally able to meet with the Senator, but all he talked about were the books he had given to other libraries and causes in New Mexico. He had no words of advice for us. He never once asked, "How can I help you?" or volunteered, "Let me see what can be done."

The City agreed to take over operation of the library in 1969. The library had greater freedom of operation under City management, and while a major portion of its money was allocated for book purchases, some was now available to pay the salary of a full-time certified librarian, the need for whom was apparent.

I had tried to convince members of the Woman's Club from the beginning of my work, that we needed a qualified librarian. Volunteer helpers were conscientious and willing, but we required the advice and knowledge only a certified librarian could provide. Celsa Quintana became librarian for the Española Library in 1972. She had been with the New Mexico State Library bookmobile for ten years prior. She had been very helpful with advice about book purchases while she served as Bookmobile librarian.

All of our work and thinking about where to locate the library and how to staff it soon led us to the logical question, "Why not think in terms of a new civic center where the library could be properly housed along with other civic offices such as the City Hall." Money was the biggest issue. We were aware that federal funds for municipal buildings were available, but preliminary designs were necessary for application. Our group soon became involved with Richard Halford and Robert Kitchen, architect consultants, regarding designs.

The work of the committee Mayor Cipriano Vigil appointed

spanned the terms of several different city councils and mayors of Española. Whoever was running for the mayoral seat came to me each time there was an election, to say they were in favor of the library and would do everything they could to help. Mayor Vigil's interest and enthusiasm about the project were matched by that of Mayor Eppie Vigil and then Richard Lucero. Councilmen during this period also gave their active support.

Life often moves in strange ways. The freak flooding of the Woman's Club building led to the City's greater awareness of and interest in the library. The City then provided funding and a building for the library. This aid in turn created outside interest and led to the offer of a valuable private collection of books to the City. The Mayor appointed a library committee and gave it the task of finding appropriate housing for such a collection, and these efforts helped to bring about a beautiful library complex which now houses the Española Public Library. This complex should make the Española Woman's Club proud of their federated project, begun so many years before. Realizing a dream often takes many years of hard work and planning.

Two people whom I came to know during this time, and to appreciate for their devoted concern for the affairs of a local community and their fine capabilities, were Bob and Ruth Trapp. Bob Trapp, editor and publisher of the *Rio Grande SUN*, was aware of the need for a library and did not want the project to fail. He always seemed to be at my elbow at the right time, lending his confident assurances and thoughtful suggestions about things to do and directions to take. He made a special effort to accommodate whenever I approached him for needed newspaper or photo coverage of events.

I came to know and admire Ruth Trapp as an intelligent and discerning woman capable of handling herself in many different situations. I appreciated her good sense and her practical know-how. I knew very quickly after asking Ruth to be on the committee, that she was someone on whom I could rely. She always followed through on work she agreed to do, and she did not hesitate to offer suggestions and to lead when she felt it necessary. We worked closely together and I greatly appreciated her efforts and her support.

I learned to admire Ruth's forthright honesty and courage. She was well informed about local people and local happenings, and when I heard people criticize some article in the *SUN* in her presence, she always rejoined,

"We tell it like it is, not the way you might want to read it or hear it."

I came across a letter Ruth wrote to me in December of 1977, while I was visiting our daughter, Julie, and her family in Mexico City. Ruth had learned that I was ill, and sent kind words of encouragement along with information about her every day activities at home. I do not think she will mind if I include some of her letter here:

> well, there you are in a strange country, so far from home, at christmas time . . .
> we shall miss you.
> just think, you get to see the genuine piñata ceremony in its native setting, and mexican hot chocolate, and a colorful mass or two. all sorts of interesting christmas customs to tell about when you get back.
> newswise: . . . frank willard, sr., was hospitalized last week with heart trouble and it was touch-and-go for awhile. jeannette came up but left sunday when things were calm again—there was not time for visiting. we went for christmas trees last sunday—went up to coyote this year and it was just overwhelmingly beautiful. skies looked like o'keeffe canvasses everywhere you turned with pedernal plunked right in the middle of it all. what a mountain that is.
> i absolutely wore [a friend] to a frazzle shopping arts and crafts shows this past month. even i have had enuf for awhile. . .
> guess i had better thaw something . . . or wash something. we will be thinking of you as you have a wonderful holiday. our best to julie, errol and the children.[57]

I will always appreciate Ruth's warm, good wishes and interest in us as a family. I also appreciate her openness to the world, and her great joy in living.

34

A STAGECOACH WEDDING

Julie became engaged to marry Errol Chavez in 1970. Their engagement came after several years of dating. Sam and I were not entirely sure we approved of the match, but we realized we had to accept Julie's decision. Errol was a local boy, the son of T. J. and Vangie Chavez, whom we had known for many years. T. J. was a Captain on the New Mexico State Police Force and an influential man in Rio Arriba County. We decided after discussion with Julie that we wanted the wedding to be one of the most memorable the Valley had ever seen.

Julie and Errol set a date of August 14, 1971, and said they wanted to hold the wedding at the historic Catholic church in Santa Cruz. They wanted an ecumenical service with both our friend, Rev. Dolph Pringle, and the Catholic priest from Santa Cruz, Father Marvin Archuleta, performing the ceremony. Everyone joined into the spirit of the occasion.

There were many things for which we had to plan. Guest lists had to be drawn up, and invitations designed and printed. Julie wanted Olga to be her maid of honor, and Sammy's wife, Sandra, to be her matron of honor. She selected as her bridesmaids Errol's sister, Loretta Chavez, and then her friends, Debbie Beetham and Susan Casselman, both from Otterbein College, and Susan Jernigan, a close friend from her years at Valley School for Girls in Tucson. We wanted to have all of the family home for this occasion, but Norman and his family would be in India at the time of the wedding and unable to attend. We were disappointed about Norman, but happy that Sammy and his family would be present. Sam's father and mother were living at the Otterbein Home in Lebanon, Ohio. His mother was not well and was being cared for in the hospital section, while his father lived in a small apartment at the Home. Both were disappointed they could not be present.

What to wear became the next order of business. Julie had a beautiful lace mantilla and a Spanish comb for her hair which she had brought home from Segovia, Spain. She wanted to use these in the wedding, but needed a Spanish fan to which she could attach her bridal bouquet and then hold as she walked. She had been unable to find a fan. A college friend, Tom White, who had been in Segovia with her, happened to call from New York City to say he would be coming to the wedding. He asked if Julie needed anything. Julie replied, "I can't find a Spanish fan."

Tom responded, "No problem." He promptly flew to Spain and purchased a beautiful one for Julie as a wedding gift. Such a wonderful friend!

We searched endlessly for Julie's wedding dress. There was nothing available locally, so we drove to Juarez, Mexico with Ivy Rosen in search of a dress. We had a lot of fun in Juarez. We did not find a dress, but we discovered some beautiful gold charm bracelets which Julie could give as gifts to her bridesmaids. We eventually found a dress for Julie back across the border in El Paso, where we were staying.

We began to think of the wedding itself and the reception to follow as planning moved ahead with clothing for the bride and for others in the wedding. Jean Garland was on the phone saying that we just had to have the reception at Swan Lake Ranch. "I have already begun to plan for it," she said, and I thought her suggestion a lovely one.

The idea of doing something special when going from the church to the reception then began to intrigue me. I was aware of the Spanish custom that the bride and groom were driven to the bride's home in a carriage following the church ceremony, with wedding guests following behind on foot to the accompaniment of a fiddler. I thought it would be lovely if we could find a carriage in which Julie and Errol could ride from the church. With this idea in mind, I tried to contact someone at the Museum of New Mexico in Santa Fe about using one of their old carriages. Several of these carriages had been outfitted for the 1st National Bank of Santa Fe's Centennial Celebration parade in 1970. I did not have much success with my inquiries at the museum. Sam and I then remembered that our good friend, Larry Meyer, was on the Board of Directors for the 1st National Bank. I called Larry and told him about the wedding plans and about our need for a carriage. Larry listened attentively to me, and then said with an air of mystery in his voice, "Isabel, what are you and Sam doing this evening?"

"Nothing important, other than pursuing information about carriages," I replied.

Larry laughed and said, "You and Sam come on down to Santa Fe this evening. I have something to show you."

We had come to expect the interesting and unusual from Larry Meyer. When we arrived that evening, Larry drove us to the storage building attached to his office. He showed us a magnificent bright red, brand new, custom built stagecoach which was an exact replica of the stagecoaches of the old West, authentic in every detail. Larry had ordered this coach for the Bank's Centennial Parade. It was not ready in time for the parade because of the time it took to custom build it, and Larry had then taken possession of the coach when it arrived. Larry casually asked as we looked at this wonderful coach, "Do you think this coach will do for the bride and groom? There is a team of four and a driver to go with it."

Sam and I were almost speechless, but we managed to catch our breath and voice a hearty, "Absolutely!" This was not a little horse drawn cart with which I feared we might end up, but a real Cinderella carriage together with a driver and a team of four. Use of the carriage was to be Larry's and his wife, Adeline's, special wedding gift to Julie. We were delighted.

I found myself beginning to run in every direction as the wedding approached. We completed plans with Ham and Jean Garland for the reception at Swan Lake Ranch, and then turned to the final touches for the wedding. Many luncheons and showers were given for Julie in the meantime, and there was an exceptional, lovely evening dinner party for her and Errol at the home of Joan and Nathan Greer in Santa Fe. The groom wanted desperately to avoid this occasion, but his groomsmen won him over. I began to wonder, "Will the bride be left standing at the altar?"

The bridesmaids were to stay with Julie at the house. We made arrangements in the Barn to accommodate everyone, and action was at its peak. I then found myself without domestic help at the last minute when my maid said she had to be home with her husband who was ill. My friend, Naomi Cutler, came to my rescue and sent her maid, Mary Medina, to work with me. I thanked Mary for coming to help me then (and I have thanked her in my mind many times since), for not only did the bridesmaids need to be fed and housed, but parents were arriving, adding to the general confusion.

My hairdresser, O'delia, made special arrangements to do my hair, and I was then dashing to the church at the last minute to make sure of flowers and ribbons for the alter and the pews. Sam was tied up at the hospital until the last minute, so I could not count on him, and Julie and the girls were saying, "Mom, you have to slow down a little." I was not quite sure how to do that.

We were finally off to the church, where we gathered in an adjoining building prior to the ceremony. We all knew, or thought we knew, how and when to enter. I was properly escorted to our family's pew following the groom's parents, and then the bridal party assembled. The organist's music changed all at once, and the procession of the bridal party began. I was on my feet too soon in my tired and nervous state, standing for the bridesmaids as they entered, and not waiting for the bride. My knees almost buckled when I saw Sam on the wrong side of Julie as he escorted her down the aisle. No one seemed to notice, and if they did, they did not let it be known. I felt badly, but I put my feelings aside. It was time for the ceremony to begin.

The ceremony at the Santa Cruz church was wonderful. My father who was a devout Presbyterian, commented on the exceptional beauty of the interior of the Santa Cruz Catholic Church and the spiritual sense of well-being he felt there. It is a large church with a ceiling close to twenty feet high, supported by hand-hewn wooden beams and hand carved corbels.

Decorations for the wedding were simple but impressive with a seven-branch candelabra decorated with white mums and lemon leaves to create an altar effect. Bouquets of white mums lined the bride's aisle, and white ribbon bows marked the pews in which members of the family were seated. The church was filled with the more than three hundred and fifty guests. Friends came from all over the state of New Mexico, and there were relatives from out-of-state in addition to the bridesmaids, groomsmen and their parents.

The wedding party was beautifully attired in every respect. Julie looked lovely. Her dress was a traditional gown of candlelight silk organza. The close fitting bodice was fashioned with a high collar and wrist length sleeves, and the full-length skirt fell to a soft chapel train. She wore a Spanish comb in her hair that held in place her floor-length silk lace mantilla. Her lace fan had a cascade of stephanotis and white rose buds centered with a white orchid.

Julie's maid and matron of honor and her bridesmaids wore floor length gowns of a rich brown organza, similar in style to that of the bride and accented at the neck, sleeves and bodice with ivory lace. The maid and matron of honor each carried arm bouquets of Golden Rapture roses, while the bridesmaids carried arm bouquets of Tropicana roses. A single rose and a Spanish comb adorned their hair.

My dress was silk with a design of small colored flowers. I wore a tiara of tiny green velvet flowers with a short veil. My shoes were green silk.

The groom's mother, Mrs. Vangie Chavez, wore a lovely dress of gray chiffon.

The groom's best man, Eric Serna, and the groomsmen, Leroy Chavez, Samuel Ziegler, Jr., Robert Gardenhire, Peter Atencio, David Otero, and Joseph Guillen, wore full formal attire as did the father of the bride and the groom's father.

Elaine Marshall of Albuquerque consented to come and play the music for the wedding. Her nuptial music included selections from Bach, Handel and Mendelssohn, and strains of the processional from Westminister Abbey filled the church as Julie's father escorted her to the alter. Elaine and her husband, Ralph, recorded the music to give to Julie and Errol as a wedding gift. Elaine played beautifully, as always.

The real excitement began as the wedding party and the guests left the church, and Julie and Errol were ushered into the waiting stagecoach. It was quite a sight and a surprise to everyone there. Guests rushed to see the coach and then rushed to their cars to follow as the coach paraded through Española. The coach did not go as far as Swan Lake Ranch where the reception was held because of the ten mile distance and the scheduled time for the reception, but the drive through town was exciting. Channel 7 News in Albuquerque had learned about the carriage and the wedding because the team of four and the driver came from a ranch south of Santa Fe where a movie was being filmed. Channel 7 called to ask permission to film, and their cameras were on hand for the event. News of the wedding was given prominent play on TV for the next two nights, with pictures of the stagecoach and team of four.

Swan Lake Ranch was an ideal location for the reception. The weather that August was very pleasant, and the sky a clear, cloudless blue. The spacious grounds at Swan Lake with the lake and the swans provided a luxurious setting. The bride's table was beautifully set with food including shrimp and other delicacies, and champagne to serve the many guests. Everyone seemed to relax and enjoy themselves. Afterwards they all gathered to watch Julie and Errol cut the three-tiered wedding cake, and there were formal toasts from the best man and well-wishers as the Sanchez Trio of roving mariachis entertained the crowd. There was a great deal of merriment, and the bride and groom were given a proper departure for their honeymoon at Las Breeses in Acapulco, Mexico.

Errol's father, T. J. Chavez, had turned to me in the reception line, and said, "This wedding will go down in history as the most beautiful wedding ever held in New Mexico."

Bride Julie Ziegler and bridegroom Errol Chavez, board a stagecoach waiting for them after their wedding on August 14, 1971, in Santa Cruz, New Mexico.

35

CITY COUNCIL BUSINESS

The people of Española elected Santiago Martinez as their new Mayor in March of 1975. Santiago's council members included Ross Chavez, Joe Suazo, Richard Quintana, Bob Savinsky, Donald Archuleta, Alex R. Gallegos, Charlie Harkins and Sam. The administration ran quite smoothly for some time with Juan Lopez as City Manager and Art Sanchez as Business Managaer. It was all "business as usual."

Bob Savinsky then dropped a bombshell on the Council on Monday, August 11th with a motion to fire City Manager Juan Lopez. Savinsky accused Lopez of mishandling a personnel issue involving the dismissal of Police Detective Don Williams, and charged Mayor Santiago Martinez, Business Manager Art Sanchez and Lopez with "unspecified" inefficiencies. Councilmen Archuleta and Chavez supported him in this motion.

Savinsky's motion did not come entirely out of the blue. There had been rumors afoot of a move among some on the Council to seek the dismissal not only of Lopez, but also of Business Manager Art Sanchez, City Attorney Tony Scarborough, Police Chief A.B. Valdez, and City Field Superintendent Arturo Trujillo. Even then, Savinsky's call for a motion sent a divisive wrench through the Council.

As Sam remembered, the motion was tabled at the August 11th meeting following a good deal of emotional discussion, but the matter was not left there. It formed the major topic of discussion at the next Council meeting on August 25th. Over three hundred townspeople attended this meeting. Most came in support of Juan Lopez. Others were simply concerned citizens who wished to see local government run in an orderly, nonpartisan fashion.

The majority on the Council, with the strong support of the Mayor, managed to kill the motion for Lopez's dismissal, and by the time the vote was taken, Savinsky, Chavez and Archuleta had joined the majority. But Savinsky then asked the Council to adopt a "Resolution of Displeasure" reprimanding Lopez and others for their actions, and wanted the resolution aired at the September 8th meeting. City Attorney Tony Scarborough defended Lopez during discussion at the meeting on the 25th of August, saying that city ordinances had been "followed to the letter." He advised Lopez to grant Police Detective Don Williams a hearing even though such was not required by city rules, but he gave no support to the request for a "Resolution."

Headlines in *The Santa Fe New Mexican* for August 26th read: "Española keeps Lopez—Ouster move buckles," and "Española anti-manager move falters." The paper recounted the tenor of the evening's meeting:

> A crowded Española City Council meeting last night saw the council unanimously vote to drop a request for dismissal of City Manager Juan Lopez, but the manager's critics indicated they will still push for a "resolution of displeasure" with Lopez at the September 8 council meeting.[58]

Sam was a supporter and friend of Juan Lopez and the other men cited, as were the majority on the Council. He was concerned that an orderly governmental process be followed and that the Council adhere to the city manager ordinance, which stated that the city manager was to be free of political encumbrance. *The New Mexican* noted Sam's feelings, saying:

> ... the present council was the best [Ziegler] had served with in his ten-year tenure, but [he] warned that if Lopez was dismissed the city would take a ten-year step backward in time and accomplishments. Ziegler warned that if Lopez was dismissed "no one would consider coming into such an explosive situation to replace him." The usually complacent councilman called for city fathers to sit down and "work things out" with the city manager and urged the council not to be hasty in making their decision.[59]

Sam was not alone. He remembered that Dom Cimino of the Cimino Car Center called the move to dump Lopez "purely personal politics and purely personal conflicts," while Jim Thompson, former City Attorney, said, "We feel some of the gentlemen on the council are more concerned about their own petty grievances against the city manager than they are about the welfare of the citizens of this community."[60] Many city employees also raised their voices in support of Juan Lopez.

Sam made a motion at the close of discussion to drop the request to dismiss Lopez, which passed without difficulty, but the ordeal had been physically and emotionally draining for all, especially for Juan Lopez.

Proper zoning for the community of Española has always been important, because zoning is necessary for orderly growth. Española did not have any zoning when Sam became a councilman. It seemed like a town without a rudder, with mobile and temporary housing interspersed in areas which should have been reserved for permanent homes. There were also no clear demarcations between "business" and "recreation" areas. Zoning would create a more orderly growth pattern, and it would protect those who had invested in their homes in anticipation that similar permanent structures would be built around them.

Zoning had been an issue for the Council for a number of years before Sam was elected. Debate about it was usually heated, with those in opposition making statements such as "Zoning is a violation of our civil rights. Only the businessmen want it," and "We don't feel zoning will improve the city. We are capable of taking care of our own property." Councilman Richard Lucero moved in 1967 to place the matter on the ballot as a referendum, but the motion did not materialize, and the issue was left to flounder.

General concern about zoning finally led to the creation of a Zoning Committee in 1968, of which Sam became chairman. The committee worked hard for the next several years trying to develop a zoning ordinance for Española. There were problems along the way. Councilman Roy Honstein urged the city in 1970 to move forward with its work on a zoning ordinance, but Mayor Richard Lucero countered that there were vacancies on the planning commission that needed to be filled before anything could be done. Robert Trapp of the *Rio Grande SUN* was a strong proponent of zoning. He wrote a number of pointed editorials during these years, urging the Council to move ahead. For example, on December 4, 1975, he scolded the Council, saying:

Zoning? Ho hum.

City Councilman Sam Ziegler hit the nail on the head Monday night when he commented that the city has spent $75,000 on zoning ordinances, but has yet to adopt one.

City fathers talked zoning during the administrations of mayors Cipriano Vigil, Epimenio Vigil and Richard Lucero. Discussions continue under the mayorship of Santiago Martinez.
For the city to have zoning, city council action is necessary. Action requires courage. Neither has been forthcoming, because zoning is a politically touchy issue and it's been impossible to get a majority on any council with the guts to tackle the issue.

In the meantime, the weird, helter-skelter growth of our city continues—with council encouragement.[61]

Then on December 25th, he applauded:

City councilmen are to be commended for . . . action taken Monday night that might not be too popular in some quarters but showed the council can face up to its responsibilities.
Councilmen turned down a proposal that a public referendum beheld on zoning . . .

. . .

Mayor Santiago Martinez indicated that regardless of the results of a zoning referendum "we know it (zoning) eventually will be good for the community."

There are times public officials have to make decisions that are unpopular with many of the voters, but they know in the long haul the community will benefit. This is one of the instances.

As Councilman Sam Ziegler declared, if the council doesn't do it, it will never get done. This council should make the decision as soon as possible.[62]

The Zoning committee brought an ordinance before the Council for consideration in January of 1976, after more than seven years of study and preparation. The ordinance was formulated following extensive consultation with lawyers and officials from other cities with such ordinances already in place, and with officers from the State Organization of Cities, a group of city officials whose sole purpose was to pool experience and knowledge in order to offer advice in situations such as ours. It appeared to be a workable plan. Sam said it was easy to understand, and would lead to the development of a more organized city while protecting individual property rights.

The ordinance outlined:

1. Permanent housing areas where buildings must be permanent homes on lots no less than 6,000 sq. ft. This area was to be off-limits to business activity.
2. Areas for trailers and mobile homes parks or "less permanent" housing.
3. "Business Area" where permanent structures could be located but not restricted to private use.
4. "Rural areas" where farming and raising of animals could be carried on along with business related to such activities.
5. Open spaces and recreational areas.

Bob Savinsky was a City Councilman with whom Sam generally agreed. But Bob was against passage of the ordinance, and he encouraged a number of mobile home owners and people living in semi-permanent dwellings to attend the Council meeting the night the ordinance was to come up for discussion and vote. Those in favor of zoning were not well-represented. Exchanges moved from calm to lively to heated during the discussion, and carried over from Council members to members of the audience, who took the opportunity to voice their opinions. City Council meetings were open meetings and usually attended by public spirited individuals. It was assumed that informed and interested people representing both the pros and cons of the issue would attend, and that it would not be a meeting stacked with individuals who had been brought there to support one point of view. Those present were a loud, rude bunch who voiced a sharp dislike for the ordinance. It had never occurred that the "pro faction" would need to do some stacking of its own.

Bob Savinsky and Sam became more riled up than others on the Council as discussion progressed. The exchanges were sharp and heated, and their argumentation ended only when there was a motion to table the discussion, which passed.

The ordinance was finally adopted by a 5-2 vote in the Council on February 9, 1976, but only after more debate with Savinsky. Savinsky and Joe Suazo were the two councilors who voted against it. Savinsky said, in a last ditch effort to postpone passage of the ordinance, that "citizens were not expecting the vote...and [he] introduced the possibility of another public hearing to air suggestions for amendments and changes."[63] City Attorney Tony Scarborough ruled that an additional public hearing was not necessary, sufficient discussion having been given through the public hearing in January. The Council accepted several changes suggested at the last month's public hearing involving mobile homes and sign regulations before taking the final vote. These changes included giving people who occupied properties that were 6,000 sq. ft. or larger two years to live in a mobile home, at the end of which time a permanent home had to be on the way or the mobile or temporary structure moved off the property.

Savinsky and Sam again seemed to be at cross-points during much of the discussion. *The New Mexican* for February 10th quoted Sam as saying:

> "I object to councilman Savinsky's allegation that we are taking our moral obligation lightly. He has put us on the spot, making us look like a bunch of jerks. I don't think anyone here is shirking his moral obligations. Anyone that votes here tonight is showing intestinal fortitude.
> "A lot of thought and prayer has gone into this. Most of us will vote according to the dictates of our conscience," Ziegler continued.[64]

The ordinance was challenged in the court immediately after it was passed. Among the challengers listed were Democratic County chairman and County Sheriff Emilio Naranjo, and Española businessmen Richard Cook, E.S. Delgado, Thomas Vigil, Leandro Quintana and Manuel E. Lujan. Mayor Santiago Martinez questioned Emilio Naranjo's motives and remarked that the challenge was "a political move." *The New Mexican* went on to note:

> Naranjo recently endorsed a slate of four candidates for Española's city council elections. Martinez said Naranjo's court action "is an effort to find things wrong with the present administration and council in order to get his candidates into office."[65]

The challenge died a natural death. No further action ensued, and the Mayor proceeded to name five local citizens to a new Planning and Zoning Commission. The members included Roman Martinez, Eddie Martinez, Josie Roybal, Leonel Gallegos, and William R. Sackett. This commission, appointed early in the game, functioned very well.

Sam was chairman of Española's Beautification Committee during the 1976 Bicentennial Year. Everyone felt the city should make a special effort to celebrate, and decided after much thought and discussion, that it would be great to do something with the figures "76." The Council gave full approval to move ahead, and our Maintenance Department under Arturo Trujillo made a large number of two feet high, six feet long "boxes" in the configuration of "7s" and "6s", which could be used as "planters."

The planters were placed on all of the traffic islands, one set for the smaller islands, and two for the larger ones. Arturo and his men really fell into the spirit of the occasion and finished these planters in record time. They were placed on the islands so they read "76" as people drove by. The workmen could hardly wait to get dirt in them and plant flowers. Red, white and blue petunias were used, and they were planted as early as possible in order to have a showing of color. Our highways were ablaze with red, white and blue once they were in full bloom. The same theme in plantings was carried out around all city buildings. A general clean-up campaign was also held late in the Spring of 1976, with many individuals and businesses coordinating efforts throughout the city. Española took on a new polish and luster.

Sam had the great honor of accepting the State Bicentennial Beautification Award. This was the award given to the community which had the best beautification and cleanup program. Governor and Mrs. Jerry Apodaca presented the award during ceremonies at the state capitol Roundhouse in mid-November of that year. Elberta Honstein, Rosemary "Kue" Hunter and I were "the three-women who spearheaded the committee that coordinated a city-wide effort to beautify and clean-up Española," 66 and we attended this special occasion along with Sam.

An "appreciation ceremony" was held at the November 15th City Council meeting to recognize the tremendous efforts local citizens had made toward the beautification of the city. The *SUN* carried a nice article about this meeting:

The monthly city council meeting was packed to capacity Monday night as Councilmember Dr. Samuel Ziegler acknowledged members of the community who helped to win the state Bicentennial Beautification Award.

Ziegler said that Española received the highest award in the state in the beautification and cleanup program.

"It all goes to show," he said, "that Española can do it if we all band together. We have one of the best settings in the country and we ought to have pride enough in our valley to fit in."

The project, Ziegler said, involved hard work throughout the summer and Arturo Trujillo, Richard Quintana, and Tony Martinez were in on helping from the beginning of the endeavor and faithfully helped all summer.

Ziegler recognized Francis Haden for designing all the flower arrangements [around the city buildings].

Several businesses were outstanding, he said. Charlie Harkins was commended for the cleanup of his business. Richard Lucero "did a fine job," he said. He also mentioned the Arrow Motel and Million Electric Company on the Taos Highway, saying "they did a good job" of keeping to the red, white and blue motif.

Paul Trujillo was commended for advising many of the youth organizations.

Phil Trujillo was recognized for supplying and helping with the trees for the median.

The Española schools, McCurdy and Holy Cross schools were commended.[67]

1976 was an exciting year around Española. There was a great demonstration of community pride and cooperation. People were enthusiastic about what was taking place, and about how nice their town could look. Española showed what it can do when we all work together toward a common goal.

Española City Council, 1970s. Sam (left, seated) served as mayor pro-tem. Connie Salazar Thompson (seated center) was mayor.

36

SAM'S BID FOR STATE POLITICAL OFFICE
THE 1978 SENATE CAMPAIGN
DISTRICT 5

Matias Chacon, Democratic State Senator from District 5, died suddenly of heart failure in February of 1977, during his second four-year term in the state senate.

Matt's death came as a shock to all of us. It meant the loss of a real political leader in Rio Arriba County and in the state of New Mexico. He had entered politics in Rio Arriba and run successfully as a Democrat in opposition to the hand-picked slate of candidates put forward by the Rio Arriba Democratic Party Chairman and local political boss, Emilio Naranjo. Those of us who knew Matt also supported him because of his courage to stand up against Emilio Naranjo.

The Rio Arriba County Commission appointed Emilio Naranjo to fill Matias Chacon's vacant seat in the Senate a week after he died. Naranjo took over the office of State Senator for District 5 in February of 1977, and began to participate in the on-going legislative session in Santa Fe.

Emilio Naranjo's appointment was of interest and concern to many of us. He had been chairman of the local Democratic Party since 1952, and had been closely involved with law enforcement, serving several terms as County Sheriff and as U.S. Marshall. He had also been the County Law Enforcement Officer, and was now County Manager for Rio Arriba. All of us were aware that it was through his control over local county commissioners, those persons elected to set policy on how the county operated, that he ran the county. Until recently, all three county commissioners had been Democrats from his slate.

Sam took care of Emilio as a patient on several occasions for minor complaints in the late 1940s. He certainly knew that he was caring for someone of importance in Rio Arriba County. When he became involved in city politics, he became very aware of the influence Naranjo tried to exert on the City Council.

Matias Chacon's death and Naranjo's assumption of his vacant Senate seat provided the stimulus Sam needed to reconsider his involvement in politics. He now had the time to undertake such an involvement because he was no longer in private practice. He felt it was the right moment for him to put in his bid for an open, more representative government in Rio Arriba.

Sam made his final decision to run against Emilio at the Annual Republican Rally, held at the Shipman Jailhouse Ranch in Nambé in mid-1977. Frances Shipman was leader of the New Mexico Republican Party, and was well recognized locally and in Washington, D.C. Sam first spoke with me at the rally and then sought out Frances. I was with him when he told her he would like to give Emilio "a run for his money." Frances immediately smiled and said, "This is interesting news. I must get word to the committee, and will let you know." Sam's talk with Frances created a political undercurrent that really rocked the rally.

Word soon got out that Emilio Naranjo's Senate seat was open for re-election and that Sam was interested in running against him. Sam officially announced his candidacy for the State Senate seat, District 5, on October 15, 1977 at a fund raising dinner at the Lucero Center in Española. Tony J. Montoya, Rio Arriba County Republican Party Chairmen, and Ethel Schwiner and Cruz Trujillo, Co-Chairpersons of the County Republican Party Organization, were there lending their support and encouragement. U.S. Senators Pete Domenici, Harrison Schmitt, and U.S. Congressman Manuel Lujan were also present along with Republican gubernatorial candidate Joe Skeen. Richard Cook of Española was Master of Ceremonies for the occasion. It was an exciting and highly successful evening. Those in attendance were very enthusiastic and generated a lot of support.

David Roybal, an influential and respected reporter and columnist for *The New Mexican*, wrote a very positive article about Sam's candidacy the day after his announcement:

> Ziegler, a physician and surgeon in the Española Valley for 30 years, said he will run to "bring dignity and honesty" to Rio Arriba County politics.

Mentioning his decades of work as a doctor in the Valley, Ziegler told the persons at Saturday's dinner, "The time has come when I'd like to serve you in another way."

His announcement drew a standing ovation from the more than 125 persons in attendance.

Domenici, aware of the Democratic strength in Rio Arriba, praised Ziegler for having the "courage" to seek election to the state senate.[68]

Two days later, Roybal wrote in his column "Rio Arriba Style," saying:

> Major fundraising efforts are part of the blitz that GOP Chairman Tony J. Montoya plans to direct at Rio Arriba Democrats in coming months.
>
> Montoya is already eyeing next year's political campaign with enthusiasm.
>
> After Saturday's dinner he talked almost as optimistically as he did last November, moments after it was learned that Republican Harrison Schmitt had upset U.S. Sen. Joseph Montoya.
>
> Tony had cause to be happy Saturday. He was pleased with the turnout at the fund-raising dinner. His work as county GOP chairman had been described as "great" and "excellent" by state Republican Chairman Garrey Carruthers and U.S. Rep. Manuel Lujan. *And, he had heard Dr. Samuel Ziegler, a respected man throughout the Valley, announce he will run under the GOP banner for the state senate.*
>
> *Ziegler, a 12-year Española city councilman, is one of the most attractive candidates to emerge from the local GOP organization in a long time."*
>
> ...Ziegler has developed a reputation as a soft-spoken conciliator in the Española City Council.
>
> He quickly made new friends Saturday when he said he hopes to bring to Rio Arriba County politics the same "honesty and dignity" that Lujan, Schmitt, and Sen. Pete Domenici have displayed at the national level.[69]

Not all responses to Sam's candidacy were positive. One phone call turned out to be a crank call. It was from someone who said he was calling on behalf of several interested persons, all of whom would be happy to support Sam if he would "see they got a case of good wine now and then." Sam responded with a polite "No, thank you." He was both amused and a little unsettled. He knew he was in for some education about the realities of campaigning and dealing with the public.

The tempo of events began to quicken with the coming of March, 1978. Sam received a letter from the New Mexico Republican Legislative Campaign Committee informing him of all the things he needed to do to ensure that his candidacy was in good order. The Rio Arriba County Republican Convention was held at the Lucero Center on Sunday, March 5th. Republican gubernatorial candidate Joe Skeen and Republican State Senator Bill Valentine of Albuquerque appeared on Sam's behalf.

This rally coincided with the City Elections just two days away on March 7th. Sam was up for re-election to the City Council along with a number of other councilmen. He ran on incumbent Mayor Santiago Martinez's "Independents for Responsible Government" slate. Charlie Bermant noted in an article in the *Albuquerque Journal* that:

> A two-year term in Ward 3 is being sought by incumbent Dr. Sam Ziegler of the mayor's slate ["Independents for Responsible Government"] and former councilman and local businessman Bob Savinsky. Ziegler has been on the council for 12 years and was a practicing physician in the Española Valley for 30 years.
>
> For the past year and a half, however, Ziegler has worked in Los Alamos. This, along with the fact he is a declared candidate for State Sen. Emilio Naranjo's seat later in the year, has provided the basis for anti-Ziegler sentiment.
>
> "I feel I can provide the value of experience without kowtowing to any machine," Ziegler said. "I'll give the people independent representation, and an honest return for their election investment.
>
> "Even though I do work in Los Alamos, I've made it a point to stay in touch here. My friends are here. My social and church life is centered in the valley."[70]

The City Council race involved a lot of door-to-door campaigning on the Mayor's slate. The ticket included Joe B. Romero, a former city police chief now running for city magistrate, and five running for councilman positions from the different wards. The councilmen were Eugene Sandoval, Henry Valencia, Consuelo "Connie" Thompson, Alex R. Gallegos and Sam.

All were elected except Joe Romero. He was defeated by incumbent Ernesto Vigil, who had been City Judge for twenty years. Ernesto was heavily supported by Democratic county Chairman Emilio Naranjo, and was the only winner from Naranjo's "For The People" ticket. This was a good omen for the Independents.

All on the winning ticket celebrated their victories at The Top of the Hill, Pres and Marie Garcia's night club in Española. Sam used the occasion to launch his campaign for the State Senate seat against Emilio, and received a great deal of support from those present.

The *SUN* carried an editorial about the municipal election entitled "Wise Decision:"

> Voters of Española deserve credit for their emphatic rejection at the polls of the ticket supported by Democratic boss Emilio Naranjo. Unfortunately, Naranjo probably took down with him a couple of good council prospects but they realized this was one of the occupational hazards of the political game.
>
> To have turned city hall over to Naranjo could well have been a disaster of the first magnitude and the solid majority for Mayor Santiago Martinez and his council candidates demonstrates that the voters were aware of this.
>
> This vote also shows the confidence they have in Martinez to continue to give an honest administration and one that faces up to its fiscal responsibilities. Taxpayers are becoming increasingly aware of governmental waste and its effect on their pocket books and Martinez sympathizes with this.
>
> Tuesday's election was indeed a critical one for the future of Española and we are confident the citizens made the right decision.[71]

These were important words for the primaries lay directly ahead.

Sam had some discussion with Matias Chacon's son, Matthew, during the celebration at The Top of the Hill about the race for the Senate against Emilio. Matthew had a following, but after he spoke with Sam, he and his family decided to throw their support behind Sam in view of Sam's twelve years experience on the City Council and his position in the community as a physician. The campaign was now getting under way. Tony Montoya and Ethel Schwiner soon came much more into the picture.

Pres and Marie Garcia were gracious, friendly and generous-hearted people whose support we appreciated throughout the campaign.

We were all encouraged by the good words in the *SUN*:

Republicans are prepared to work hard for Ziegler, probably the strongest candidate they've put forth in years.[72]

The Primary Election took place on June 6th. Sam received his Certificate of Nomination as the Republican candidate for State Senator from District 5 shortly thereafter. He was unopposed in the primary, but there were three on the ballot for the November election: Emilio Naranjo and Sam from the Democratic and Republican parties respectively, and a third party candidate, Antonio "Ike" DeVargas, Chairman of the La Raza Unida Party. DeVargas's campaign was very much a grass roots movement. DeVargas was a Marine veteran who did not like the local "dictatorship" in Rio Arriba under Emilio Naranjo that he found upon his return from Vietnam, and had decided to try and do something about it.[73]

Local papers wrote articles immediately after the primary which set a general tone for the campaign and marked the undercurrents. The *Rio Grande SUN*'s editorial for June 8th, stated, for example:

Monday's deluge perhaps could have been an omen for Anti-Naranjo Democrats in Rio Arriba County, for what didn't fall Monday [June 5] certainly crashed down around their ears Tuesday [June 6]. Predictions that "This is the Year" fell flat as Democratic boss Emilio Naranjo marched his loyal troops to the polls for another primary triumph.

There is no magic to this. It is simply good, sound grassroots politics whose basic premise is "get out the vote."

Emilio is still the Professor of Practical Politics in New Mexico, and until another Professor comes along, who is willing and able to devote the time, effort and money to it and get the anti-Naranjo vote to the polls, Emilio will continue delivering his regular lectures. [74]

This same edition of the *SUN* rightly noted that the Republicans could not overlook the candidacy of Ike DeVargas and the presence of a third party on the ballot:

> . . . observers are preparing for the scrap between Naranjo and Republican Sam Ziegler this fall in the general election.
> . . . Virtually all of the votes DeVargas will get [however] will come off of Ziegler's support, and DeVargas will certainly pull some votes. . .
> *Raza Unida, who has kept Emilio in and out of court for the past few years, may well guarantee that he stays in the state senate.* [75]

There appeared to be much room for optimism at the same time. David Roybal of *The New Mexican* wrote, for example:

> Looking ahead now to the general election, county Republicans went through a quiet primary campaign with only the District 1 commission post contested.
> The party has some attractive candidates set to compete in the election. . . There is Dr. Samuel Ziegler who is challenging Naranjo for the District 5 State senate seat; . . .[76]

There was constant campaign activity from mid-June on, with many long, tiresome hours of work. The Republican candidates usually traveled as a group and included Joe Lujan running for County Assessor, Manuel "Gordo" Sena running for County Sheriff, and Sam. Others involved were Tony Montoya, Ethel Schwiner, Ramona Vigil Chavez, a faithful campaign volunteer, and often Cruz Trujillo, the Honorary Campaign Chairman from Tierra Amarilla. Ethel's husband, Jim Schwiner, usually drove. I also generally went along with the group to campaign.

There was a large GMC van for transportation. We covered Rio Arriba County like a blanket, seeking out the most remote areas from Arroyo Seco in the south to Chama and Dulce in the north, and from Chimayo in the east to Youngsville and Coyote in the west. Felipe Suazo who was running for County Commissioner, joined us when traveling to the Los Ojos and Chama areas.

Much of the local campaigning was done after work in the evenings, reserving the weekends for day-long excursions into more distant areas. Chimayo or Alcalde or Velarde were all easily accessible in a short time, and there was campaigning in small groups in private homes until nine or ten o'clock at night.

The group made a number of trips to Youngsville, Gallina, Regina and Lindrith in the mid-western part of the county, and we were amazed how many homes in these sparsely populated areas had what appeared to be vicious dogs to protect them.

People often turned out to be patients of Sam's in many of the communities and on the isolated farms. People would run out and throw their arms around him, exclaiming, "Dr. Ziegler! We are so glad to see you and know that you are running." But then they would say, "Dr. Ziegler, we are afraid to vote for a Republican." People rarely said why they were afraid, but sometimes they would comment that they thought they would not get their welfare or social security checks if they did not vote for Naranjo. Naranjo seemed to have tight control over money funds. People believed he was the one who saw they received their money. They would be responsive to our explanations and our requests for support, but in most instances, their fears overcame their desire to vote for our group.

There was an exciting luncheon at the home of Roy and Elberta Honstein in Fairview on July 26th. The Honsteins sponsored the affair for Republican women and did it in fine style. The food was delicious and the conversation stimulating. Those invited were women from Española and Rio Arriba County who had been active in local political, business and social affairs. Sam was considered the "guest of honor," and gave his usual pitch. The featured guest was Francine I. Neff, former Treasurer of the United States. She spoke about the financial position of the U.S. government and was most informative.

Sam's mementos from this occasion are several one and two dollar bills which bear Francine I. Neff's signature. He talked with a number of women after the luncheon about issues pertinent to the campaign.

During this time, Sam received an undated letter from Antonio "Ike" DeVargas, the La Raza Unida candidate. The letter disturbed him. DeVargas wrote to question Sam's motives and to intimate that he was in the race only to represent the wealthier interests in the county. He wrote:

> As you know, I'll be one of your opponents in the race and am deeply concerned about your motive for entering the race at all. First of all, I don't believe you have any knowledge of the very special needs that the people here have. Secondly, I believe that you will represent the same interests that Emilio does, specifically the Cooks, the Dentons, the Brashars, & Bill Mundy to name a few. These interests do not reflect the needs of the people of the county and they along with Emilio are at the heart of Land, Water And [*sic*] economic problems of this county. Thirdly, I know that you were not even nominated to this candidacy by your Party's central committee. I understand that you nominated yourself which gives me reason to suspect that you may have been moved by desire to insure [*sic*] Emilio Naranjo's position & thus maintain the status quo.
> Obviously, this is an intolerable situation and it would be outragious [*sic*] for it to continue, therefore I propose that you resign your candidacy and end the charade. This is the only right thing for you to do, anything less is a disservice to the voter of Rio Arriba County. You must know of course that you can't ride on Domenici & Lujan's coattails here.[77]

Sam felt compelled to respond to DeVargas's letter and wrote to DeVargas on July 11th:

> I feel I owe you the courtesy of an answer to your recent undated letter, even though you did not grant me the courtesy of receiving it before a copy [of your letter] was given to the press.
> In the first paragraph of your letter, you state three reasons why I should drop out of the race. I hope you are better informed on the pertinent issues of the campaign than you are about me. All

three of your reasons could not be further from the true facts.

I fail to see why the situation is intolerable. My candidacy has been well received throughout Rio Arriba County and New Mexico in general. Withdrawal from the Senatorial race is unthinkable, for me. I look forward to a well-fought, clean and honorable race. [78]

DeVargas sent no further challenges Sam's way, nor did Sam encourage him to withdraw from the race. He knew DeVargas was adamant about running and carrying forth his cause against Emilio. It is of note that had DeVargas not injected himself into the race, Sam's chances of victory would have been much brighter.

I sent out a mailing during the summer, trying to add my own personal support to Sam's efforts:

Dear Friends,

Throughout this campaign, I have wanted to write to you about my husband, Sam Ziegler, and his race for the State Senate, District 5.

I have been his wife for 38 years and know him well. He is honest and truthful—always giving consideration to problems before making decisions. Sam cares about others, and is tireless in his efforts for them.

He is truly a fine man. As your State Senator, I know that you can trust him to help create the kind of state you and I want for our families.

Please vote for Sam on Election Day, Tuesday, November 7th. [79]

Sam and his campaign crew targeted Ojo Caliente, Tres Piedras and several small communities just below the Colorado border, including Los Pinos and San Miguel for campaign visits early one Saturday late-July. We had to drive north to Antonito, Colorado and then west on State road 17 for about ten miles where they cut south on a poorly graded dirt road just across the border to reach Los Pinos and San Miguel. These communities did not have more than twenty or thirty people each. They were supposedly strongly Democratic, but according to information Tony

Montoya had received, they were also very unhappy with Emilio.

Our group were warmly received and Sam met several of his patients. We spent a number of hours discussing local needs. The primary thing people here complained about was the condition of their road. They said that Emilio promised them road maintenance, but never did anything until just before election day. They wanted someone who would take a real interest in their community. We went into these small villages not to tear down the opponent, but to let people know that they were interested in them and their needs, and that we would try to represent them in the legislature in an honest and sincere way.

People responded to their words, and as we were leaving, they assured us of their support. We handed out "Sam Ziegler for Senate" bumper stickers, and personally stuck stickers on all of the useable transportation in both villages. Certainly, a huge number of friends were not made in the two small communities, but we hoped we had gained some real advocates. Tony Montoya was again fantastic and amazed the group with how many contacts he had.

The group this day included Ramona Vigil Chavez, Gordo Sena, Joe Lujan, Tony Montoya, Cruz Trujillo, Sam and myself. We spent a pleasant, comfortable and productive day together. Some of the talk as we drove was about the campaign, some was just light and frivolous, with occasional more serious conversation about the national political scene.

The darkness of the night began to settle in as we made our way back. Joe Lujan was driving the van. Cruz Trujillo, who had made a great hit in the small communities we had just visited, was beside Joe in the front seat. Tony Montoya, Sam and I were in the middle seat, with Ramona and Gordo in the back. We took time to cut across from U.S. Highway 285 at Tres Piedras to Tierra Amarilla on U.S. Highway 84 in order to check with some supporters there. It began to rain as we passed Ghost Ranch and headed south toward Abiquiu. Visibility was poor at times. Then, just as we passed Abiquiu, Cruz Trujillo suddenly shouted, "Watch out for the cows!" Joe swerved the van and we saw a white cow run past on the right side. The next thing we knew there was a loud "Whammm!" The van struck a cow we could not see with such force that it took us fifteen minutes to find it after we had screeched to a halt and gotten out to see what had happened. The night was pitch black, and it was raining hard. We finally discovered the cow off to the right of the road deep in a ditch. It had been killed upon impact

Gordo was a cattle man, and was able to bleed it and save the meat for the owner.

The front of the van was so badly damaged that the van was no longer serviceable. Cruz Trujillo exclaimed once he got his voice back what a frightening experience it had been for him. We were all shaken, but none of us appeared injured except Ramona and Gordo, who had suffered some whiplash injury.

We did not have to wait long in the darkness and rain. As luck would have it, a State Policeman traveling north to Chama appeared out of the darkness within minutes of the accident and stopped to help. He took us to a little bar at the inter-section of the Chama Highway and the El Rito road (U.S 84 and State Road 94) after assessing the situation, and then radioed State Police Headquarters in Española for transportation for us back to town. A tow truck soon arrived.

Campaigning in August was as intensive as that in July. Travel was by private cars in convoy now that the van was no longer useable.

Several trips were made to visit the Jicarilla Apaches in Dulce and we were able to spend time with key people at their City Hall. Ramona Vigil Chavez was instrumental in making initial contacts here. Dulce had always gone Democratic, but after meeting with people there and talking to them about the philosophy of open government with proper representation as opposed to heavy-handed rule by a small group, they seemed to understand the difference and appeared more open to supporting Sam.

August 12th was a busy day with an early morning drive of ninety miles to Chama where we rode in the Chama Fiesta Parade in Bill Mundy's buggy. Ben Maestas and Sam had lunch with Senator Domenici at noon, and absorbed some of his wisdom.

Our daughter, Julie, her children, Lisa and the twins, Dustin and Duane, and Sam's father, then ninety-four years old, were along on this occasion. Sam's father had come from Ohio for a visit during the campaign. He got a kick out of riding on the float in Chama parade. He was still surprisingly active, and enjoyed accompanying us on many of our visitations and meetings with senior citizens and others in the area. He had written a letter to Sam some days earlier. He said:

The enclosed is for your birthday, August 22. It is a contribution for your political campaign fund. It is small compared to the investment you are making, but it is contributed by a father who believes in his son and has confidence that he will always do what he knows and believes to be true and right.

I hope and pray that you may win in the election, but if not be prepared to take defeat like a man. It may be God's plan to have you serve in some other and larger way.[80]

We rushed back from Chama to Santa Clara Pueblo in Judy Rowley's new van and spent time with our friends, Joseph Lonewolf, Grace Medicine Flower, Teresita Naranjo and Sandy Salazar, eating too much of their delicious Santa Clara Day food. We went from there to a Benefit Dance at the Española High School Prather Gymnasium for Joe Salazar, who was running for County Commissioner. Joe was a long standing patient and good friend of Sam's. We gave him all the support we could. We dragged home about midnight, exhausted but feeling as though we had had a productive day.

August 19th was an exciting and very different day for us. We spent most of it in Abiquiu, campaigning and attending the 50th Wedding Anniversary of Frank and Dorothea Martinez. We mingled with numerous patients and friends on this special occasion. A few days later we were at Alva Simpson's Rancho de Abiquiu planning for the big September 10th Republican Bar-B-Que, which all big-wigs were to attend. Alva and Julianna Simpson, Birky Cole, who was the Simpson's secretary and hostess, Joe Medina, Tony Montoya, Cruz Trujillo, and Jim and Ethel Schwiner were there. It was a productive day spent dealing with all of the logistics for the big day. Catering, beer trucks, cold drinks of all kinds, a dance band, and other matters all had to be considered.

At the end of the first week in September, David Roybal of *The New Mexican* wrote of the campaign to date:

One of the more interesting general election races here is Naranjo's match up for the District 5 State Senate seat with Republican Samuel Ziegler and Antonio DeVargas.

DeVargas contends Naranjo's record is riddled with corruption, and he intends to continue his dogged pressure on the county political boss. It is doubtful that Naranjo will be able to completely disregard that pressure, much of which grows out of valid complaints.

But for now he talks only of Ziegler. He said a few days ago, "The race is going to be based on what he had done as a councilman and what I have done for the county in the 45 days as a state senator for Rio Arriba."

"He's a nice man. I have respect for the man." Naranjo said of Ziegler late last week. But he confidently claimed voters will choose him over Ziegler once records are compared.

Ziegler has repeatedly pledged to "bring dignity and honesty" to Rio Arriba County politics.

"I'm going to run a campaign on what I have to offer," he said soon after announcing his candidacy. As Naranjo boasts of his record, so too is Ziegler proud of his.

But records not always determine the outcome of political races. There is more to a successful campaign than a simple presentation of one's record.

For Ziegler, DeVargas and the other underdogs of Rio Arriba's political races this year, the directions which their campaigns take after Sunday are more important.[81]

I am spending considerable time talking about Sam's decision to enter politics at this level because the events were an interesting and enlightening experience for me and my entire family. I was quite proud of Sam taking on this challenge, and I wanted to support him in every possible way. I knew Sam was sincere and honest in wanting to improve conditions in the Valley. My only concern had been that the pressure of campaigning and the barbs being thrown would be too stressful, But Sam seemed to thrive and was totally immersed in his campaign.

September 10th was a big day at Rancho de Abiquiu. Great festivities were staged by the State Republican Party Organization on behalf of Rio Arriba County. The "festivities" began about 1:00 p.m. when a number of us gathered at the Española airport to meet the aircraft carrying our honored guests. It was an exciting moment for us as we greeted the passengers. U.S. Senators Pete Domenici and Harrison Schmitt were first out of the plane. It was especially exciting to greet Senator Schmitt, who not long before had been one of the first men to walk on the moon. U.S.

Congressman Manuel Lujan followed, then gubernatorial candidate Joe Skeen, New Mexico Republican Party Chairman Garrey Carruthers, Jack Simmons and others.

We set out from the airport for Rancho de Abiquiu, State police and City police leading the caravan. More people joined as the convoy progressed north on State Rd 84 through Hernandez, Medanales and on to Abiquiu. We must have had a parade a mile long by the time we passed through Abiquiu. We were warmly greeted for this special New Mexico Republican Rally by our hosts Alva and Julianna Simpson and some three thousand early arrivals, that welcomed us enthusiastically at Rancho de Abiquiu.

The band started playing, setting an exciting pace for people to greet and talk and enjoy food.

The atmosphere was vibrant. A woman, believed to be a patient of Dr. Sam's, grabbed him by the arm and took him whirling to the area for dancing. From then on, it was an exciting and fun political afternoon and evening.

David Roybal of *The New Mexican* wrote of this event:

> The rally was the first major 1978 general election campaign effort of Rio Arriba County Republicans.
>
> State candidates, after landing in separate planes about noon at the small Española airport, were driven to the Simpson ranch as part of a large auto caravan that followed a police escort through Española.
>
> Dr. Samuel Ziegler, opposing Naranjo ... expressed satisfaction with the larger-than-expected turnout at Sunday's rally.
>
> "Rio Arriba County and northern New Mexico is coming alive," he told persons who cheered and danced with candidates as they were introduced.[82]

The *Albuquerque Journal* estimated the crowd at three thousand, and noted that Domenici, while on his way back to Albuquerque following the rally, had said, "the large crowd at the barbeque was a 'tribute to our organization in Rio Arriba county. I think we may win some offices up there in the election.'"[83]

A campaign mailing was distributed on Sam's behalf early in October. It really helped to kick the campaign into high gear. It read:

Dear Citizens of Rio Arriba,

"Sam Ziegler, a change that makes sense." Sam Ziegler, a fresh and active change from the tired old ways of the past. That is what Sam Ziegler means for you and your family.

Let us all "thank you," but let us say "good-bye" to the kind of representation that has lost touch, that doesn't respond, that just doesn't care anymore.

Sam Ziegler has lived here and worked here and is aware of the problems of Rio Arriba. We are asking you to vote on Tuesday, November 7, for Sam Ziegler—A Change That Makes Sense." Sam Ziegler, a Senator we can be proud of.

Sincerely,
Ramon Velarde Avenicio and Rebecca Lucero
Josie Velarde   Tony J. Montoya
Dolph & Gwen Pringle   Pablo & Ramona Chavez
Ethel Schwiner Horace & Nathalia DeVargas
Cruz Trujillo   Kue Hunter
Joe & Judy Vigil   Gene Finch [84]

The culmination to much of the campaigning came on October 7th, when the State Republican Organization held a $75-a-plate dinner at the Albuquerque Convention Center. President Ronald Reagan and George Bush, Sr. were present along with gubernatorial candidate Joe Skeen and over one thousand well-wishers and contributors. This evening had an air of intense excitement for us. The Master of Ceremonies, Garrey Carruthers, Chairman of the State Republican Party, began introducing important Republicans from different areas of the state as the evening's activities began. Out of the clear blue sky and much to Sam's surprise, Carruthers asked him to come up on the stage and be recognized. As he approached the head table, Carruthers introduced him as "Sam Ziegler, whom we compliment for having the courage and the fortitude to run against Emilio Naranjo." Sam received a standing ovation.

I came away from all this excitement much encouraged about Sam's chances in the election to come. I was very proud of his performance during the busy campaigning, and I managed, somehow, to have President Reagan autograph a napkin for me.

In late October 1978, Sam delivered a radio address to help shift his campaign into high gear:

> Good Morning. This is Dr. Sam Ziegler, your candidate for State Senator, District No. 5. Throughout this campaign, my fellow Republican candidates and I have run a positive campaign, allowing you to judge us on what we have to offer in terms of honesty, sincerity, experience and a real desire to serve the people of Rio Arriba County and northern New Mexico.
>
> The time has come, however, to set the record straight. You have heard that if the Democrats do not get in, you will lose your low income housing. This is absolutely not true. You have heard if the Democrats do not get in, you will lose your Welfare benefits. This is absolutely not true. You have heard that if the Democrats do not get in, your food stamps will be taken away from you. This is absolutely not true. You have heard that the Democrats are the ones who "passed the Indigent Hospital fund."… This is absolutely not true. The general public, you as taxpayers, voted that fund in, out of the goodness of your hearts, and you meant it to be used to alleviate suffering and privation. You did not mean it to become a political football in the hands of the Democrats.
>
> My opponent has questioned my work, Dr. Sam Ziegler's work, on the City Council for the past twelve years. I was elected to the City Council four times by overwhelming majorities. This is certainly an indication of accomplishment and approval of service to a community. One only has to look at the progress that has come about in Española over the past 12 years to see the many things that have been done. This is due to a City Council working together unselfishly, and for the people of Española and northern New Mexico… I can point to a new neighborhood facility, a new City Hall and Criminal Justice complex, a balanced city budget as evidence of some of the things that have

been accomplished in cooperation with my fellow councilmen.

I would like to define my stand, on right-to-work legislation. It is the divine right of everyone to have the opportunity to earn a living for himself and his family. It is an infringement on man's freedoms, as guaranteed by our constitution, to force him to join an organization in order to get a job. I am not anti-union. I know in the past unions have done much for the working man. This is a highly emotional issue and I will study all such legislation thoroughly and if such an issue comes to vote, I will honestly and truly try to reflect the feelings of those I represent. Remember! Right-to-work does not mean one cannot belong to a union. It merely protects your right to choose.

I have been accused of being a liar because I said I was for lower taxes and still voted for a ½ cent increase in the gross receipts tax. As a representative of our people, I feel this slight increase in tax shared by outlying community residents was more preferable to the good people of this Valley than a much more burdensome increase in water and sewer rates, and certainly preferable to contaminated wells and raw sewage on the surface. I am strongly in favor of taking the gross receipts tax off of food, medical care, prescription drugs and medical supplies, and this I will work for. I am not a liar. There is always an honest reason for what I say and have done.

I have continued to work for my living during my campaign. I campaign during my off hours and my employer gets full return for his dollar. My opponent has campaigned constantly for several months. Have we, as taxpayers, continued to pay him a salary as the County Manager while he campaigned? Friends, I am tired of being ripped off as a resident in Rio Arriba County. I hope you are also tired of being ripped off as a taxpayer in Rio Arriba County. It is high time for a change and I know most of you feel the same way.

This is Dr. Sam Ziegler asking for your support for myself for State Senate.[85]

Emilio Naranjo, at least publicly, was very quiet while we were busy campaigning throughout Rio Arriba. He generally refused interviews with local newspapers even to make clear his own views on various issues of importance in the county. His general silence may have been due, in part, to his numerous legal problems which had begun to emerge early in the year and which came to a head in late September and October.

Charges against Emilio Naranjo of vote fraud, illegal use of Democratic Party funds and county monies, and misuse of absentee ballots were common in Rio Arriba. With regard to absentee ballots, there was a standing joke around Española about how many "dead people" voted on election day. Charges of this kind continued through the summer and into the fall and provided constant themes during the campaign.

Sam started off his final push in the campaign with a radio announcement in Spanish which our daughter, then Julie Chavez, read:

> *Me llamo Julia Chavez. Quiero decir unas palabras de parte del hombre quien sera la proxima Senador del Estado de Nuevo Mexico del Condado de Rio Arriba, Distrito 5.*
>
> *Este Hombre ha didicado treinta anos de su vida a la gente de Rio Arriba. Es un hombre de honradez y integridad quien ha demonstrado interes sincero para la bienstar de la gente de este tierra por su trabajo como un doctor y un consejera de la cuidad de Española.*
>
> *Este Hombre es mi Padre, Dr. Samuel Ziegler.*
>
> *Vengan a votar conmigo el Dia 7th de Noviembre para el Dr. Samuel Ziegler y el mejor gobierno.*

(My name is Julia Chavez. I want to say a few words in behalf of the man who will be the next State Senator from Rio Arriba County, District 5.

He is a man who has dedicated 30 years of his life to the people of Rio Arriba. He is a man of honesty and integrity who has shown real concern for the welfare of the people of this area through his work both as a physician and as an Española city councilman.

This man is my father, Dr. Sam Ziegler.

Cast your vote along with me on November 7 for my father, Dr. Sam Ziegler. Cast your vote for Dr. Ziegler and for better government).[86]

The *SUN* wrote an opinion about the race for the Senate at the beginning of October, which again set forth one of the main problems Sam had in the race:

> While Democratic Chairman Emilio Naranjo expresses confidence he'll win in a 3-man race for the state senate, he's working hard just the same. Word is he's going door-to-door in the north and if he's ever going to collect on past political debts, this is the year to do it.
>
> His two opponents, Republican Dr. Sam Ziegler and La Raza's Ike DeVargas should split the anti-Naranjo vote and allow old "Null and Void" to serve legitimately in the state senate.
>
> . . . if it weren't for the votes DeVargas obviously will pull, [Ziegler] would have a shot at the senate seat. Every vote DeVargas gets, will be a strong anti-Naranjo vote that would have gone to Ziegler.
>
> The race for the state senate seat held by Naranjo through appointment by the county commission is actually the only interesting one in the county at this stage. [87]

The New Mexican published its Rio Arriba County endorsements on November 1ˢᵗ. It stated:

> Rio Arriba County voters on Nov. 7 can determine whether controversial political boss Emilio Naranjo will retain control over the county government.
>
> We believe he should not.
>
> Naranjo has manipulated county government for more than 25 years by controlling county commissioners, the persons who are elected to set policy on how the county is operated. Commissioners in Rio Arriba, however, have done exactly what Naranjo wants. Any person who attends just one county commission meeting can see that.
>
> Thus, the county's nearly $3 million budget is spent the way Naranjo wants it to be spent.
>
> It was determined earlier this year that two persons Naranjo pushed as county commissioners stole taxpayers' money while in office. Naranjo shrugged off the charges. [88]

The New Mexican's endorsement of Sam as a candidate was most welcome:

> We believe Republican, Dr. Sam Ziegler, a respected physician
> in the county for 30 years and an Española city councilman
> for 12 years, would be a better representative for the county.
> Ziegler would surely offer a welcome change from Naranjo's
> often self serving approach to Government. [89]

This endorsement was echoed in the *Rio Grande SUN* the following day:

> In the critical 3-way race for State Senator from Rio Arriba,
> the SUN indorses Republican Sam Ziegler. In his more than 30
> years in the county as a physician, Ziegler has displayed a compas-
> sion for the people and his campaign has been in that theme—what
> he can do for the people.
>
> He opposed Democrat Emilio Naranjo whose compassion
> for the people has been demonstrated in our courts. . . His interest
> in being state senator is not what he can do for the people, but what
> he can get out of it for himself.
>
> Antonio (Ike) DeVargas, La Raza candidate is intelligent
> and capable and a longtime foe of the Naranjo machine. But when
> he says if the race were between Ziegler and Naranjo he would vote
> for Naranjo, we must look askance at his candidacy.[90]

And so it went down to election day. It was a tiring but exciting week leading up to November 7th. Election Day itself was also an interesting experience. I relaxed at home in the early morning, then went to vote with Sam after picking up our son, Norman, who had come down from Denver for the occasion. We made regular rounds of the polling places, checking with our people. I also worked our precinct voting area on Riverside Drive with close friends Nathalia DeVargas, Stella Volk, Dee Jeffers and Kue Hunter. Nathalia was wonderful and was not shy about standing up for Sam. Many friends came by at different times to lend a show of support.

It was a tiring day and by the time the polls closed, we settled ourselves in the quietness of our home to await the results, with Norman, T.J. and Vangie Chavez, Horace and Nathalia DeVargas, and Joe and Belle Becker joining us. It was some time before all of the results from the different polling places were in because of the distances in Rio Arriba County. The early reports showed Sam doing pretty well, but not quite good enough. Our son, Sam Jr., called that evening to say that his thoughts were with us.

Headlines in the local paper the next morning confirmed our worst fears. "Naranjo scores 'greatest' win in Rio Arriba" greeted us in *The New Mexican,* and the *Rio Grande SUN* ran with the headline "Democrats Score Easy Rio Arriba Win." *The New Mexican* wrote:

> Emilio Naranjo Tuesday won another election in Rio Arriba County, and he savored the victory.[91]

And:

> Having lost much hope by 9 p.m. Tuesday, Sam told one well wisher that perhaps "the good Lord" would still help. He was trailing Naranjo then by more than 800 votes. It was mostly the northern precincts, where totals are smaller and where Naranjo generally does well, that were unreported at that time.[92]

All was not negative on reflection. Phone calls from friends were soon forthcoming with words of encouragement.

"Next time, Sam."

"Good work, Sam. You almost did the impossible."

Larry Calloway of *The New Mexican* noted:

> Sen. Emilio Naranjo…scored a *surprisingly narrow victory* in his bid for a full elected term in the [Senate]. Naranjo… got 4,906 votes in the overwhelmingly Democratic county to 3,783 for Republican Samuel Ziegler, MD, and 740 Raza Unida candidate Antonio DeVargas.[93]

The New Mexican ran an editorial the following day, which made room for second thoughts and hope for the future. It said:

It is political patronage at its purest, most simple form which keeps Naranjo in power.

. . .

The problem is that with dependence comes the loss of independence. The strong man invariably takes away some of the power and right of the people.

. . .

There may come a time when people in Rio Arriba County realize that fixed speeding tickets, token payments from the county medical indigent fund and menial public jobs are not worth the price of closed, corrupt government.[94]

Dr. Sam alongside his father, Rev. Samuel G. Ziegler, of Dayton, Ohio. Taken in fall of 1978 in the living room at the Ziegler home.

Dr. Ziegler was elected to the Española City Council in 1966. A Republican, he ran twice, unsuccessfully, for State Senator in heavily Democratic Rio Arriba County.

37

FIRST WOMAN PRESIDENT OF THE CHAMBER

I served on the Board of Directors of the Española Valley Chamber of Commerce in 1978. Several members of the Chamber including its president, Dom Cimino, approached me toward the end of the year to ask if I would be interested in serving as president the coming year. The question took me by surprise. There had been several women on the Board, but no woman had ever served as the Chamber's president in its forty-two year history. The position was a demanding and challenging one which would require a significant commitment of time. I knew that the Chamber carried a sizeable debt and that the Chamber needed to be promoted with local business people. I thanked those who approached me and told them I would consider the matter closely. I gave it a great deal of thought, and after talking with Sam, I said that I would be honored to serve. Before I knew it, I was unanimously elected to be the Chamber's first woman president!

I must say that all of the people on the Board were complimentary of my selection as president, and several came to me to say that they felt a real precedent had been set. I received letters of congratulation from a number of people, among them James Hoffman, President of the Chamisa Broadcasting Company, Inc. (KDCE Radio 950). I appreciated Jim's kind offer of support and assistance. He wrote:

> Congratulations and best wishes on your recent election to the Presidency of our Chamber of Commerce.
>
> As in the past, we at KDCE and KBSQ-FT will provide whatever assistance we can to the Chamber and to you as you enter into this new and challenging position. Again, congratulations from all of us.[95]

Diane Baker, Executive Director of the Santa Fe Chamber of Commerce, sent her best wishes as well. She wrote:

> Congratulations. . . Being the president of the Española Valley Chamber of Commerce will be challenging, but I'm also sure—"rewarding."
>
> Wishing you the best possible success.[96]

I had a reasonable idea of my responsibilities as president from my experience on the Board. I also had some notions about what I wanted to accomplish. There was a fine group of business people on the Board with whom I was to work, and I had every anticipation of a productive year. I was appreciative of the time and effort that local business people, who were much involved with their own affairs, devoted to the Chamber and to community work, and I hoped to do well by them in my new capacity.

The Chamber was in the process of hiring a manager when I took over. Ruby Reif, the Chamber's acting secretary, worked closely with me on correspondence and projects needing special attention until John Arrington came on board as the new Manager. We realized an additional helper was also needed to cover the workload at the Chamber's office and to greet travelers and visitors when they stopped for information. Margie Montoya was hired to fill this position.

The Chamber serves an important role in supporting local businesses and encouraging new business. One of the first projects I undertook was paying personal calls on the owners of new businesses in town and welcoming them on behalf of the Chamber. This was a difficult task for me as a woman. Visiting construction sites and adobe brick factories and the like were not activities to which I was accustomed. My comfort level grew with time, but it took some effort and adjustment. I felt the need for support in these ventures, and asked Ruby Reif to join me. We made a good team representing the Chamber to the public. Local business people responded to our welcome and to our invitation to join the Chamber. We began to see an increase in membership which rose from seventy-five to one hundred and twenty-one by early fall of the year.

The increased membership and interest in the Chamber paid other dividends. The Chamber had a debt of some $6,000. A local bank became aware of the increased interest in the Chamber, and stepped forward to offer a loan to the Chamber to settle its debt. The Chamber readily accepted the offer with the full backing of the Board, and was able to pay off the loan with the additional revenues generated from new membership dues. We were all proud of the achievement.

Dan Herrera from *The New Mexican* interviewed me shortly after I assumed office and asked how I saw my role and that of the Chamber. I commented about the growth I saw coming to the Valley and about our need to plan and guide this growth:

> There are people who are interested in keeping [Española] a country town, but it keeps changing… I think when they put in the four-lane highway through Riverside, that was it. The highway changed the whole character of the town right then.[97]

Many of us were concerned about the possible loss of "our polished turquoise sky and clean air" in the midst of all the change. I emphasized to Dan the Chamber's role in encouraging clean industry. The need for additional amenities for local residents was also evident, and I said to Dan:

> We need to take care of…the people who live here… Otherwise people will continue to go out of town instead of shopping [in Española].[98]

I felt strongly that more department stores, and restaurants with good family dining to balance the fast food businesses already in town, would give Española a greater appeal.

I was aware that Española was strategically located at the "hub" of northern New Mexico. All the major roads moving north and south passed through town and branched out to other areas of historical, cultural, recreational and business interest. This position made Española an ideal location for businesses which provided amenities for residents and visitors, and which promoted tourism.

The Chamber played a central role in promoting Española as the "hub" of the north, but it had no means of "advertising" our strategic location. There was a need for local maps with exact business locations, and a color brochure which would publicize the Valley's points of historical and cultural interest, and its scenic beauty. I suggested and encouraged the preparation of maps and a brochure as a special project soon after I became president, and received full support from the Board.

Funds to accomplish these projects came from two sources. The Española City Council agreed to institute a Lodger's Tax. The initiative for this tax came from the Chamber Manager, John Arrington. The Chamber Board appointed a committee of four local business people to work with John. The four members were Dorila Lujan, C.L. Hunter, Bill Smith, and Joe Suazo. The City received their presentation well and moved ahead quickly to approve the tax. Other monies came from a matching state grant from the Cooperative Promotional Funds. These sources provided the more than $7,000 which was needed.

We moved ahead quickly with the color brochure that everyone felt would stimulate tourism and be a great asset for local businesses. John Arrington concentrated on details for funding. Bob Trapp compiled the historical information to be used, while Belle Becker formulated the basic design. John kept a constant vigil with the Delgado Agency in Santa Fe to see that the preparation of the brochure progressed as desired. We made numerous trips to Santa Fe for final additions and corrections. A presentation to the public was ready by early February. The brochure went on display at the Chamisa Inn, where John Arrington spent a day talking with local business people and others who came to see it and offer their comments. We had 50,000 brochures ready for distribution by May. The project was viewed as a great success.

Spring and summer were taken up with a city beautification project and the Oñate Fiesta. Mayor Santiago Martinez declared April 22-29 "Española Clean-Up Days." Nancy Bell from Amantes de Flores was chairperson for the Clean-Up Committee. She was responsible for contacting the schools and community organizations about the clean-up and enlisting their participation. Nancy outdid herself in her tireless efforts to coordinate clean-up teams in designated areas, see that the judges made their rounds, and then organize the awards. This was no small task, and the Chamber appreciated Nancy's energy and enthusiasm. "Clean-Up Days" remains an on-going project in Española, and has been well-received.

Our Oñate Fiesta in mid-June took place with all the usual fanfare. The Chamber was scheduled to have a float in the Fiesta Parade. Designing and assembling a float was no easy task because most of the Chamber members were busy preparing floats to represent their own businesses. I discussed the Fiesta request for a float with the Board. It was decided that we call Dr. Anthony Garcia to come to our rescue. I had known Anthony since he was a young man. He is the eldest child of Manuel and Marie Garcia, all of whose children Sam delivered. We had followed his career with interest from his schooling in Santa Fe at St. Michael's to his becoming a dentist and establishing a practice in Santa Fe, and then his opening a lovely flower shop called "Delta Plants and Flowers" at his restaurant *Anthony's at the Delta* in Española. He is a creative man, and I knew he would be of help.

Anthony readily agreed to undertake the project. We decided our theme should be "Española," which means "Spanish Lady." Anthony designed a beautiful float, and with the help of a few dedicated Board members, decorated it elegantly with crepe paper and flowers. When all was ready, Anthony arranged a graceful seating of lovely Spanish ladies for the parade through town. The Chamber was most appreciative of his efforts.

An added highlight our Fiesta in 1979 was the visit of the Spanish Ambassador, H. E. Jose Llade y Fernandez Urrutia, and his wife, Pilar. The Mayor of Española and members of the City Council and Chamber of Commerce were present to greet the Ambassador and his wife at a reception at the Sanctuario de Chimayo, and then to join them for dinner at Rancho de Chimayo. The Ambassador and his wife were also on hand to view the Fiesta Parade.

Our fall that year began with the Chamber sponsoring the Labor Day Jerry Lewis Muscular Dystrophy Association Telethon. I was in charge of organizing volunteers and arranging for phones and communications at the Chamisa Inn. We had over thirty volunteers who gave very generously of their time, and we collected $3,600 in pledges by the end of the day. We were all excited when Channel 7, KOB TV in Albuquerque, called requesting that the president of the Chamber and a member come to Albuquerque to be interviewed about the Chamber's activities for the Telethon. Belle Becker willingly agreed to go with me, and we spent several hours at the TV Station being filmed and talking about what we had done. It was 11:00 p.m. before we were on our way back to Española. I thought we had spoken well for the Chamber, but we never saw any clips of this interview on the news. How disappointing!

The Chamber Board met every Wednesday morning at 7:00 a.m. for breakfast at the Chamisa Inn in Riverside. I found that the members of the Board took these meetings seriously, and were interested in facilitating efforts to improve business affairs in the Valley.

Matters discussed included a broad range of topics. The need for better litter control dominated one meeting at which we voted to enlist the active support of local officials in the enforcement of the City's Litter Ordinance. This vote involved follow-up contact with Municipal Judge Vigil, Chief of Police A. B. Valdez, and the Española City Council.

Another meeting was devoted to discussion about a program to improve the local airport, which the Chamber supported. The Chamber also sent a letter to New Mexico Governor King about preventative measures to be instituted in case of flood threats. The Rio Grande spring runoff was unusually high that year.

The Chamber recognized the need for radio and newspaper advertising to help promote the Valley. This advertising went along with the color brochure and its distribution. The Chamber had additional discussion about new ways to direct visitors to the Chamber's Information Center, again as a means of promoting the Valley. Groups wishing to have seminars and small conventions in town were in need of information about lodging and meeting places. The Chamber worked closely with them and with the Taos ski areas during ski season, to provide information about overflow lodging and accommodations.

Another matter the Chamber considered was the City's fire rating. It formulated a letter to the City Council encouraging the hiring of men to remain on twenty-four hour duty at the Fire House. Their presence would help upgrade the City's fire rating and thereby, reduce fire insurance rates for local residents.

Most Board meetings were orderly, with all those present anxious to promote the community in positive ways. There were, occasional heated exchanges. I remember one meeting when a member of the Board spoke up saying, "I have a comment and a complaint. I do not feel that a person should serve on this Board if they go out-of-town to buy their cars." The speaker proceeded to level an accusation at another member of the Board. His comment came out of the blue. Silence followed. The member who was accused then rose to state her reasons for "buying her car elsewhere," and words flew back and forth. The accusation fortunately had come toward the end of the meeting, so there was not much time for discussion. I suggested that each member give the matter thought, and that if the majority felt it merited further consideration, I would appoint a committee to come up with recommendations. My concern was that the confrontation would reach the media, but fortunately, no representative was present, so the issue quieted down. Members of the Board later suggested that the Valley should come first when buying anything, but if pricing was out of reason, then one was certainly free to go elsewhere.

The Chamber did sponsor speakers and programs for local business people. These included a seminar that District Attorney Eloy Martinez presented on handling bad checks, and a quarterly meeting devoted to tourism with David Santillanes, the State Director of Tourism, providing the discussion. U.S. Senator Harrison Schmitt came to the Valley to meet with local business people and discuss their needs and problems in preparation for the White House Conference on Small Business, set for January 13-17, 1980. Senator Schmitt contacted me about arrangements for the meeting. We gathered in the conference room at the Chamisa Inn on January 6, 1980 with a sizeable crowd in attendance.

The Senator was particularly interested in minority issues having to do with problems of business development and with the participation of women. He had asked that we save a chair for an Hispanic lawyer who requested time to speak. The lawyer arrived late, rushing into the room following Senator's introduction, and requesting that he be allowed to speak first because he needed to leave for Washington. Senator Schmitt very kindly assented.

The lawyer began by saying he appreciated the opportunity to talk with Senator Schmitt and local Hispanic business people, then stated that he did not feel enough was being done for the good of Hispanics and that Washington needed to be told. His talk proceeded from there and was rapid and overly long. Heads seemed to droop lower and lower as he continued. I fear he rapidly lost his audience. Senator Schmitt finally managed to say time was slipping by, and asked for questions or comments from those present. There were none, and the lawyer dashed out of the room as quickly as he had entered.

Senator Schmitt then rose to explain in more detail his reason for coming. He asked again for comments. One successful Hispanic business person in the front row immediately spoke up, saying they were angry and did not need anyone telling people in Washington that Hispanics in New Mexico were neglected and needed help. They spoke with pride about their own business and family, and received a standing ovation from those present when they finished. The meeting ended soon thereafter, and everyone seemed to leave in good spirits. I was not certain what had been accomplished, but I was pleased to see the forceful response that had been given.

I had another occasion to contact Senator Schmitt. The Chamber learned of a proposed 24.6% increase in the rates for electricity for the Valley. I sent a letter to the Senator saying:

> The members of the Board are totally opposed to this unjustified increase and are asking you to do everything in your power to see that the Federal Government does not approve such an increase.[99]

Senator Schmitt wrote back that he was pleased that the Department of Energy, after review of the proposed rate adjustment, had revised the rate downwards. Further study was necessary, but:

> You may be assured of my continued efforts to ensure that the rate for power will be established as low as possible consistent with sound business principles and legislative requirements.[100]

It is said that a good leader is one who is able to allocate responsibilities equitably among the members of the group or organization with whom they work, and set reasonable expectations for results. I tried to do this as president, always keeping in touch to provide needed assistance and make sure projects were moving ahead. Much of what I did was the time-consuming, non-glamorous work of follow-through which required dedication to the task at hand and a genuine interest in the business people of the community. I found that I grew into the job as I worked, and came to appreciate the time and energy past-presidents had devoted to the Chamber.

There were constant telephone calls to make about general business matters, and special calls to Board members when a matter of concern was to be discussed and voted upon. There were also frequent checks with secretaries preparing notices to be mailed and flyers to be posted for meetings sponsoring outside speakers, follow-ups on arrangements, and preparation of speeches and reports for weekly and quarterly Board meetings. I held executive meetings of the Board on several occasions when important matters came up needing discussion and decision-making. The Lodger's Tax, the brochure, concerns or questions about membership and finances all took time and thought along with dictating correspondence and keeping in touch with local radio and TV stations about advertising. The Chamber Manager, John Arrington, and I were in regular communication about Chamber concerns, and I often made special requests of my vice-president, Vic "Butch" Archuleta, when I needed help contacting business people whom we hoped to recruit to fill a vacancy on the Board. These contacts often involved quick calls to Butch at Becker's store to see if he were free, a hurried trip to see someone only to find they were not available, and then attempts to set a follow-up visit. All the hours of "behind the scenes" work with projects, business contacts, promotions, and routine Chamber functions made for a busy year.

Time passed quickly for me. I felt good about my work as president. I felt that the Chamber as a group had done an outstanding job helping to support and promote local business affairs. I learned much about the community that I had not been aware of before, and gained more respect for the people of the Valley as I worked with the Chamber and handled its responsibilities. It was time well-spent because the Chamber's activities were an investment in the future of the community.

Roy Honstein, a former president of the Chamber, and his wife, Elberta, offered to update our list of past-presidents of the Chamber. This information was to go in the Annual Banquet program. Past-presidents were encouraged to provide framed photographs of themselves which would be placed on display in one of the rooms of the Chamber's office. The Honstein's efforts interested and encouraged past members to attend the Annual Banquet in January. We had a record crowd with excellent media coverage, which was a fine culmination to my year as president.

One of the more pleasurable functions of the Chamber is its sponsorship of awards for Woman of the year, Man of the Year, and Organization of the Year. Decisions regarding these awards are made in December, with the awards themselves announced in January at the Chamber's Banquet.

An "anonymous committee" of three members of the Chamber makes the selections from among the nominations. The president selects the three members secretly, and they do their work in secret, reporting back only to the president.

Requirements for candidates were that they have an outstanding history of long, unselfish and dedicated service to the Española Valley which had contributed to the happiness of the people and the betterment of the community, and that the service given should have been unrewarded financially. No person whose service was rendered while in a salaried position could be eligible, even though their accomplishments may have been outstanding.

The awards given during my year were:

Woman of the Year—Rosita Rayburn. Rosita had come to Española with the Farmer's Stabilization Program and was recognized for her outstanding work with the Boy and Girl Scouts.
Man of the Year—Mark Sanchez, for fulfilling a promise that benefited all in the community. Mark was a recovered alcoholic recognized for his personal attention to and counseling of referrals to Alcoholics Anonymous and the Hoy Alcoholism Program, Inc. of Española. Mark had been sober for nine years in 1979, and has been a recovered alcoholic now for more than twenty-nine years.
Organization of the Year—3HO ("Healthy, Happy, Holy"), a non-profit educational and scientific foundation established near Española in 1969 by Yogi Bhajan, chief religious and administrative authority for the Sikhs in the Western Hemisphere.

We were fortunate to have Harold Brock serve as Master of Ceremonies at the Annual Banquet when I passed my gavel on to the new president, Jose V. ("Butch") Archuleta. Harold's wit and fine facility for reparteé kept the evening's entertainment in full swing. I discussed the evening's agenda with Harold prior to the banquet, and I remember him saying to me with a grin, "Now, Isabel. I know you will have a report to give of the Chamber's activities over the past year. You can talk as long as you like, and as long as you have something interesting to say. But remember that most people will get up to go home around 9:00 p.m."

I said my "Goodbyes" that evening and wished the Chamber much success for the coming year. The Board gave me a beautiful plaque in parting, with the inscription:

ISABEL H. ZIEGLER
PRESIDENT
1979
ESPAÑOLA VALLEY
CHAMBER OF COMMERCE

38

IT'S RETIREMENT TIME AND LIVING TREASURES

In a ceremony held at the Española Hospital on July 15, 1974 Arthur and Phoebe Pack honored Sam as the first physician of the hospital. It was a memorable occasion for us all. Many of our family and friends were there. I know Sam was both pleased and humbled by this recognition. Arthur spoke of the "tremendous enthusiasm" Sam had brought to the planning of the hospital. He said, "We must give credit where credit is due—to the man who put his lifeblood into the hospital and has been doing it ever since."[101] This recognition marked a fulfillment for Sam for his many years of service and dedication. I remember that occasion well as I watched and listened to the words of respect and praise for Sam and his work.

Two years later on October 1, 1976 Sam closed his office in Española and joined the Occupational Medical Group at the Los Alamos National Laboratory. The Group ran a comprehensive medical clinic that cared for all work-related illnesses and accidents, performed regular employee physical exams and did comprehensive physical evaluations of all new employees.

The surgery crew at the Española Hospital paid a special tribute to Sam when he left. It was a very touching moment. Verla Flading read a poem she had written as good-byes were said. She was now Head Nurse at the hospital and had been Sam's chief surgical nurse, a role into which Kay Sanchez moved. Kay was present on this occasion along with Rose Reese, Ruth Dunn, Barbara Martin, Mary Alire and others.

Saying good-byes was a sad time and a disconcerting experience as we closed up the office and cleaned out the files.

Sam would talk for hours at night as he thought through and rationalized his decision to retire. A day at the hospital usually started at 7:00 a.m. with surgery scheduled, then perhaps a delivery followed by hospital rounds, then to the office to see patients. He often had to return to the hospital at the end of the day and was not home until 9:00 p.m., only to have to return to the hospital again at midnight. This left little time at home for the family. We took it in our "stride," but Julie remarks, even today, about the few, special moments that she might have with her father as they sat together in a nice big chair. The boys also joke about having to ask their father if they could make an appointment in order to talk with him. They actually did do this, only to have to cancel because of the hospital calling.

These were exhaustive days for Sam, but he loved his practice and caring for his patients. The years from 1946-1976 were considered "golden years" of medicine, when the majority of physicians practiced as single practitioners or with one or two other physicians, as Sam had done. Although trained as a surgeon and obstetrician, he became a general practitioner out of necessity, and he grew to enjoy his role as a family doctor with very close relationships over many years with individual patients and their families. I know how gratifying it was for him to hear a patient say, "He is MY doctor." I also know he felt as much loyalty to his patients as they felt for him.

All these years later, I still have people stop and speak with me about Sam. They will say, "We miss Dr. Ziegler so much. He always found time to talk to us, and the minute I walked into his office I felt better, just knowing I was going to see him." My thanks to all these people for their appreciation.

When Sam finally made the decision to retire and join the Group at Los Alamos, I don't think I had ever seen him so relaxed. He worked regular hours Monday through Friday from 8:00 a.m. to 5:00 p.m., and had evenings and weekends off except for an occasional emergency call. He really luxuriated in this time for himself and our family.

Sam eventually took on more responsibility when he became the leader of the Occupational Medical Group, but he was mentally and physically rested now and could handle the additional demands. His Group was responsible for the care of some eleven thousand employees of the Lab, and of the Zia Company which handled maintenance for the Lab.

Another change took place when I applied and joined the Los Alamos National Laboratory in 1980. I was an assistant Buyer in the Materials Management Division. This included buying everything from food to ammunition.

Even though we were both working, we were pleased with the change since it gave us time to think about and pay attention to our children. Julie seemed settled and happy in Barcelona, Spain with her three children. We heard of occasional ups and downs between her and Errol, but for the most part, they appeared to be supportive of each other. Errol's job with DEA kept him constantly busy, and after two years in Barcelona, he and the family were moved once again, this time to Mexico City.

Julie and Errol and the children came home on a visit when the twins must have been about eighteen months old. Julie and Errol then left with their daughter, Lisa, on a trip to California, leaving Sam and me to baby sit the twins. We were more than happy to help. We had not seen our grandchildren in some time, and this gave us a chance to get reacquainted. We got baby beds from the hospital for the twins and placed them in the back room of our house.

We put the twins to bed that first night and went into the TV room to watch a TV program before going to bed ourselves. About the time I thought the twins should be asleep, I heard strange sounds coming from the back room. I went into the kitchen several times to listen, but each time everything seemed quiet.

The third time I heard a strange sound, I finally went out into the back room as quietly as I could and turned on a light to investigate. I found the twins sitting up in bed covered with glitter. Glitter was in their hair, on their hands, all over the beds and on the floor. Glitter everywhere!

Without thinking, we had placed one of the baby beds close to the shelves along the wall where I kept items I used in my craft work. Duane was in the bed closest to the shelves, and was busy reaching for bottles and passing them on to Dustin after opening them and investigating. They were having a wonderful time playing with the contents of all these bottles and emptying them all over the bed and themselves. Amidst the jumble were an assortment of beads, buttons and bobbles along with all that glitter!

I immediately called Sam to help. We picked up the twins and set them on the floor at one side so we could strip the beds. We then put the boys in the tub to be washed from head to foot. The beds had to be completely changed, and the electric sweeper pulled out to help clean up all of the glitter and beads. I was worried the boys might have gotten glitter in their eyes or swallowed something, but they seemed alright.

The twins kept us very busy babysitting. We had to maintain a constant vigil. They would be by us in the TV room jabbering away in twin talk, and all at once, one would go in one direction and the other in another direction. Caring for twins was a new experience for us and, indeed, "Never a dull moment!"

Sam and I retired from work at the Los Alamos National Laboratory on October 3, 1986, Sam from his position as Group Leader for Occupational Medicine in the Health, Safety and Environment Division, and I from my position as Administrative Services Specialist in the Procurement Office of the Materials Management Division. Many friends gathered for a party at our daughter's home in Española on October 25th. It was a lovely affair. Richard Lucero, Mayor of Española, attended and during a brief but very touching ceremony, read a proclamation which spoke of our lives and work in Española. The Mayor concluded with these words:

> Now, therefore, let it be resolved that the City Council and the Mayor on behalf of the City congratulate the Zieglers for their dedication and loyalty to the community and wish them the very best in their retirement. Therefore, we proclaim this day, October 25, 1986, as Sam and Isabel Ziegler Day in the Española Valley.[102]

Sam's active participation in a work environment was now over, but I remember well the wonderful and challenging involvements we both had along the way. Sam is no longer with us now, but I know he shared my sentiments. I have our family, three fine children, seven grandchildren and nine great-grandchildren. They have all made Sam and me very proud. I have many friends throughout the area. I continue to live in Española and all of northern New Mexico is around me. There is still the beauty of the Sangre de Cristo and the Jemez mountains.

I reflect on the many experiences that have shaped and enriched my life as I look back over the years. Sam shared my feelings and his words reflect mine as well. Here's what he had to say:

> I remember with great joy the confidence and energy I had as a young surgeon, and feel deeply my agony and fatigue as an experienced family physician who worked "twenty-six" hour days.

I laugh when I see myself bumping into the rear end of a horse as I walked home one dark night from McCurdy Clinic, and feel again the excitement of purchasing our first new car from Clyde Hunter at Hunter Motor Company in Española.

I am proud to be the husband of a beautiful woman who was not sure she could accept life in northern New Mexico, and then was named Woman of the Year in the Española Valley and became the first woman president of the Española Chamber of Commerce.

I reflect back on the good humor and forceful acumen of a man like Major General Charles Corlett, and picture the simple honesty and sincerity of the husband of a patient who came into my office late one afternoon and placed a handful of crumpled bills on the counter to settle a long overdue account.

I well remember being the father of a much wanted baby girl and in my excitement, sending announcement telegrams to relatives with the wrong name. I feel great pride now being the father of a lovely woman who is a successful business woman, is fluent in Spanish, and has a fine family with three lovely children.

I think of the fun I have had watching my sons grow and mature, and am glad of the chance to put my arms around one son who is a Registered Nurse, has earned a PhD and is a fine artist, and shake the hand of the other son who has become a successful businessman, and who retired from the Navy a Captain. Both are responsible family men with accomplished children.

I hear the soft words of our devoted friend, Caroline Dozier, whose eyes were always filled with love when she was with our daughter, Julie, and I see the look of amazement and joy on Ben Talachi's face when he witnessed his rain dance bring a downpour from a cloudless sky.

I still hear the first magical cries of the newborn, and know the satisfaction that comes from saving the life of an accident victim.

I feel the weight of caring for a three-day-old baby with an abdominal cyst and an older man with a liver mass, on both of whom I successfully operated.

I recall the excitement I experienced treating Greta Garbo, and the stimulation that came from sharing an evening with Georgia O'Keeffe, balanced against the measured concern I felt for an elderly patient whose thanks for care I gave shown through expressive eyes and an occasional wrinkled smile.

All that we have experienced has been a true adventure into the human condition and the human soul.[103]

The Española Hospital celebrated its 50th Anniversary on May 9, 1998. Fifty years ago, the hospital was only a thirty-two bed facility with one physician and a small, dedicated staff of nurses and other administrative personnel and caretakers. Today it is an imposing hospital equipped with the latest technology and equipment, and staffed by a well-trained and knowledgeable medical and surgical staff.

It was the Packs' dream a half-century ago that the hospital which they gave to the community bring modern medicine to northern New Mexico and be a place people could come to be healed. I do not think they were disappointed.

The community is fortunate to have this great facility, and more recently, a nineteen million dollar addition. I am sure that the next half-century will see it continue to be a haven for the relief of pain and suffering.

On Sunday, October 4, 1998 Sam and I were recognized along with three other individuals as "Living Treasures" by a Santa Fe program that honors elderly local people who have performed significant community service during their lives.

We gathered with many others in the courtyard of the Palace of the Governors that Sunday afternoon. It was a wonderful, touching moment, filled with much heartfelt emotion.

Bob Trapp, editor and publisher of the *Rio Grande SUN*, was at the ceremony with his wife, Ruth. Bob wrote eloquently about the occasion and the people honored. I close with his fine words which we shall long remember:

Some real good people were honored Sunday afternoon in Santa Fe.

Recognized as "Living Treasures" in a Santa Fe program honoring elderly people for a lifetime of achievement, were Dr. Sam and Isabel Ziegler, Española; Dr. Valerie McNown of Pojoaque and artisans Eliseo and Paula Rodriguez of Santa Fe.

All five were certainly worthy of the honor, but the impacts the Zieglers and Dr. McNown have had on Northern New Mexico over the years are of particular note.

Drs. Ziegler and McNown are unique individuals. In their professions, he a surgeon and she a pediatrician, each could have become extremely wealthy had they chosen to practice in larger cities or wealthier environments.

They chose Northern New Mexico, at the time one of the poorer regions in the United States, partly because of their love of the area but more so because they saw a need for their talents and services.

One wonders if either totaled up the pay they accepted in chili or apples or bills discounted or simply written off because it was apparent to them the patient would never be able to pay. We don't see enough of that dedication of self-sacrifice in today's profit-driven society.

Attendees at the Sunday event spoke simply, eloquently and emotionally of the impact the Zieglers and Dr. McNown had on their lives and the lives of their families. The "Living Treasures" might have been a bit embarrassed at listening to the many accolades, but the organization that sponsors this annual event deserves credit for recognizing "Living" treasures.

Individuals deserving such honors should be recognized during their lifetime, not posthumously.

Isabel Ziegler, while her husband was busy in his field, spent years in community service, working in a variety of community projects. These included a personal project for beautification of the city and helping develop the Española public library from its early days as a Woman's Club library to the current facility in the Lucero Center.

She served as her husband's office staff in the early days of his practice when Ziegler, a trained surgeon, found himself treating anything from skinned knees to bloody automobile accident victims. In short, a general practitioner rather than a surgeon.

All three are among the rare individuals who put more into a community than they take.

Many kind words were heard Sunday but a couple about Sam Ziegler not mentioned, we'll recount here:

In 1956, four young people with an idea but no money thought they would start a newspaper in Española. The enthusiasm was there, but the money wasn't.

So the four talked local businessmen into loaning them some "seed" money, which together with what cash they had and a loan from the Española State Bank, launched the *Rio Grande SUN* in October, 1956—42 years ago this week.

Among those taking a chance on these greenhorns were Drs. Sam Ziegler, Merle Yordy and Michael Pijoan. Each loaned us $250 a grand total of $750, a lot of money in 1956.

As the *SUN* gradually became solvent, the doctors were repaid and upon getting his check for $250 (plus 5% simple interest), Sam Ziegler wrote a complimentary letter acknowledging that the debt was paid and complimenting us for surviving those early years.

We're not sure in later years as he entered politics, Dr. Ziegler was as enthused about the *SUN*, but any differences created by politics did not affect our friendship or mutual respect.

Another untold story was, while his years on the Española city council were acknowledged, his two runs for the state senate were not. While he lost both times, the fact that he dared challenge the entrenched Democratic machine attested not just to his political courage but his genuine desire to change and improve the lot of Rio Arribans who had suffered under one-man rule for several decades.

As a Republican, in a county where Democrats outnumbered Republicans 6-1, he faced daunting odds but his first campaign saw him earn more votes than any Republican had since the early 1950s.

His campaigns were scrupulously clean while some of his detractors were not, but he insisted on keeping the high road. Sam Ziegler was one of the few political candidates we have seen in our 42 years we could describe without qualms as honest and sincere who was seeking public office to serve and not to profit.

Finally, Drs. Ziegler and McNown have destroyed, in our mind at least, the image of doctors spending two or three days a week on the golf course. To the best of our knowledge, Sam never picked up a golf club until well into his retirement and Valerie McNown may never have done so.

Northern New Mexico is by far a better place because of these "Living Treasures."[104]

In October, 1998, Sam and Isabel Ziegler were recognized as "Living Treasures" by a Santa Fe program honoring citizens for a lifetime of achievements.

NOTES

1. Arthur Pack, We Called It Ghost Ranch (Abiquiu, New Mexico: Ghost Ranch Conference Center, 1966), pp. 83-84.
2. Mary A. Evans, "Mrs. Evans Recalls Early Days in Española Valley," Rio Grande SUN Historical Edition, 1962, Section Five, p. E-15.
3. Bill Martin and Molly Radford Martin, *Bill Martin, American* (Caldwell, Idaho: The Caxton Publishers, Ltd., 1959), p. 190.
4. *Ibid.*, p. 216. See also: "'Night Riders' Captured, Jailed!" *Rio Grande SUN Historical Edition*, 1962, Section Five, p. E-2, for a description of McKinley's capture and jailing as related by Carlos Manzanares, former sheriff of Rio Arriba.
5. Pack, *We Called It Ghost Ranch*, pp. 32, 41.
6. "Samuel Stauffer McBride," *Rio Grande SUN Historical Edition*, 1962, Section Five, p. E-4.
7. Arthur was the manager of the Grocery Department at Bond Willard Mercantile.
8. Frank was the co-owner of Bond Willard Mercantile.
9. Hubert was superintendent of the Española Public Schools.
10. Clyde was the owner of Hunter Motor Company.
11. Howard was the owner of the M&S Garage and Oldsmobile dealership.
12. Mr. Cook was the owner of the Española Mercantile.
13. For more information about *colcha*s, see for example: Susan H. Ellis, *New Mexico Colcha Embroidery* (8609 La Sala de Sur NE, Albuquerque, New Mexico, 1980), 3rd Printing, pp. 2-11; William Wroth (Ed.), *Weaving & Colcha from the Hispanic Southwest* (Santa Fe, New Mexico: Ancient City Press, 1985), pp. 3-10, 69-77.
14. For more information about the early Women's Club, see the pamphlet given to the public at the dedication of the new Lucero Center and Public Library in Española on March 10, 1974.
15. From B. B. Dunne's column, "Paso Por Aqui," in *The New Mexican*. A clipping from our personal file dating from 1947. Complete references are missing. *Italics added.*
16. *The Santa Fe New Mexican*, Saturday, May 8, 1948, pp. 1, 12.
17. The land on which the house is situated was part of a Grant of lands made under different decrees between the years 1694 and 1706. The Grant was issued by Diego DeVargas and Pedro R. Cubero, the Governor and Captain General respectively of the Province of New Mexico, to Joseph Mascarenas and others,

who were placed in possession at different times. They and their heirs and assigns occupied the land from about the year 1705 to 1900, when there were proceedings in the Court of Private Land Claims to confirm titles to the land. The land was later surveyed, and in 1910 a United States Patent was issued. This patent was finally placed in the record in 1944. *Abstract of Title*, No. 17, Española Abstract and Title Co., p. 4.

18. Letter from Georgia O'Keeffe to Mrs. Samuel Ziegler, dated January 29, 1970, Abiquiu, New Mexico.

19. Card from Georgia O'Keeffe to Mrs. Samuel Ziegler. The note on the card is undated, but is from the late 1970s, mailed from Abiquiu, New Mexico.

20. Letter from Georgia O'Keeffe to Dr. Samuel Ziegler, dated October 8, 1965, Abiquiu, New Mexico.

21. Albert Rosenfeld, "Modern Medicine—where 'the clock walks'," *Collier's*, February 3, 1956, p. 26.

22. Rosenfeld, "Modern Medicine -," p. 29.

23. Rosenfeld, "Modern Medicine -," p. 26.

24. Letter from Dr. Earl L. Malone, 302 West Tilden, Roswell, New Mexico to Dr. Samuel R. Ziegler, dated January 16, 1956.

25. Letter from Miguel Gutierrez, Governor of Santa Clara Pueblo to Dr. Samuel Ziegler, dated January 21, 1956, Española, New Mexico.

26. J. M. Scarborough, District Judge, First Judicial District, "Statement Concerning The Article On The Española Medical Center," *The* Española *Valley News*, January 25, 1956, p. 1.

27. Albert Rosenfeld, "A Reply To The Statement Made By Judge Scarborough," *The* Española *Valley News*, Wednesday, February 8, 1956, p. 1.

28. Monroe Courtright, "Article In Magazine Causes Concern In New Mexico Town," *Public Opinion*, Westerville, Ohio, Thursday, February 2, 1956, pp. 1, 8.

29. Letter from Rev. Samuel G. Ziegler to Dr. Samuel R. Ziegler, dated April 20, 1956, Dayton, Ohio, pp. 1-4.

30. "Spring Bonnets," *The New Mexican*, Thursday, April 20, 1961, p. 5.

31. Letter from Elmo Tipton to Sam and Isabel Ziegler, dated November 1, 1996, Santa Ynez, California.

32. Alan C. Vedder, *Furniture in Spanish New Mexico* (Santa Fe, New Mexico: The Sunstone Press, 1977).

33. Ruth Laughlin, *The Wind Leaves No Shadow* (New York: Whittlesey House, 1948).

34. The new highway include sections of U.S. Highway 285/84 coming into Riverside from Santa Fe, and U.S. 291/68 moving from Riverside toward Alcalde.

35. "Artist With Dirt On Hands Beautifies Area 'Island'," *The New Mexican*, Monday, March 30, 1964, p. 3.

36. "Glen Ramsey, Mrs. Ziegler Are Valley's Top Citizens, *Rio Grande SUN*, Thursday, January 21, 1965, p. 1.

37. Steve Terrell, "Jacques Cartier remembered," *The New Mexican*, Wednesday, December 4, 1991, p. B1.

38. Letter from Norman Ziegler to the family, dated Friday night, February 17, 1961, George School, Newtown , Pennsylvania, p. 1.

39. Letter from Isabel Ziegler to Paula Williams, dated June 16, 1972, Española, New Mexico, p. 1.

40. Letter from Olga Velasco Scott to Isabel Ziegler, dated October 15, 1996, Houston, TX, p. 1.

41. *Ibid.*, p. 2.

42. Letter from Olga Velasco Scott to Norman Ziegler, dated November 30, 1996, Houston. TX, p. 1.

43. *Ibid.*, p. 4.

44. Letter from Samuel Ziegler, Jr. to the family, dated November 3, 1961, Westerville, Ohio, p. 2.

45. Postcard from Norman Ziegler, addressed to Dr. and Mrs. S. R. Ziegler, Box W, Española, New Mexico, USA (Outside the Iron Curtain), dated August 25, 1962, Prague, Czechoslovakia.

46. Letter from Janis Harvey Hamrick to Isabel Ziegler, dated May 26, 1996, Lancaster, Ohio, p. 2.

47. Letter from Janet Harvey Hussong to Isabel Ziegler, dated June 4, 1996, Dayton, Ohio, p. 1.

48. *Ibid.*

49. Letter from Janis Harvey Hamrick . . , p. 2.

50. *Ibid.*, p. 3.

51. "Española's 'Las Conquistadoras' Release Vocal Album; Proceeds Donated to Hospital Fund," *Santa Fe News*, Thursday, August 17, 1967, p. 1.

52. "Eppie Beats Cippy in Mayor Race, Five Elected on 'Citizen' Slate." *Rio Grande SUN*, Thursday, March 3, 1966, p. 1.

53. *Ibid.*

54. "Council, Mayor Tested," *Rio Grande SUN*, Thursday, May 8, 1969, p. 1.

55. "Council, Mayor Accept Challenge," *Rio Grande SUN,* Thursday, May 15, 1969, p. 1.

56. "Lucero Wins Second Term," *Rio Grande SUN*, Thursday, March 5, 1970, p. 1.

57. Letter from Ruth Trapp to Isabel Ziegler, dated December of 1977, Española, New Mexico.

58. E. E. Dominguez, "Española keeps Lopez—Ouster move buckles," *The New Mexican*, Tuesday, August 26, 1975, p. A1.

59. *Ibid.*, p. A10.

60. "Citizens Speak Out For City Manager," *Rio Grande SUN*, Thursday, August 28, 1975, p. 1.
61. "Zoning Merry-Go-Round," *Rio Grande SUN*, December 4, 1975, p. 2.
62. "Council Commended," *Rio Grande SUN*, December 25, 1975, p. 2.
63. E. E. Dominguez, "Española council adopts zoning law," *The New Mexican*, Tuesday, February 10, 1976, p. A1.
64. *Ibid.*
65. E. E. Dominguez, "Española mayor charges politics behind zone suit," *The New Mexican*, Thursday, February 19, 1976, p. A1.
66. "Beautification Awards," *The New Mexican*, Wednesday, November 17, 1976, p. A6.
67. *Ibid.*, p. A8.
68. David Roybal, "Councilman to see senate post," *The New Mexican*, Sunday, October 16, 1977, p. D8.
69. David Roybal, "Rio Arriba Style," *The New Mexican*, Tuesday, October 18, 1977, p. A10. Emphasis added.
70. Charles Bermant, "Española's Opposing Slates Make Final Pitches," *Albuquerque Journal*, Sunday, March 5, 1978, p. E4.
71. "Wise Decision," *Rio Grande SUN*, Thursday, March 9, 1978, p. A2.
72. "Rio Arriba Democrats Prepare For Lively June Primary," *Rio Grande SUN*, Thursday, April 13, 1978, p. A1.
73. For information about DeVargas, see: David Roybal, "Naranjo rights trial starts in Albuquerque," *The New Mexican*, Wednesday, October 11, 1978, pp. A1-2; "Three Seek County's Senatorial Post," *Rio Grande SUN*, Thursday, November 2, 1978, p. A4.
74. "Chalk Up Another," *Rio Grande SUN*, Thursday, June 8, 1978, p. A2.
75. "The LAND of Disenchantment," *Rio Grande SUN*, Thursday, June 8, 1978, p. A2. Emphasis added.
76. David Roybal, "Naranjo organization apparent winner in RA," *The New Mexican*, Thursday, June 8, 1978, p. A2.
77. Letter from Antonio Ike DeVargas to Dr. Sam Ziegler, c/o Española City Council. The letter is undated, but signed at the bottom by both DeVargas and G. D. LaMadera.
78. Letter from Samuel R. Ziegler, MD to Mr. DeVargas, dated July 11, 1978, Española, New Mexico.
79. Campaign mailing, Summer, 1978, paid for by Ziegler for Senate, Gene Finch, Treasurer.
80. Letter from Rev. Samuel G. Ziegler to Sam Ziegler, dated August 1, 1978, Española, New Mexico.
81. David Roybal, "Hopefuls plan RA campaign," *The New Mexican*, Thursday, September 7, 1978, p. A12.

82. David Roybal, "Skeen foresees growth in state," *The New Mexican*, Monday, September 11, 1978, p. A1.
83. Robert V. Beier, "3,000 Hail GOP at Abiquiu," *Albuquerque Journal*, Monday, September 11, 1978, p. A2.
84. Campaign mailing, October, 1978, paid for by Ziegler for Senate, Gene Finch, Treasurer.
85. Radio address delivered during late October, 1978, paid for by Ziegler for Senate, Gene Finch, Treasurer.
86. Radio ad taped by our daughter, then Julia Chavez, and aired on local radio during the final days of the campaign, paid for by Ziegler for Senate, Gene Finch, Treasurer.
87. "The LAND of Disenchantment," *Rio Grande SUN*, October 5, 1978, p. A2.
88. "New Mexican *Opinion*: Rio Arriba endorsements," *The New Mexican*, Wednesday, November 1, 1978, p. A4.
89. *Ibid.*
90. "The Legislature . . ," *Rio Grande SUN*, November 2, 1978, p. A2.
91. David Roybal, "Naranjo scored 'greatest' win in Rio Arriba," *The New Mexican*, Wednesday, November 8, 1978, p. A1.
92. *Ibid.*, p. A2.
93. Larry Calloway, "GOP makes seven-seat gain in House," *The New Mexican*, Wednesday, November 8, 1978, p. A5. Emphasis added.
94. "Naranjo's power" in New Mexican Opinion, *The New Mexican*, Friday, November 10, 1978, p. A4.
95. Letter from James F. Hoffman, President, Chamisa Broadcasting Company, Inc., KDCE Radio 970, to Isabel Ziegler, Española Valley Chamber of Commerce, dated January 11, 1979.
96. Letter from Diane Baker, Executive Director, Santa Fe Chamber of Commerce, to Isabel Ziegler, Fairview Station, dated February 12, 1979.
97. Dan Herrera, "Chamber president foresees growth for Española," *The New Mexican*, Monday, February 12, 1979, p. B-1.
98. *Ibid.*
99. Letter from Isabel H. Ziegler, President, Española Chamber of Commerce, to Hon. Jack Schmitt, dated November 16, 1979, Española, New Mexico.
100. Letter from U. S. Senator Harrison Schmitt to Mrs. Isabel Ziegler, Española Valley Chamber of Commerce, dated February 1, 1980, Washington, D. C.
101. "Española Hospital honors physician," *The New Mexican*, Tuesday, July 16, 1974, p. B1. For further discussion of this day, see also: "First Physician Honored," *Española Hospital Noticias,* Vol. 6, No. 7, Fall Issue, 1974, p. 1; Susan Scott-Mayer, "Plaque Honors Dr. Ziegler," *Rio Grande SUN*, Thursday, July 18, 1974, pp. 1, 8.

102. Hollie Sowerwine, "Ziegler Feted By Friends Upon Retiring From Lab," *Rio Grande SUN*, Thursday, November 6, 1986, p. C-1.
103. Samuel R. Ziegler, MD and Isabel H. Ziegler, As Told To Norman P. Ziegler, PhD, RN, *"For The Soul Is Dead That Slumbers"* (3209 West 70th Street, Shreveport, LA: K's Kopy It, First Printing, June, 1999), p. 658.
104. Robert Trapp, "Living Treasures Impacted Everyone," *Rio Grande SUN*, Thursday, October 8, 1998, p. A-7.

CPSIA information can be obtained at www.ICGtesting.com
Printed in the USA
BVOW072059300412

288970BV00001B/9/P